MW01254396

HOLLYWOOD CELEBRITIES 2:
MORE OF MY FAVORITE STARS

"In my first non-fiction book, *Hollywood Celebrities: Where Are They Now?*, I attempted to bring their fans important and interesting information regarding fine child stars and other actors of yesteryear that we all loved and miss very much—although some of them are still active in their show business careers today."—Author

Here in this book Ron Ebner—author of *The Winds of Hell*, *Nova*, *Plague World*, *Sociopaths: America's Psycho Killers* and *Sociopaths 2: America's Psycho Killers: Updated and Expanded* and two short story collections—has gone on to gather information about additional actors and former actors, including:

Michael Ansara, Macaulay Culkin, John Denver, Andy Devine, Fats Domino, Dan Haggerty, Paul Hogan, Al Jolson, Peter Lorre, Roddy McDowall, Audie Murphy, Haley Joel Osment, Sabu, Buffalo Bob Smith, Jimmie Walker, Vera Miles, Natalie Wood, updates of Mouseketeers and many more. Plus updates for stars listed in the first edition, a special investigation into John Wayne's mysterious death and a section on the Dead End Kids.

Also included is a section on Famous Wrestlers and the cast of "Godspell."

The experiences of these actors go way beyond what we, the Hollywood uninitiated, have been exposed to—some wonderful events, others terrible in the extreme. Read through these pages and find out what has happened to some of my favorite Hollywood celebrities.

HOLLYWOOD CELEBRITIES 2: MORE OF MY FAVORITE STARS

BY

RON EBNER

CONTENTS

1. More of My Favorite Stars—page 11-238

2. The Mysterious Death of John Wayne—229

3. A Tribute to the Dead End Kids—234

4. A Tribute to the Cast of "Godspell"—242

5. Famous Wrestlers—250

In remembrance of

RAY BRADBURY
and
DON GRADY

Two fine talents who are now, I believe, still
doing their thing in a better world.

WHATEVER HAPPENED TO...?

ALBERONI, SHERRY
1946-

Update: I'm pleased to write that Sherry has received the Disney Legend Award at the D23 Expo. This honor was bestowed upon her July 18, 2015 for the talented work she provided during the four-year production (1955-59) of TV's Mickey Mouse Club. She joins other former Disney celebrities such as Annette Funicello, Tommy Kirk, and Kevin Corcoran. Congratulations, Sherry!

ANSARA, MICHAEL
1922-2013

Stage, screen, and voice-over actor possibly best known for his role of Cochise on TV's "Broken Arrow." Michael George Ansara was born on April 15, 1922 in a small village in the middle east then known as the French Mandate for Syria and the Lebanon. His family immigrated to America in 1924 and settled in Lowell, Massachusetts; ten years later they moved to California. It was there that Michael decided to become an actor when he took acting classes to overcome his shyness (imagine the forceful presence of Michael Ansara as shy!). He also earned a B. A. at Los Angeles City College.

(Photo, l. John Lupton and Michael Ansara in Broken Arrow*)*

He began his prolific career (after numerous uncredited roles) by appearing in a small part on "Family Theatre" called "Hill Number One: A Story of Faith and Inspiration" in 1951 and several episodes of "Alfred Hitchcock Presents" in 1956. But it was the lead role for the six-foot-two-inch actor as the famed Chiracahua Apache chief Cochise in ABC's classic western, "Broken Arrow," that skyrocketed his career. That fine show aired from 1956 to 1958. This western series also starred John Lupton as Indian agent Tom Jeffords. "Arrow" became a cult favorite but Michael stated, "I was not enthused with the role as my character lacked any depth or challenge."

While doing "Arrow" 20-th Century Fox, where the show was being filmed, arranged a publicity date (very common in Hollywood) for Michael with actress Barbara Eden; they married in 1958 and he appeared a number of times on Barbara's show, "I Dream of Jeannie." Unfortunately the marriage ended in divorce in 1974 (they had a son, actor Matthew Ansara). Michael had been married before to Jean Byron from 1955 to 1956 (divorced). He married Beverly Kushida in 1977.

Sticking with westerns and ABC, Michael went on to star in "Law of the Plainsman" (1959-60) where he played an Apache named Sam Buckhart who was appointed U. S. Marshal. His character typically roams the west hunting bad guys and righting wrongs—formula for the time and fans loved it, though not enough to keep it on the air.

(Photo, l. Michael as U. S. Marshall Sam Buckhart in a shot from "Law of the Plainsman," *c. 1959.)*

In 1962 Michael starred with Ramon Novarro in a Broadway show.

Michael appeared in the following motion pictures: "Action in Arabia" (1944) with George Sanders, "Kim" (1950) with Errol Flynn, "Brave Warrior" (1952) with Jon Hall, "The Robe" (1953) with Richard Burton, "The Egyptian" (1954) with Victor Mature, "The Lone Ranger" (1956) with Clayton Moore, "The Ten Commandments" (1956) with Charlton Heston, "The Comancheros" (1961) with John Wayne, "Harum Scarum" (1965) with Elvis Presley, "The Pink Jungle" (1968) with James Garner, "Guns of the Magnificent Seven" (1969) with Yul Brynner, "Dear Dead Delilah" (1972) with Agnes Moorehead, "Day of the Animals" (1977) with Christopher George, "Access Code" (1984) with Martin Landau, "Border Shootout" (1990) with Michael Forest, "The Long Road Home" (1999) with T. J. Lowther, "Batman: Vengeance (voice-over)" (2001) with Kevin Conroy.

Some of the many TV shows he appeared in were: "Terry and the Pirates" (1952) with John Baer, "Soldiers of Fortune" (1955) with John Russell, "The Adventures of Rin Tin Tin" (1956) with Lee Aaker, "The Rifleman" (1959; here Michael played U. S. Marshal Sam Buckhart, later his series spun off from this) with Chuck Connors, "Wagon Train" (1961 & 1963) with Ward Bond, "The Outer Limits: Soldier" (1964) with Lloyd Nolan, "Voyage to the Bottom of the Sea" (1964 & 1966) with Richard Basehart, "Bewitched" (1966) with Elizabeth Montgomery, "Daniel Boone" (1966) with Fess Parker, "Gunsmoke" (1966 & 1967) with James Arness, "Star Trek" (1968) with William Shatner, "Lancer" (1970) with James Stacy, "Hawaii Five-0" (1972) with Jack Lord, "Police Story" (1973-74) with Scott Brady, "Kojak" (1976) with Telly Savalas, "Buck Rogers in the 25th Century" (1979-80) with Gil Gerard, "Hardcastle and McCormick" (1985) with Brian Keith, "Rambo" (1986) with Neil Ross, "Star Trek: Deep Space Nine" (1994-96) with Avery Brooks, "Batman Beyond" (1999) with Will Friedle.

Michael received a star on the Hollywood Walk of Fame on February 8, 1960; it's located at 6666 Hollywood Boulevard.

Though he often play brooding, desperate villains, Michael actually was a man easy to get along with and possessed of a generous nature. He often said about acting that, "One of the best things about being an actor—traveling throughout the world, meeting all kinds of people and learning about other cultures."

Sadly, Michael died of complications from Alzheimer's disease on July 31, 2013 at his home in Calabasas, California. He was interred with his son, Matthew Ansara, at Forest Lawn Memorial Park in the Hollywood Hills, Los Angeles, California.

ARNESS, JAMES
1923-2011

This big man—big in stature and big as a quality actor—was born as James King Aurness on 26, 1923 in Minneapolis, Minnesota to Rolf Cirkler Aurness and Ruth Duesler. He was certainly best known for his portrayal of U. S. Marshall Matt Dillon on the long-running (1955-1975) CBS TV western, "Gunsmoke," which also starred Amanda Blake (1929-89) as Kitty Russell, Milburn Stone (1904-80) as Doc Galen Adams, Ken Curtis (1916-91) as Festus Haggen, Dennis Weaver (1924-2006) as Chester Goode, Buck Taylor (1938- , son of actor Dub Taylor) as Newly O'Brien and a guest cast of hundreds. The series was created by director Norman Macdonnell and writer John Meston. Interestingly, Matt Dillon was played on CBS radio (1952-61) by William Conrad of "Cannon" fame and as the narrator for "The Fugitive" and "The Invaders." The radio show also starred Howard McNear (Floyd the barber on "The Andy Griffith Show") as Doc Charles Adams, Georgia Ellis as Kitty, and Parley Baer (also on "The Andy Griffith Show" as the mayor) as Chester Proudfoot. The narrator for "Gunsmoke," George Walsh, began on radio in 1952 and moved to TV to do the show right up until it ended in 1975.

"Gunsmoke" director Charles Warren chose James Arness to play the role of Matt Dillon on the TV show because Jim had done a picture for Warren earlier and because—according to James Stewart—John Wayne had recommended Jim for the part.

The show was cancelled at the end of its 20th season because it had dropped in the "sacred, all powerful" Nielsen rating down to only one of the top 30. The cast hadn't been told and had no idea; they read about the cancellation in the trade papers. That's why there was no final, wrap-up show. *(Photo, r. Jim as Matt Dillon)*

Jim was also well known for his appearance as the crusty, never-take-any-crap, mountain man Zeb Macahan in the popular western "How the West Was Won" (TV miniseries in 1977, regular series from 1978-79). The show also starred Bruce Boxleitner, Eva Marie Saint, Fionnula Flanagan, Kathryn Holcomb, William Kirby Cullen, and Vicki Schreck.

Actor Peter Graves (1926-2010) was Jim's younger brother.

Jim graduated from high school in 1942 and went to work at various trades including loading and unloading boxcars at the Burlington freight yards in Minneapolis and logging in Pierce, Idaho. He wanted to be a fighter pilot during WWII but his six foot seven inch frame kept him out of aircraft. Instead Jim served in the Army as a rifleman with the 3rd Infantry Division and was severely wounded in in the leg in Anzio, Italy; he recuperated at Army 91st General Hospital in Clinton, Iowa. This purple-heart recipient suffered the rest of his life from chronic leg pain which was sometimes noticeable when seen walking on the "Gunsmoke" show.

(Photo, l. Cast of Gunsmoke, *1967: Amanda Blake in front; back, l-r: Milburn Stone, Ken Curtis, James Arness)*

Jim attended Beloit College in Wisconsin and began his acting career as a radio announcer for station WLOL in Minneapolis in 1945. But acting piqued his interest and he hitchhiked to Hollywood. Jim went to RKO Studios and the first thing they did was shorten his name to "Arness." His first movie was "The Farmer's Daughter" (1947) with Loretta Young. He got a bit part as the rampaging, alien monster in "The Thing From Another World" (1951) with Kenneth Tobey and appeared with veteran actor James Whitmore in the classic horror film, "Them!" with Edmund Gwenn and Joan Weldon (written by George Worthing Yates, a veteran of science fiction films).

A close friend of John Wayne, Jim appeared in several of the Duke's movies such as "Hondo" (1953) with Geraldine Page and "Island in the Sky" (1953) with Andy Devine and Lloyd Nolan.

(Photo, l. The interior of the real Long Branch Saloon, Dodge City, Kansas taken sometime between 1870-1885) (1949)

Some of the many movies he appeared in include: "Battleground" with Van Johnson, "Wagon Master" (1950) with Ben Johnson, "Sierra" (1950) with Audie Murphy, "Carbine Williams" (1952) with James Stewart, "Big Jim McLain" (1952) with John Wayne, "Many Rivers to Cross" (1955) with Robert Taylor, "Gun the Man Down" (1956) with Angie Dickinson, "The Macahans" (1976) with Bruce Boxleitner, "The Alamo: Thirteen Days to Glory" (1987) with Brian Keith, "Gunsmoke: Return to Dodge" (1987) with Amanda Blake, "Gunsmoke: The Last Apache" (1990) with Richard Kiley, "Gunsmoke: To the Last Man" (1992) with Pat Hingle, "Gunsmoke: The Long Ride" (1993) with James Brolin, "Gunsmoke: One Man's Justice" (1994) with Bruce Boxleitner.

Some of Jim's TV roles include: "Lux Video Theatre: The Chase" (1954) with Frances Bavier, "Front Row Center: The Challenge" (1956) with Ray Collins, "McClain's Law" (1981-82) with Marshall Colt, "Red River" (1988) with Bruce Boxleitner.

In 1948 Jim married Virginia Chapman; they divorced in 1960. He married Janet Surtees in 1978 and they were together until his death. Jim was inducted into the Hall of Great Western Performers of the National Cowboy and Western Heritage Museum in 1981.

Jim wrote about his career in "James Arness: An Autobiography," released in September 2001. He enjoyed poetry, sailboat racing, and surfing.

Sadly, Jim died of natural causes on June 3, 2011 at his Brentwood home, Los Angeles, California and is interred at the Forest Lawn Memorial Cemetery in Glendale, California.

BAIRD, SHARON
1942-

Update: In my last book, "Hollywood Celebrities: Where Are They Now?," I gave Sharon's mother's maiden name as Nikki Marcus. Sharon has asked me to indicate that it was actually Nicoletta (nickname, Nicki) Marcus. And she wanted me to add that, in addition to her other film credits, she also appeared in the fine children's film, "Pufnstuf," as Shirley Pufnstuf. It came out in 1970 and also starred Jack Wild, Billie Hayes, Martha Raye, "Mama" Cass Elliot, and Billy Barty.

In addition, I'm pleased to write that Sharon has received the Disney Legend Award at the D23 Expo. This honor was bestowed upon her July 18, 2015 for the talented work she provided during the four-year production (1955-59) of TV's Mickey Mouse Club. She joins other former Disney celebrities such as Annette Funicello, Tommy Kirk, and Kevin Corcoran. Congratulations, Sharon!

BEERY, WALLACE
1885-1949

This fine film actor is probably best remembered for his portrayal of the one-legged pirate, Long John Silver, in the 1934 film version of Robert Louis Stevenson's classic novel, "Treasure Island." This version also starred Jackie Cooper, Otto Kruger, Nigel Bruce, and Lionel Barrymore. He is also well known for his role of the alcoholic former heavyweight boxing champion Andy Purcell in the 1931 tearjerker, "The Champ" with Jackie Cooper, Irene Rich, and Roscoe Ates. Wally won an Academy Award for Best Actor in that movie that was nominated for the Academy Award for Best Picture. His 1932 contract with MGM stipulated he be paid $1 more than any other actor at the studio, making him the highest paid actor in the world at that time. Wally was the brother of actor Noah Beery Sr. and the uncle of actor Noah Beery Jr. (of TV's "Rockford Files" fame).

(Photo, r. Wallace Beery as Long John Silver with parrot friend Cap'n Flint in Treasure Island, *1934)*

Wallace Fitzgerald Beery was born on April 1, 1885 on a farm in Clay County, Missouri to Noah Webster Beery and Frances Margaret Fitzgerald. The family left the farm in the 1890s and moved to Kansas City, Missouri where father Beery became a police officer. Wally wasn't happy with school or the piano lessons he had to take so he ran away from home at age 16 and joined the Ringling Brothers Circus as an assistant elephant trainer. After two years with the circus he left after being clawed by a leopard.

Wally moved in with his brother Noah in New York City in 1904 and became a baritone singer in comic opera. He also worked on Broadway in Summer Stock. In 1907 he starred in "The Yankee Tourist." He continued acting in Chicago and in Niles, California. In 1915 Wally acted in his first silent film opposite his future wife, Gloria Swanson, "Sweedie Goes to College." His marriage to Gloria didn't last long because of his drinking and abuse. Some of Wally's other silent films include Sir Arthur Conan Doyle's dinosaur classic, "The Lost World" (1925) where he played Professor Challenger; the movie also starred Bessie Love and Lewis Stone; "Robin Hood" (1922) and "The Last of the Mohicans" (1920).

When the sound era in film came around, Wally's deep, resonant voice and gruff manner combined with his bulky, six foot frame made him a natural for villainous roles and was soon under contract with MGM. He starred as the convict Butch in "The Big House" (1930) with Chester Morris, a highly successful film. In fact, during the 1930s Wally was one of Hollywood's Top 10 box office stars.

He made a number of comedies with Marie Dressler and Marjorie Main. Wally's career began to decline somewhat in the 1940s he was always top-billed and none of his movies lost money. He didn't work well with children and was complained about by child actors Jackie Cooper and Margaret O'Brien, although Mickey Rooney seemed to like working with him.

In 1939 Wally almost got the role of The Wizard/Prof. Marvel in "The Wizard of Oz" but because of other film commitments had to turn it down.

Some of Wally's film roles include, "Volcano" (1926) with Bebe Daniels, "Min and Bill" (1930) with Marie Dressler, "Tugboat Annie" (1933) with Marie Dressler, "Viva Villa!" (1934) with Fay Wray, "China Seas" (1935) with Jean Harlow, "Slave Ship" (1937) with Warner Baxter, "20 Mule Team" (1940) with Leo Carrillo, "Barnacle Bill" (1941) with Marjorie Main, "Jackass Mail" (1942) with Marjorie Main, "Salute to the Marines" (1943) with Fay Bainter, "Bad Bascomb" (1946) with Margaret O'Brien, "The Mighty McGurk" (1947) with Dean Stockwell, "A Date With Judy" (1948) with Jane Powell, "Big Jack" (1949) with Marjorie Main.

In 1935 Wally turned down the role of Capt. Bligh in "Mutiny on the Bounty" because he didn't want to work with Clark Gable. Odd because, according to Wally, they were good friends outside the studio and had a lot in common.

He married actress Gloria Swanson in 1916; they divorced in 1919. In 1924 Wally married Rita Gilman; they had one child and divorced in 1939.

Wally owned and flew his own planes and in 1933 was commissioned a Lieutenant Commander in the U. S. Navy Reserve. During the filming location for "Treasure Island" on Santa Catalina Island he flew daily from his home in Beverly Hills.

Sadly, Wally died of a heart attack at his Beverly Hills home on April 15, 1949. He was buried at Forest Lawn Memorial Park Cemetery in Glendale, California. The inscription on his grave marker reads: "No man is indispensable but some are irreplaceable."

BENDIX, WILLIAM
1906-1964

This radio, film, and TV actor first played either a tough cop or a rough gangster type, but he could do comedy equally well. He was born William Bendix on January 14, 1906 in Manhattan, New York City, New York to Oscar Bendix and Hilda Carnell. After dropping out of high school, Bill was a batboy for the New York Yankee and said that he had seen Baby Ruth hit at least a 100 home runs at Yankee Stadium. Fitting, because in later life—as an actor—Bill got to play "The Bambino" in "The Babe Ruth Story" (1948), released by Allied Artist and co-starring Claire Trevor and Charles Bickford.

Bill went to work as a grocer in the City until the Depression when work was tough to find. He moved on to acting in 1936 in the New Jersey Federal Theatre Project, part of Pres. Roosevelt's New Deal program sponsored by the Works Projects Administration to employ most anyone in the acting field. In 1939 he went on the stage in William Saroyan's "The Time of Your Life." This got him seen by Hal Roach and signed him to a film contract. That got him into "Wake Island" (1942) and an Academy Award nomination. Moving into film noir, Bill played Jeff, a brutal employee of a no-goodnik named Nick Varna (Joseph Calleia) in Dashiell Hammett's "The Glass Key" (1942), which also starred Brian Donlevy, Alan Ladd, Bonita Granville, Veronica Lake, and Richard Denning.

That film got Bill attention, but he did even better as Gus, a wounded and dying American sailor during WWII in Alfred Hitchcock's "Lifeboat" (1944), an excellent movie that also starred Tallulah Bankhead (rumor has it that Miss Bankhead never wore panties under her dresser and some of the guys on the crew actually complained about it!), Walter Slezak, John Hodiak, Henry Hull, and Hume Cronyn. In 1949 Bill got to clown it up with class-act singer Bing Crosby in a funny adaptation of Mark Twain's "A Connecticut Yankee in King Arthur's Court,

" with Rhonda Fleming and Sir Cedric Hardwicke.

(Photo, l. Cast of The Life of Riley: *Lugene Sanders, William Bendix, Marjorie Reynolds, Wesley Morgan)*

Then in 1944, Bill began acting in a role for which he is probably best remembered by appearing on radio as Chester A. Riley in "The Life of Riley." It was a hit until 1951, and Bill's exclamation of indignation "What a revoltin' development THIS is!" was one of the most famous catchphrases of the 1940s. Unfortunately for viewers, when the show went to TV in 1949, Bill wasn't available to play Riley because of a film contract commitment for the film version of "Life of Riley." The part went, instead, to Jackie Gleason, who won an Emmy for his work. Despite Jackie's great ability to be funny, the show was not popular because fans missed William Bendix as Chester A. Riley. Thus, in 1953 when Bill became available, he once again got to play the bumbling aircraft riveter for TV fans and was a hit from 1953-58. The show also starred Marjorie Reynolds as Riley's wife Peg, Tom D'Andrea as Riley's neighbor and friend Jim Gillis, Lugene Sanders and daughter Babs, Wesley Morgan as son Junior, Gloria Blondell as Honeybee Gillis, Sterling Holloway as inventor Waldo Binney, and wrestler Henry "Bomber" Kulky as friend Otto Schmidtlapp.

Some of Bill's roles in film include: "They Drove By Night" (1940) with Humphrey Bogart, "Who Done It?" (1942) with Abbott & Costello,

"Guadalcanal Diary" (1943) with Lloyd Nolan, "The Hairy Ape" (1944) with Susan Hayward, "Two Years Before the Mast" (1946) with Alan Ladd, "The Blue Dahlia" (1946) with Veronica Lake, "The Life of Riley" (1949) with Rosemary DeCamp, "Detective Story" (1951) with Kirk Douglas, "Blackbeard the Pirate" (1952) with Robert Newton, "Battle Stations" (1956) with John Lund, "The Deep Six" (1958) with Alan Ladd, "Johnny Nobody" (1961) with Nigel Patrick.

Some TV roles include: "Lights Out: The Hollow Man" (1952) with Doris Dowling, "Wagon Train: Around the Horn" (1958) with Ward Bond, "Riverboat: The Barrier" (1959) with Darren McGavin, "The Untouchables: The Tri-State Gang" (1959) with Robert Stack, "Overland Trail" (1960) with Doug McClure, "Mister Ed: Pine Lake" (1961) with Alan Young, "Burke's Law" (1963-64) with Gene Barry.

Bill married Theresa Stefanotti in 1927; they had two children and were together until his death. He received two Stars on the Hollywood Walk of Fame: for radio at 1638 Vine Street and for television at 6251 Hollywood Boulevard in Hollywood, California.

(Photo, l. William Bendix and Sterling Holloway from The Life of Riley*)*

Sadly, Bill died of pneumonia on December 14, 1964 in Los Angeles, California. He is buried at the San Fernando Mission Cemetery in Mission Hills, Los Angeles.

One of Bill's quote's sums up his life and the kind of man he was: "I've had a long, varied, pleasant, eventful career. I don't hate anybody and I don't have any bitter thoughts. I started out without any advantages, but I've been lucky and successful and I've had fun."

BISSELL, WHIT
1909-1996

He may have not been a big man (5'8") but during his career Whit appeared in more than 200 films and scores of TV shows. He was born as Whitner Nutting Bissell on October 25, 1909 in New York City, New York. He went to Hollywood in the 1940s. One of the classic "B" movies he appeared in was "I Was a Teenage Werewolf" (1957). He played the quintessential mad doctor who turned troubled teenager Michael Landon into the wolf man, a role which gave Michael his big break into Hollywood stardom. In the follow-up film Whit gets to play Prof. Frankenstein in "I Was a Teenage Frankenstein" (1957) with Phyllis Coates (of TV Superman fame as Lois Lane), Robert Burton, and Gary Conway. Two more classic horror films of the 50s in which Whit appeared were "Invasion of the Body Snatchers" (1956) with Kevin McCarthy, Dana Wynter, King Donovan, Carolyn Jones and "Creature From the Black Lagoon" (1954) with Richard Carlson, Julia Adams, and Richard Denning.

In his youth Whit was an avid yachtsman and an accomplished fencer (not building; sticking). He attended the University of North Carolina and it was there that he began acting with the Carolina Playmakers. He tried his hand on the Broadway stage before moving on to Hollywood and his long career as a character actor.

His first film was "Holy Matrimony" (1943), a comedy with Monty Woolley, Gracie Fields, and Alan Mowbray.

Whit appeared in several science fiction classics involving time travel, in George Pal's "The Time Machine" (my personal favorite) (1960) with Rod Taylor, Yvette Mimieux (her bio is elsewhere in this book), Alan Young, and Sebastian Cabot; the TV movie "The Time Machine" (1978) with John Beck, Priscilla Barnes, and Rosemary DeCamp; and in 1993 Whit came back to replay his original role as Walter Kemp in a short with Rod Taylor called "Time Machine: The Journey Back," with Alan Young.

Some of Whit's other film roles include, "The Sea Hawk" (1940) with Errol Flynn, "Brute Force" (1947) with Burt Lancaster, "He Walked By Night" (1948) with Richard Basehart, "Tokyo Joe" (1949) with Humphrey Bogart, "The Red Badge of Courage" (1951) with Audie Murphy (look for a biography of Audie elsewhere in this book), "Lost Continent" (1951) with Cesar Romero, "Riot in Cell Block 11" (1954) with Neville Brand, "The Caine Mutiny" (1954) with Humphrey Bogart, "Target Earth" (1954) with Richard Denning, "Johnny Tremain" (1957) with Hal Stalmaster, "Birdman of Alcatraz" (1962) with Burt Lancaster, "5 Card Stud" (1968) with Robert Mitchum, "Airport" (1970) with Burt Lancaster, "Soylent Green" (1973) with Charlton Heston, "Flood!" (1976) with Robert

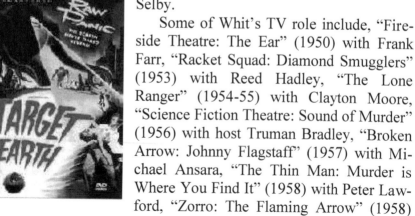

Culp, "The Night Rider" (1979) with David Selby.

Some of Whit's TV role include, "Fireside Theatre: The Ear" (1950) with Frank Farr, "Racket Squad: Diamond Smugglers" (1953) with Reed Hadley, "The Lone Ranger" (1954-55) with Clayton Moore, "Science Fiction Theatre: Sound of Murder" (1956) with host Truman Bradley, "Broken Arrow: Johnny Flagstaff" (1957) with Michael Ansara, "The Thin Man: Murder is Where You Find It" (1958) with Peter Lawford, "Zorro: The Flaming Arrow" (1958) with Guy Williams, "One Step Beyond: Brainwave" (1959) with host John Newland, "Cheyenne" (1957-60) with Clint Walker, "The Roaring 20's: Brother's Keeper" (1960) with Dorothy Provine, "The Ri-fleman" (1959-61) with Chuck Connors, "Tales of Wells Fargo" (1957-62) with Dale Robertson, "Lawman" (1958-62) with John Russell, "The Outer Limits: Nightmare" (1963) with Martin Sheen, "The Fugitive: Scapegoat" (1965) with David Janssen, "The Invaders: Dark Outpost" (1967) with Roy Thinnes, "Cannon: Scream of Silence" (1971-73) with William Conrad (see Bill's bio elsewhere in this book), "Petrocelli: The Pay Off" (1976) with Barry Newman (see Barry's bio in this book), "Project U. F. O.: Sighting 4023" (1976) with Caskey Swaim, "Falcon Crest: Power Play" (1984) with Jane Wyman.

In 1938 he married Adrienne Marden; they had two children and divorced in 1954. Whit married Dilys Mary Shan Jukes in 1954; they had one child and divorced in 1958. In 1967 Whit married Jennifer Raine; they were together until her death in 1993.

Whit received a life career award from the Academy of Science Fiction, Fantasy & Horror Films in 1994.

Sadly, Whit died of Parkinson's disease on March 5, 1996 in Woodland Hills, Los Angeles, California. He is buried in Westwood Village Memorial Park Cemetery in Los Angeles.

BRADBURY, RAY
1920-2012

This giant of science fiction/fantasy writers was born as Ray Douglas Bradbury on August 22, 1920 in Waukegan, Illinois to Leonard Bradbury and Esther Moberg. Perhaps best known for his disturbing look into the future in the novel, "Fahrenheit 451" (1953), as well as "The Martian Chronicles" (1950) and "The Illustrated Man" (1951). Many of his works were made into popular films.

He was an avid reader as a child in Waukegan. Later, in some of Ray's fictional works, Waukegan becomes "Green Town," Illinois. In 1934 the family moved to Hollywood, California and Ray soon grew to love it. He attended Los Angeles High School and was part of the drama club. At the age of 14, Ray had a habit of roller-skating around Hollywood in the hope of meeting celebrities. Some of those he did meet this way include special effects genius Ray Harryhausen and radio star (at that time) George Burns. That worked well as Ray got his first writing assignment at that age writing for the Burns and Allen show!

He began writing at the age of 11, putting his words on used butcher paper when that was the only paper he could get during the Depression. Some of his favorite authors Ray read in his youth include some of my favorites: H. G. Wells, Jules Verne, Edgar Rice Burroughs, and Edgar Allen Poe. He loved the radio show "Chandu the Magician" (starring Gayne Whitman) and could remember entire scripts. At age 16 Ray joined the Los Angeles Science Fiction Society so he could be around people of similar interest.

He met veteran sci fi writer Robert A. Heinlein in 1937, and Mr. Heinlein influenced Ray in the humanistic style of science fiction and fantasy writing.

Ray's first published story was "Hollerbachen's Dilemma" which appeared in the January 1938 issue of "Imagination." Ray published and wrote most of the stories for his own fanzine, "Futuria Fantasia." Ray's first paid work was "Pendulum" which was published in the pulp magazine "Super Science Stories" in November 1941. He earned $15.

His first collection of short stories, "Dark Carnival," was published by Arkham House (owned by the famous horror writer, August Derleth) in 1947. Ray's short story, "Homecoming," won one of the O. Henry Prize Stories of 1947.

He first wrote "The Fireman" as a novella; it was later published as a novel of 50,000 words as "Fahrenheit 451" (the temperature at which paper ignites).

If you're thinking about it, should you go ahead and write? And should you go to college to learn how? Ray always said, "You can't learn to write in college. It's a very bad place for writers because the teachers always think they know more than you do—and they don't."

On writing "Fahrenheit 451" Ray said, "I wasn't trying to predict the future. I was trying to prevent it."

Ray married Marguerite McClure in 1947; they had four daughters and were together until her death in 2003. The best man at Ray's wedding was Ray Harryhausen. They were close friends for over 70 years. Ray had many friends, one close friend being Gene Roddenberry, the creator of "Star Trek."

In 2004 Ray received a National Medal of Arts and he was given a star on the Hollywood Walk of Fame at 6644 Hollywood Boulevard in 2002. Other honors for Ray include an asteroid named in his honor, "9766 Bradbury," and an Apollo astronaut named a crater on the moon "Dandelion Crater" after Ray's novel, "Dandelion Wine." He also received the Grand Master Award from Science Fiction Writers of America in addition to many others.

Many of Ray's works became movies. Some of those include: "It Came From Outer Space" (1953) with Richard Carlson, "The Beast From 20,000 Fathoms" (1953) with Paul Hubschmid, "Moby Dick" (screenplay, 1956) with Gregory Peck, "Fahrenheit 451" (1966) with Julie Christie, "Something Wicked This Way Comes" (1972) with Ben Clennell, "The Screaming Woman" (1972) with Olivia de Havilland, "Something Wicked This Way Comes" (1983) with Jason Robards, "The Halloween Tree" (animated, 1993) with Leonard Nimoy, "It Came From Outer Space II" (1996) with Brian Kerwin.

Many of Ray's works appeared on TV as well. Here are some: "Lights Out: Zero Hour" (1951) with John O'Hare, "Tales of Tomorrow: Homecoming" (1953) with Edith Fellows, "Steve Canyon: The Gift" (1958) with Dean Fredericks, "Alfred Hitchcock Presents" (1956-62) with host Alfred Hitchcock, "The Twilight Zone: I Sing the Body Electric" (1962) with host Rod Serling, "Out of the Unknown: The Fox and the Forest" (1965) with Frederick Bartman, "Curiosity Shop: The Groom" (1971) with Mel Blanc, "The Martian Chronicles" (mini-series, 1980) with Rock Hudson, and many others.

Unfortunately, Ray suffered a stroke in 1999 that left him partially dependent on a wheelchair for getting around. But nothing kept him from his work and he continued to write every day just as he had done for many decades. He used to attend science fiction conventions but gave that up in 2009. Sadly, Ray died on June 5, 2012 in Los Angeles, California after a long illness. He was interred at Westwood Village Memorial Park Cemetery in Los Angeles, California.

The New York Times called Ray Bradbury "the writer most responsible for bring modern science fiction into the literary mainstream." He was a genius at what he did and other writers will remember and continue to learn from him for quite a long time.

BRADY, PAT
1914-1972

Actor, singer, and musician Pat Brady was born Robert Ellsworth Patrick Aloysious O'Brady on December 31, 1914 in Toledo, Ohio to vaudeville performers John O'Brady and Lucille Brewer. He became famous as western legend Roy Rogers' comic sidekick in movies and on TV. He got an early start in show business when, at the age of four, Bob O'Brady set foot on stage in a road show production of "Mrs. Wiggs of the Cabbage Patch." That did it! Little Bob liked it so much he became addicted to show business for life.

Pat also had an interest in music and that was how he met the future Roy Rogers. Bob Brady was performing as a bass guitarist at Sam's Place in Sunset Beach, California in 1935 when he met and became friends with Leonard Slye, a young country and western singer and member of the very popular Sons of the Pioneers. When Len became film legend Roy Rogers he suggested Bob as his replacement in the band. However, since the band already had Bob Nolan and felt that one "Bob" was enough, Bob Brady became Pat Brady.

Pat first starting acting in film with the Sons of the Pioneers opposite western star Charles Starrett for Columbia in 1937 ("Outlaws of the Prairie"). He went to Republic in the early 40s and played comic relief for Roy Rogers as a character named Sparrow Biffle. Long friends by 1951 when Roy went to TV he naturally took Pat with him. Sparrow became Pat Brady (actor and character) in more than 100 episodes of The Roy Rogers Show. Baby Boomer kids have long remembered Pat furiously driving his Jeep, nicknamed "Nellybelle," across the desert either in pursuit or driving away from outlaw danger—sometimes with Roy's faithful dog, Bullet, running just behind.

(Photo, l., Roy Rogers, Trigger, Bullet, and Pat Brady with Nellybelle).

Pat served as a tanker in the 4th Armored Division (my old unit in the late 60s—author) during World War II from 1943-46 and earned two Purple Hearts. He went back with the Sons of the Pioneers until 1948 when their contract was up with Republic, then joined the Riders of the Purple Sage. Pat co-starred with Roy Rogers and Dale Evans on Roy's show from 1951-57; he rejoined The Sons of the Pioneers in 1959, replacing character actor Shug Fisher, and stayed with it until 1967 when he moved to Colorado Springs, Colorado.

Some of the movies Pat appeared in include: "West of Cheyenne" (1938) with Charles Starrett, "Texas Stagecoach" (1940) with Bob Nolan, "Sons of the Pioneers" (1942) with Roy Rogers, "Hands Across the Border" (1944) with Roy Rogers, "Eyes of Texas" (1948) with Andy Devine, "Trigger, Jr." (1950) with Dale Evans, "Pals of the Golden West" (1951) with Roy Rogers.

TV appearances include: "Wagon Train" (1959) with Ward Bond, "G. E. True Theater: The Day of the Hanging" (1959) with Noah Beery Jr., "Walt Disney: The Saga of Windwagon Smith" (1961) with Rex Allen, "30 Minutes at Gunsight" (1963) with Marty Robbins.

Unfortunately, like so many servicemen (and other professions), Pat returned from the war with a drinking problem; it caused him and his family a lot of grief down through the years. One day in 1971 he injured himself (possibly while intoxicated) and subsequently checked himself into a rehab (The Ark in Green Mountain Falls, Colorado on February 26; he died there on February 27, 1971. Pat was buried at the Evergreen Cemetery in Colorado Springs, Colorado in the military section, plot 139-B.

BURGESS, BOBBY
1941-

Update: I'm pleased to write that Bobby has received the Disney Legend Award at the D23 Expo. This honor was bestowed upon him July 18, 2015 for the talented work he provided during the four-year production (1955-59) of TV's Mickey Mouse Club. He joins other former Disney celebrities such as Annette Funicello, Tommy Kirk, and Kevin Corcoran. Congratulations, Bobby!

BURR, LONNIE
1943-

Update: Lonnie has released an updated and expanded edition of his previous book, "Confessions of an Accidental Mouseketeer." This one is called just, "The Accidental Mouseketeer." It has lots more info and photos. Well worth the read. Go to his site at mouseketeerlonnieburr.com and order a signed copy. And check out Lonnie's interview on "Stu's Show" last October 28, 2015; lot of good poop concerning his career and the estrangement between Lonnie and the rest of the Mouseketeers.

CAREY JR., HARRY
1921-2012

Son of the famous actor Harry Carey, Harry Carey Jr. was a well-respected, quality supporting actor. Six foot one inch "Dobe" was born on his parents 1000-acre ranch on May 16, 1921 in Saugus, California as Henry George Carey. Dobe (he was given that nickname by his father because the boy's red hair reminded him of the adobe soil on the ranch) grew up among cattle and horses and learned to speak the Navajo language from the many Indians who worked on his father's ranch. During WWII he enlisted in the Navy and served in the Pacific as a medical corpsman at first, but later was transferred (against his wishes) back to the States to serve under his father's good friend, John Ford, in making training and propaganda films.

After the war, Dobe moved into acting. After a few bit parts, he got to work with John Wayne in Ford's, "Red River" (1948) that also starred Montgomery Clift, Joanne Dru, and father Harry Carey. In 1948, Dobe was back with John Wayne again in "3 Godfathers" that also starred Pedro Armendáriz and Ward Bond. Dobe even appeared in a TV series for Walt Disney Studios entitled, "The Adventures of Spin and Marty" which appeared on the TV show "The Mickey Mouse Club" in 1955.

Dobe appeared in many films. Some of them include: "Rolling Home" (1946) with Jean Parker, "She Wore a Yellow Ribbon" (1949) with John Wayne, "Rio Grande" (1950) with John Wayne, "The Wild Blue Yonder" (1951) with Wendell Corey, "Niagra" (1953) with Marilyn

Monroe, "Island in the Sky" (1953) with John Wayne, "Mister Roberts" (1955) with Henry Fonda, "The Searchers" (1956) with John Wayne, "The Great Locomotive Chase" (1956) with Fess Parker, "Noose for a Gunman" (1960) with Jim Davis, "Cheyenne Autumn" (1964) with James Stewart, "The Rare Breed" (1966) with James Stewart, "The Devil's Brigade" (1968) with William Holden, "Dirty Dingus Magee" (1970) with Frank Sinatra, "Cahill, U. S. Marshall" (1973) with John Wayne, "The Long Riders" (1980) with David Carradine, "Gremlins" (1984) with Phoebe Cates, "The Whales of August" (1987) with Bette Davis, "Back to the Future Part III" (1990) with Michael J. Fox, "Last Stand at Saber River" (1997) with Tom Selleck.

(Photo, l. Harry Carey Jr. in Red River, *1948)*

Some of Dobe's TV roles include: "Waterfront: The Race" (1954) with Preston Foster, "The Lone Ranger: Return of Dice Dawson" (1955) with Clayton Moore, "Broken Arrow" (1958) with Michael Ansara, "Tombstone Territory: Holcomb Brothers" (1960) with Pat Conway, "Men Into Space: Shadows on the Moon" (1960) with William Lundigan, "Tales of Wells Fargo: Gunman's Revenge" (1961) with Dale Robertson, "Whispering Smith: Safety Valve" (1961) with Audie Murphy (see Audie's bio in this book), "Have Gun—Will Travel" (1958-63) with Richard Boone, "Lassie" (1961-63) with Jon Provost, "Wagon Train" (1959-65) with John McIntire, "Bonanza" (1959-67) with Lorne Greene, "Cimarron Strip: The Sound of a Drum" (1968) with Stuart Whitman, "The Virginian" (1967-70) with James Drury, "The Streets of San Francisco: The Hard Breed" (1974) with Karl Malden, "Gunsmoke" (1959-74) with James Arness, "Police Woman: Sons" (1978) with Angie Dickinson, "Little House on the Prairie: A New Beginning" (1980) with Michael Landon, "Knight Rider: Not a Drop to Drink" (1982) with David Hasselhoff, "William Tell" (1987-88) with Will Lyman, "B. L. Stryker: Auntie Sue" (1989) with Burt Reynolds.

Dobe married Marilyn Fix—the daughter of actor Paul Fix—in 1944; they have four children and remained together until Harry's death.

In 1987 Dobe was awarded the Golden Boot by the Motion Picture & Television Fund Foundation and in 2003 he got the Silver Spur Award from Reel Cowboys. Dobe also was awarded a Star on the Hollywood Walk of Fame 6363 Hollywood Boulevard in 1960.

On family and friends, Dobe once said: "I loved Duke (John Wayne) and he loved me. The thing is, I don't think he ever forgave me for being the son of Harry Carey. Harry Carey was his absolute hero."

Dobe published a book called "Company of Heroes: My Life as an Actor in the John Ford Stock Company" in 1996.

Sadly, Harry Carey Jr. died of natural causes on December 27, 2012 in Santa Barbara, California. He was interred at the Westwood Memorial Park Cemetery in Los Angeles, California.

CARRADINE, JOHN
1906-1988

This well-known character actor, best remembered for his roles in horror and western movies, was born Richmond Reed Carradine on February 5, 1906 in New York City, New York to parents William Reed Carradine and Genevieve Winifred Richmond. Father William was a correspondent for the *Associated Press* and mother Genevieve a surgeon. John was born in Greenwich Village but grew up in Kingston, New York. Unfortunately, his father died when he was only two years old and his mother later remarried a man who often needlessly beat him.

John attended the Episcopal Academy in Merion Station, Pennsylvania where he developed his eloquent diction and powerful memory retention. But his decision to become an actor occurred when he was just 11 years old and saw a stage production of Shakespeare's "The Merchant of Venice." He made his own stage debut in New Orleans, Louisiana, in 1925 in "Camille." His travels took him to Los Angeles, California, where John managed to get some work in theater. It wasn't long before he became friends with actor John Barrymore and landed a job as a set designer for the legendary director, Cecil B. DeMille. His classic baritone voice caught DeMille's attention and he hired him to do voice-overs in several of DeMille's movies, including "The Sign of the Cross" (1932).

(Photo, l. John Carradine as Dracula)
    In 1930, the six-foot-one-inch-tall, aristocratic-appearing actor auditioned for "Dracula" but was beat out by the soon-to-become legendary horror actor, Bela Lugosi. He also lost the title role in "Frankenstein" (1931) to Boris Karloff, but later got to play Dracula in "House of Frankenstein (1944) and "House of Dracula" (1945). He had been working as John Peter Richmond but legally changed his name to John Carradine in 1937.

One of John's stand-out roles was as the ill-fated preacher Casey in John Ford's 1940 classic, "The Grapes of Wrath" which starred Henry Fonda, Jane Darwell, Charley Grapewin, and John Qualen (look for a great, dramatic scene with John as the destitute and crazed Muley Graves). He gave another fine performance as Maj. Cassius Starbuckle in Ford's western epic, "The Man Who Shot Liberty Valance" (1962), which starred John Wayne, James Stewart, Vera Miles, Lee Marvin, Edmond O'Brien, and Andy Devine.

In the 1940s John toured with his own Shakespearean company to perform in "Macbeth" and "Hamlet." And he was on Broadway in "The Madwoman of Chaillot" (1945) and "A Funny Thing Happened on the Way to the Forum" (1962).

John married his first wife, Ardanelle Cosner, in 1935; they had two children, Bruce (adopted) and David and divorced in 1944. He married actress Sonia Sorel in 1944 and they had three children, Christopher, Keith, and Robert; they divorced in 1957. In 1957 John married Doris Grimshaw who died in a fire in her apartment in 1971; they were separated at the time. He married Emily Cisneros in 1975; they were together until his death in 1988.

During John's prolific career, he appeared in at least 225 movies, though he claimed many more. Films include: "Tol'able David" (1930) with Noah Beery, "The Invisible Man" (1933) with Claude Rains, "The Black Cat" (1934) with Boris Karloff, "Les Misérables" (1935) with Charles Laughton, "The Prisoner of Shark Island" (1936) with Warner Baxter, "Captains Courageous" (1937) with Spencer Tracy, "The Hurricane" (1937) with Jon Hall, "Kidnapped" (1938) with Freddie Bartholomew, "The Hound of the Baskerville's" (1939) with Basil Rathbone, "Western Union" (1941) with Randolph Scott, "Revenge of the Zombies" (1943) with Gale Storm, "Bluebeard" (1944) with Jean Parker, "A Christmas Carol" (1947) with Somar Alberg. "The Egyptian" (1954) with Jean Simmons, "The Ten Commandments" (1956) with Charlton Heston, "The Unearthly" (1957) with Myron Healey, "The Cosmic Man" (1959) with Bruce Bennett, "Tarzan the Magnificent" (1960) with Gordon Scott, "Cheyenne Autumn" (1964) with Richard Widmark, "The Wizard of Mars" (1965) with Roger Gentry, "Munster, Go Home!" (1966) with Fred Gwynne, "Blood of Dracula's Castle" (1969) with Paula Raymond, "Bigfoot" (1970) with Joi Lansing, "Blood of Ghastly Horror" (1971) with Tommy Kirk, "The Shootist" (1976) with John Wayne, "The White Buffalo" (1977) with Charles Bronson, "Vampire Hookers" (1978) with Bruce Fairbairn, "Frankenstein Island" (1981) with Robert Clarke, "Antony and Cleopatra" (1983) with James Avery, "Buried Alive" (1990) with Robert Vaughn.

Some of John's TV appearances include: "The Adventures of Ellery Queen" (1951) with Lee Bowman, "The Adventures of Ozzie and Harriet" (1954) with Ozzie Nelson, "Climax!" (1955-56) with William Lundigan, "Cheyenne" (1957) with Clint Walker, "Matinee Theatre" (1956-57) with John Conte, "Have Gun – Will Travel" (1958) with Richard Boone, "Sugarfoot" (1958) with Will Hutchins, "Bat Masterson" (1959) with Gene Barry, "The Rifleman" (1959) with Chuck Connors, "Gunsmoke" (1955-59) with James Arness, "Wanted: Dead or Alive" (1960) with Steve McQueen, "Wagon Train" (1958-60) with Ward Bond, "The Red Skelton Hour" (1956-62) with Red Skelton, "The Alfred Hitchcock Hour" (1965) with Vera Miles, "Branded" (1965-66) with Chuck Connors, "The Big Valley" (1969) with Richard Long, "Bonanza" (1961 and 1969) with Lorne Greene, "Love, American Style" (1973) with Rosemary DeCamp, "Kung Fu" (1972-75) with David Carradine, "Captains and the Kings" (1976) with Ray Bolger, "McCloud" (1977) with Dennis Weaver, "Vega$" (1978) with Robert Urich, "Fantasy Island" (1982) with Ricardo Montalban, "The Twilight Zone" (1986) with host Rod Serling.

John was inducted into the Hall of Great Western Performer of the National Cowboy and Western Heritage Museum in 2003. He was also awarded a Star on the Hollywood Walk of Fame on February 8, 1960; it is located at 6240 Hollywood Boulevard.

About his acting career, John once said, "I've made some of the greatest films ever made—and a lot of crap, too!"

Sadly, John Carradine died of natural causes on November 27, 1988 in Milan, Lombardy, Italy. He was buried at sea as a Naval Sea Burial between the California coast and Santa Catalina Island.

CHARLES, RAY
1930-2004

This genius of modern pop music was born Ray Charles Robinson on September 23, 1930 in Albany, Georgia to Bailey Robinson and Aretha William. "The High Priest of Soul" was a singer, songwriter, musician, and composer and, for the most part, created the genre of soul music by combining rhythm and blues and gospel into music that Ray composed for Atlantic Records. While he was with ABC Records in the 1960s, Ray was one of the first Afro-American musicians to be granted artistic control by a mainstream record company.

While Ray was still an infant, the family moved to his mother's hometown of Greenville, Florida. Ray learned to play the piano by watching and being shown by musician Wylie Pitman at the Red Wing Café. He was only three when he started to play. Because of glaucoma, Ray began to lose his sight at the age of three or four and was completely blind by seven. But that didn't hold him back. Even though he didn't want to go, Ray attended the Florida School for the Deaf and the Blind in St. Augustine, Florida from 1937 to 1945 and it was there that he developed his musical talent. At first Ray played classical music on the piano, but he was more interested in playing the jazz and blues he heard on the family radio. Every Friday the South Campus Literary Society was wowed by the child prodigy Ray Robinson who played the piano and sang popular songs for the people who came. Soon he assembled his own band, RC Robinson and the Shop Boys, and Ray sang his own arrangement of "Jingle Bell Boogie." He also sang on local radio.

After leaving school, Ray moved to Jacksonville, Florida. He played the piano for bands at the Ritz Theatre in LeVilla for $4 a night. To look for more opportunities in a bigger city, at the age of 16 Ray moved to Orlando, Florida. Things were picking up but the following year, 1947, Ray moved to Tampa where he got two jobs. The first was playing piano for Charles Brantley's Honeydippers; the second as a member of a country group called The Florida Playboys. This is when he began the habit of wearing his iconic sunglasses and modeled himself after the popular singer, Nat King Cole. Around this time he made his first four recordings: "Wondering and Wondering," "Walking and Talking," "Why Did You Go?," and "I Found My Baby There."

In the early 50s, Ray recorded two rhythm and blues singles under the name of Ray Charles for Swing Time Records, "Baby, Let Me Hold Your Hand" and "Kissa Me Baby." Both became big hits.

In 1952, Ray began recording for Atlantic Records. By 1959 he had reached the Billboard Top Ten with some of his many fine songs. In 1956 Ray had recruited and all-girl singing group named the Cookies; he renamed them The Raelettes and had them back him on all his recordings.

Ray's contract with Atlantic expired in 1959 and he signed with ABC-Paramount Records. The first hit single Ray released through ABC (1960), "Georgia on My Mind," received national acclaim and two Grammys. He earned another Grammy with his follow-up hit, "Hit the Road, Jack." In 1962, Ray created his own record label, Tangerine Records. By 1965 Ray's heroin habit was getting him in trouble with the law and so he decided to go to a rehab in Los Angeles. The following year found him out and back on the charts with "I Don't Need No Doctor" and "Let's Go Get Stoned." He recorded Buck Owens' "Crying Time" and reached no. 6 with that one.

Unfortunately for Ray, by the end of the 60s his kind of music was getting beat out by psychedelic rock. But he hung in there with r & b and gospel music. In 1972 he released an album called "A Message From the People" with his gospel-influenced version of "America the Beautiful." Some didn't like Ray's version of a national treasure but many more loved it. A 1975 release of Stevie Wonder's hit "Living for the City" was a big hit for Ray and got him another Grammy.

In November 1977 Ray went on TV as the host of "Saturday Night Live." Then in 1979 Ray's "Georgia On My Mind" was proclaimed Georgia's state song.

In 1983 Ray signed with Columbia Records and recorded a string of country albums. Among working with other country artists, Ray recorded a hit duet with his lifelong friend, Willie Nelson: "Seven Spanish

Angels." Ray appeared at the presidential inauguration of Ronald Reagan in 1985 and sang his version of "America the Beautiful" at Game 2 of the World Series between the Arizona Diamondbacks and the New York Yankees in 2001. In 2003, Ray performed at the Montreal International Jazz Festival. His last public appearance was on April 30, 2004 at the dedication of Ray's music studio as an historic landmark in Los Angeles, California.

(Photo, l. Here's Ray with President Ronald Reagan and First Lady Nancy in 1984)

In 1951 Ray married Eileen Williams; they divorced in 1952. In 1955 he married Della Beatrice Howard; they divorced in 1977. With other women of Ray's acquaintance, he had 12 children.

During his long career, Ray appeared in film and on TV. Some of these include: "Shindig!" (1965) with many other musical talents, "In the Heat of the Night" (1967) with Sidney Poitier, "Spirits of the Dead" (1968) with Brigitte Bardot, "The Johnny Cash Show" (1970), "Ash Wednesday" (1973) with Henry Fonda, "Hudson & Halls" (1976) with Lynsey de Paul, "Saturday Night Live" (1977) with Don Pardo, "Any Which Way You Can" (1980) with Clint Eastwood, "The Blues Brothers" (1980) with John Belushi, "Limit Up" (1989) with Dean Stockwell, "Quantum Leap" (1990 & 1993) with Scott Bakula, "The Nanny" (1997 & 1998) with Fran Drescher, "

Ray was awarded a Star on the Hollywood Walk of Fame at 6777 Hollywood Boulevard.

In 2003, Ray had hip replacement surgery and was planning to go back on tour until he began suffering from other ailments. Sadly, Ray died at his home in Beverly Hills, California on June 10, 2004 from acute liver disease. He was interred at the Inglewood Park Cemetery in Inglewood, California.

Ray possessed one of the most recognizable voices in American music and his contributions to the art certainly have no equal. He influenced other highly successful artists, such as Elvis Presley, Van Morrison, Billy Joel, Aretha Franklin, and Stevie Wonder, to name a few. He certainly became a legend during his own lifetime and will long be remembered.

COLBERT, ROBERT
1931-

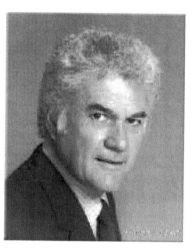

Actor Robert Lewis Colbert was born on July 26, 1931 in Long Beach, California. Bob served in the Army and while stationed at Okinawa worked evenings as a disc jockey for Radio Free Asia station KSBK in Suri; during the day he was a company clerk with an MP unit. His first appearance acting came after a woman in Air Force Special Services heard him sing and asked him to appear in one of their shows, "The Caine Mutiny Court-Martial." That did it; Bob was hooked on acting. When he returned to the States he performed on stage and was seen by actor Mickey Shaughnessy who recommended him to a talent agent. Before long he was contracted by Warner Bros.

Bob is probably best remembered for his role as Dr. Doug Phillips, a scientist on the Irwin Allen, science fiction TV classic "The Time Tunnel," on ABC from 1966-67, which starred James Darren and Whit Bissell (for bios of Jimmy and Whit see their names elsewhere is this book), Lee Meriweather, and John Zaremba.

According to Bob during his career he never pushed to become a big star but was instead content to be under contract with Warner Bros. and work steadily. He never had a desire for major stardom and consequently be mobbed by adoring fans. He also stated that he very much enjoyed working with other cast members and the crew of "The Time tunnel" and wished it had lasted longer than it had.

(Photo, l. Here's Bob in a scene from The Time Tunnel, *1966)*

Some of Bob's film appearances include: "Under Fire" (1957) with Rex Reason; "Have Rocket – Will Travel" (1959) with The Three Stooges (Moe Howard, Larry Fine, Joe DeRita); "A Fever in the Blood" (1961) with Angie Dickinson; "The Mayor" (1965) with Chad Everett; "The Lawyer" (1970) with Barry Newman; "The Killer Who Wouldn't Die" (1976) with Mike Connors; "Scorpion" (1986) with Robert Logan; "Grand Tour: Disaster in Time" (1992) with Jeff Daniels.

Some of his many TV appearances include: "The Alaskans" (1960) with Roger Moore; "Sugarfoot" (1959 & 1960) with Will Hutchins; "Cheyenne" (1960) with Clint Walker; "Maverick" (1960-61) with James Garner; "The Roaring 20's" (1962) with Dorothy Provine; "Bronco" (1959-62) with Ty Hardin; "Wagon Train" (1962 & 1963) with John McIntire; "77 Sunset Strip" (1960-64) with Edd Byrnes; "Perry Mason" (1965) with Raymond Burr; "Hawaii Five-0" (1969) with Jack Lord; "Death Valley Days" (1963-70) with host Stanley Andrews; "Alias Smith and Jones" (1972) with Ben Murphy & Pete Duel; "Quincy, M. E." (1978) with Jack Klugman; "Knight Rider" (1984) with David Hasselhoff; "Simon & Simon" (1985) with Gerald McRaney & Jameson Parker; "Dallas" (1987) with Larry Hagman; "In the Heat of the Night" (1991) with Caroll O'Connor; "Baywatch" (1994-95) with David Hasselhoff.

Bob married dancer/songwriter Dottie Harmony in 1961; divorced in 1976. They had two children. He is now semi-retired but does cameo appearances and photo signings at science fiction and western conventions.

COLE, TOMMY
1941-

Update: I'm pleased to write that Tommy has received the Disney Legend Award at the D23 Expo. This honor was bestowed upon him July 18, 2015 for the talented work he provided during the four-year production (1955-59) of TV's Mickey Mouse Club. He joins other former Disney celebrities such as Annette Funicello, Tommy Kirk, and Kevin Corcoran. Congratulations, Tommy!

CONRAD, WILLIAM
1920-94

This actor, producer, and director was involved in radio, film, and TV for over 50 years. His fine resonant voice is fondly remembered for his portrayal on radio as the character Marshall Matt Dillon, a role he created on the popular radio version of "Gunsmoke" from 1952-61. But Bill will probably be best remembered as the corpulent but effective private investigator Frank Cannon on the popular action TV series, "Cannon." This show ran 1971-76, a Quinn Martin production than aired on CBS. In 1981 he once again played a PI on the action show, "Nero Wolfe," which ran on NBC and co-starred Lee Horsley (TV's Matt Houston). Unfortunately, it didn't do as well as "Cannon" and only ran for 14 episodes. Bill did better on his next crime drama as prosecutor J. L. McCabe on "Jake and the Fatman." This one ran 1987 to 1992 on CBS and co-starred Joe Penny as "the Fatman's" investigator, Jake Styles.

Of course, no one can forget his base voice ominously narrating other QM shows such as "The Fugitive," and "The Invaders." (Bill did the opening and closing narration while the announcer was Dick Wesson for both series—not Hank Simms as is sometimes erroneously reported. He did other QM shows like "Cannon" and "The Streets of San Francisco.")

Bill was born John William Cann Jr. on September 27, 1920 in Louisville, Kentucky to movie theater owners John William Cann and Ida

Mae Upchurch. While he was in high school the family moved to Southern California. In Fullerton College Bill majored in drama and literature. He soon began his career in show business as an announcer, writer, and director for local radio station KMPC.

Bill was a fighter pilot in the U. S. Army Air Corps during WWII and later a producer/director of the Armed Forces radio service. He mustered out with the rank of captain.

He appeared on radio as far back as 1940 in the horror anthology series, "The Hermit's Cave," that ran in Los Angeles for four years. Bill has stated that he probably played more than 7500 roles on radio during his career. No mean feat.

In film, Bill usually got to play the heavy. One of his best remembered, early roles was as Max, one of the hit men sent to eliminate Burt Lancaster's character in the 1946 film noir, "The Killers," which also starred Ava Gardner, Edmond O'Brien, and Albert Dekker. But he got to play a good guy, the local district commissioner in George Pal's "The Naked Jungle" (1954) with Charlton Heston, Eleanor Parker, and Abraham Sofaer.

In 1961 Bill moved to Warner Bros. to produce and direct. He made the film noir masterpiece, "Brainstorm" (1965) which starred Jeffrey Hunter, Anne Francis, and Dana Andrews. He was also the executive producer of "Countdown," a sci fi thriller released in 1968 which starred Robert Duvall and James Caan.

(Photo, below. William Conrad as Cannon, 1972)

Fans of William Conrad might remember it was his distinctive voice that narrated the fondly-remembered, Clio Award-winning 1971 public service announcement about pollution that featured Iron Eyes Cody as the weeping Indian beset by inconsiderate litter bugs. Fans might also remember that Bill narrated the popular animated series, "Rocky and Bullwinkle" from 1959 to 1964.

Some of Bill's on-screen performances include, "Four Faces West" (1948) with Joel McCrea, "Cry Danger" (1951) with Dick Powell, "The Conqueror" (1956) with John Wayne, "-30-" (1959) with Jack Webb,

"Geronimo" (narrator 1962) with Chuck Connors, "Brainstorm" (1965) with Jeffrey Hunter, "The Brotherhood of the Bell" (1970) with Glenn Ford, "Cannon" (1971) with Linda Day George, "Attack on Terror" (narrator 1975) with Ned Beatty, "Night Cries" (1978) with Susan Saint James, "Battles: The Murder That Wouldn't Die" (1980) with Lane Caudell, "Shocktrauma" (1982) with Philip Akin, "Killing Cars" (1986) with Senta Berger.

Some of Bill's TV roles include, "The Rough Riders: The Governor" (1958) with Kent Taylor, "Bat Masterson: Stampede at Tent City" (1958-61) with Gene Barry, "77 Sunset Strip: The Target" (1963-64) with Efrem Zimbalist Jr., "The Name of the Game: The Power" (1969) with Robert Stack, "O'Hara, U. S. Treasury" (1971) with David Janssen, "Tales of the Unexpected" (narrator 1977) with Bill Bixby, "Police Squad: Testimony of Evil" (1982) with Leslie Nielsen, "Murder, She Wrote: Death Takes a Curtain Call" (1984) with Angela Lansbury.

In 1943 Bill married June Nelson; they were together until her death in 1957. In 1957 Bill married fashion model Susan Randall; they had one son, Christopher and were together until her death in 1979. He then married Tipton "Tippy" Stringer (widow of TV newscaster Chet Huntley) in 1980; they were together until his death.

Sadly, Bill died from congestive heart failure on February 11, 1994 in Los Angeles, California. He was buried in the Lincoln Terrace section of Forest Lawn Cemetery, Hollywood Hills, near Los Angeles.

Bill was posthumously elected to the National Radio Hall of Fame in 1997.

CORCORAN, KEVIN
1949-2015

Update: Sadly, I have to report that former child star, director and producer Kevin Corcoran passed away on October 6, 2015 in Burbank, California from colorectal cancer. He is survived by his wife, the former Laura Soltwedel. Kevin was a vital part of the Walt Disney Studios during the 1950s and 60s, playing the mischievous and high-strung younger brother opposite actor Tommy Kirk in five movies,

Here's Kevin and Spike (who played Old Yeller) in the 1957 film of the same name.

including "Old Yeller" (1957) and "The Shaggy Dog" (1959). Nick-named "Moochie" (by Walt Disney) in several of his productions, Kevin starred in "Toby Tyler, or Ten Weeks With a Circus" (1960) and "Johnny Shiloh" (1963). After retiring from acting in the late 60s, Kevin continued to work in the picture business (as he called it) as an assistant director and producer.

We'll miss you, Moochie.

CRANE, BOB
1928-1978

Actor, radio personality and professional drummer, Bob was born Robert Edward Crane in Waterbury, Connecticut on July 13, 1928.

Bob began his career in show business as a disk jockey for WLEA in Hornell, New York in 1950. After he moved to Los Angeles he got his own show at KNX radio. Bob had such a dynamic, on-air persona as the host that it wasn't long before he became known as "The King of the Los Angeles Airwaves." His was the number-one rated morning show and he had smash guest stars such as Marilyn Monroe, Bob Hope, Frank Sinatra, and Ronald Reagan.

Since he was working for CBS, Bob soon became noticed by some of their top executives who gave him guest appearances on "The Dick Van Dyke Show." Later, Donna Reed suggested Bob as a regular role on her TV sitcom, "The Donna Reed Show" as Dr. David Kelsey (1963-65). In 1965 he was offered and accepted the lead role in his own TV series, the World War II sitcom "Hogan's Heroes," which ran until 1971. This 5'10" leading man was on a roll and both Bob (he was nominated for an Emmy twice) and the show became very popular.

In 1973 he starred in and toured for five years with a play called "Beginner's Luck." Bob once again got his own show, "The Bob Crane Show," in 1975 but it was cancelled after just three months.

He enlisted in the National Guard in 1948 and was honorably discharged in 1950. In 1949 he married high-school sweetheart Anne Terzian; they had three children and divorced in 1970. While filming

"Hogan's Heroes" Bob met and married Patricia "Patti" Olson (stage name Sigrid Valdis) in 1970. They had one son and adopted a daughter and remained married (though separated) until his death in 1978.

(Photo, l. Bob and wife Patti Crane)

One interesting aspect of this actor's life that seems to be dwelt upon is Bob's incredible sexual addiction. As he never denied it and no one who knew him did either, I mention it here for what it's worth; it has been suggested that it may have contributed to his death. Bob even had a large video collection of his sexual escapades that he had been putting together since about 1956.

Some of the movies in which Bob appeared were, "Return to Peyton Place" (1961) with Carol Lynley, "The New Interns" (1964) with Dean Jones, "The Wicked Dreams of Paula Schultz" (1968) with Elke Sommer, "Arsenic and Old Lace" (1969) with Helen Hayes, "Superdad" (1973) with Kurt Russell.

TV appearances include, "Disneyland: The Survival of Sam the Pelican" (1954) with Kurt Russell, "Twilight Zone" (1961) with Dean Jagger, "The Alfred Hitchcock Hour" (1963) with William Conrad, "The Red Skelton Hour" (1967) with John Banner, "Night Gallery" (1971) with host Rod Serling, "Love, American Style" (1969-71) with various actors, "Police Woman" (1974) with Angie Dickinson, "Ellery Queen" (1976) with Jim Hutton, "Quincy M. E." (1977) with Jack Klugman.

Lastly, we must mention the violent and mysterious circumstances surrounding Bob's death. While "Hogan's Heroes" was on the air, it is alleged that Richard Dawson—one of Bob's co-stars—introduced him to John Henry Carpenter, a member of the video department at Sony Electronics. Bob was interested in photography and Carpenter had access to video recording equipment; thus, he was able to tape Bob in at least several of his sexual encounters.

Supposedly he was friends with Carpenter for a number of years but it was said they had a falling out. While his play, "Beginner's Luck," was running in Scottsdale, Arizona, Bob was allegedly bar hopping with Carpenter looking for women to pick up on June 28, 1978. Some sources say that had an argument (one source said that Carpenter wanted to have sex with Crane) and Bob told him their friendship was at an end. Sometime during the early morning hours of June 29, the actor was brutally bludgeoned (some say with a video camera tripod; the actual murder weapon was never found) on the left side of his head and a VCR cable wrapped around his neck (post mortem)—murdered while he slept in his Winfield Apartments, hotel room in Scottsdale. His body was discovered that afternoon by a friend who came to see him—actress Victoria Berry Wells (she was co-starring in Crane's stage play, "Beginner's Luck," at that time).

The eye of police suspicion turned upon former friend John Henry Carpenter. His rental car had blood smears (actually just a few spots) in it that matched Bob Crane's blood type (only 10% of the population had that type; unfortunately, more accurate DNA testing did not exist at that time). Carpenter was investigated but due to insufficient evidence, charges were never filed.

Police reopened the case in 1992 but, though DNA testing was now available it could not be used because so little of the original blood sample remained. In spite of mostly circumstantial evidence Carpenter was brought to trial in 1994. He was found not guilty and maintained his innocence until he died in 1998. Officially, the murder remains unsolved.

Bob Crane's remains were interred at Oakwood Memorial Park in Chatsworth, California on July 5, 1978. However, in 1999 his widow, Patricia Olson had him exhumed and moved to Westwood Village Memorial Park in the Westwood Village area of Los Angeles, California, not too far from Natalie Wood's grave. When she died in 2007, Olson was buried next to him under her stage name, Sigrid Valdis.

CROTHERS, SCATMAN
1910-1986

This actor, singer, dancer, and musician was born Benjamin Sherman Crothers on May 23, 1910 in Terre Haute, Indiana to Benjamin Crothers and Donnie Donel. He got his nickname in 1932 when the Scatman auditioned for a radio show in Dayton, Ohio. The director didn't think his given name was catchy enough, so Benjamin thought up the name, "Scat Man," for his style of singing. At the time a type of vocal jazz was known by the handle, "scat singing," an improvisation style with nonsense syllables. Ella Fitzgerald was considered one of the greatest of scat singers. Later, Benjamin's nickname was shortened to "Scatman" by Arthur Godfrey.

He is probably best known for his role at the psychic Dick Halloran in Stanley Kubricks' hit horror movie, "The Shining" (1980) with Jack Nicholson (a close friend of Scatman) and Shelley Duvall. Also as Louie the Garbage Man on TV's "Chico and the Man" (1974-78) with Jack Albertson and Freddie Prinze.

Scatman started his musical career at the age of 15 as a drummer in a band in a speakeasy in Terre Haute; he also played guitar. Interestingly, gangster Al Capone often frequented that establishment. Scatman moved to Oakland in the 1930s, and to Los Angeles, California in 1952. His first movie appearance was in "Meet Me at the Fair" (1953) with Dan Dailey.

He appeared in four of Jack Nicholson's films, including the hit "One Flew Over the Cuckoo's Nest" (1975) which also starred Louise Fletcher and Will Sampson (see Will's biography in my first book, "Hollywood Celebrities: Where Are They Now?").

Some of the films in which Scatman appeared include: "Yes sir, Mr. Bones" (1951) with Chick Watts, "East of Sumatra" (1953) with Jeff Chandler, "The Gift of Love" (1958) with Lauren Bacall, "Tarzan and the Trappers" (1958) with Gordon Scott, "The Sins of Rachel Cade" (1961) with Angie Dickinson, "The Patsy" (1964) with Jerry Lewis, "Alvarez Kelly" (1966) with William Holden, "Hello, Dolly!" (1969) with Barbara Streisand, "The AristoCats" (voice over, 1970) with Phil Harris, "The King of Marvin Gardens" (1972) with Jack Nicholson, "Win, Place or Steal" (1974) with Dean Stockwell, "Linda Lovelace for President" (1975) with Linda Lovelace, "The Shootist" (1976) with John Wayne, "Scavenger Hunt" (1979) with Richard Benjamin, "Bronco Billy" (1980) with Clint Eastwood, "Zapped!" (1982) with Scott Baio, "Twilight Zone: The Movie" (1983) with Dan Akroyd, "The Journey of Natty Gann" (1985) with John Cusack.

Some of Scatman's TV roles include: "Climax!: One Night Stand" (1955) with host William Lundigan, "Alfred Hitchcock Presents: Don't Interrupt" (1958) with host Alfred Hitchcock, "Bonanza: The Similar" (1961) with Lorne Greene, "Dragnet 1967: The Missing Realtor" (1967) with Jack Webb, "Harlem Globetrotters" (voice over, 1970-71) with Eddie "Rochester" Anderson, "Kojak: The Corrupter" (1973) with Telly Savalas, "Kolchak: The Night Stalker: The Zombie" (1974) with Darren McGavin, "Sanford and Son: The Stand-In" (1975) with Redd Foxx, "Petrocelli: Jubilee Jones" (1976) with Barry Newman, "The Incredible Hulk: My Favorite Magician" (1979) with Bill Bixby, "Magnum, P. I.: Lest We Forget" (1981) with Tom Selleck, "Hill Street Blues: The End of Logan's Run" (1984) with Daniel J. Travanti, "This Is Your Life: Scatman Crothers" (1984) with host Ralph Edwards, "The Transformers" (voice over, 1984-86) with Frank Welker.

He married Helen M. Sullivan in 1937; they had one child and stayed together until his death. Scatman was awarded a Star on the Hollywood Walk of Fame at 6712 Hollywood Boulevard in 1981.

Unfortunately, Scatman was a heavy smoker all his life and was diagnosed with lung cancer in 1985. He died of pneumonia at his home in Van Nuys, California on November 22, 1986. Scatman is buried at Forest Lawn Cemetery in Hollywood, California.

CULKIN, MACAULAY
1980-

Macaulay Carson Culkin, one of the most famous American child stars (#2 after Shirley Temple), was born on August 26, 1980 in New York City, New York to Christopher Culkin and Patricia Brentrup; the pair never married. At the age of four, Mac (or Mack) appeared on stage in "Bach Babies" at the New York Philharmonic. He did numerous roles on stage, in TV and film during the 80s including a kidnapping victim on "The Equalizer: Something Green" (1988) with Edward Woodward. Mac was the first child star to receive $1,000,000 for a role (a supporting one, at that) for his part in "My Girl" (1991) with Jamie Lee Curtis.

Probably best remembered for his portrayal of Kevin McCallister in

"Home Alone" (1990) with Joe Pesci and Daniel Stern. Out of a possible 200 kids who auditioned for the part of Kevin, director Chris Columbus said that no one else came near Mac's ability to become the character. The movie was a blockbuster and grossed over $285 million in the U. S. alone. It was followed with the equally good "Home Alone 2: Lost in New York" (1992) also with Joe Pesci and Daniel Stern.

(Photo, l. Macaulay Culkin in a shot from Home

Alone, *1990)*

A real change of character came for Mac when he stopped being cute and became the youthful psychotic murderer, Henry, in "The Good Son" (1993) with Elijah Wood and Wendy Crewson. He earned $5,000,000 for that one!

Unfortunately, good roles started to elude him after he turned 14 (an old story for child stars in Hollywood) and he pretty much retired after that, though came back in 2003 to do a few more roles. In 1998 Mac married Rachel Miner; they were divorced in 2000.

Some of Mac's other movie roles include, "Rocket Gibraltar" (1988) with Burt Lancaster, "Uncle Buck" (1989) with John Candy, "Only the Lonely" (1991) with Maureen O'Hara, "Getting Even With Dad" (1994) with Ted Danson, "Richie Rich" (1994) with Edward Herrmann, "Party Monster" (2003) with Wilson Cruz, "Saved" (2004) with Jena Malone, "Sex and Breakfast" (2007) with Kuno Becker, "Adam Green's Aladdin" (2016) with Adam Green.

A few of his TV appearances include, "Wish Kid" (voice 1991) with Quinn Culkin, "Frasier" (voice 1994) with Kelsey Grammer, "Will and Grace" (2003) with Eric McCormack, "Kings" (2009) with Ian McShane, "Robot Chicken" (voice 2005-10) with Seth Green, "The Jim Gaffigan Show" (2015 and 2016) with Jim Gaffigan.

Must mention that early in April 2016 there were online reports of Mac's death. However, they were wholly fictitious, another fake celebrity death to appear online in a string of such reports coming form an unknown source(s). I'm glad to state that Mac is currently (as of April 10, 2016) alive and well.

After having made enough money by the age of 12 to never have to work again, Mac says now that he won't take just any role and hasn't for a long time. He did "Party Monster" because it intrigued him. He now lives in an expensive New York City apartment he owns and spends most of his time painting, writing, and "whatevering," as Mac puts it.

When you're as rich as he is, you can do pretty much whatever you want without working anymore. Cool, Mac.

DANO, ROYAL
1922-94

Well known character actor Royal Edward Dano, Sr. was born on November 16, 1922 in New York City, New York to Caleb Edward Dano and Mary O'Connor Dano. He left home at the age of 12 and traveled throughout the south and into the west.

Eventually, after attending New York University, this 6'2" aspiring actor performed as part of the Army's 44th Special Service Provisional Company during World War II; he rose to the rank of Sergeant. Later he appeared on Broadway in "Finian's Rainbow." He was nominated as one of the Promising Actors of 1949. Being tall with a gaunt face and a lean build, Mr. Dano usually found himself being cast in roles during his 42-year career as gloomy or sinister characters (as in "Something Wicked This Way Comes)—difficult parts he always did well.

His first credited movie role was as The Moocher in Joseph Pevney's fine murder mystery, "Undercover Girl," (1950) with Alexis Smith and Scott Brady. Mr. Dano does well and his character learns the hard way not to become "one of the guys" of a gangster mob.

During his career Mr. Dano appeared in many westerns and mysteries. He once played Abraham Lincoln in a five-part presentation entitled "Mr. Lincoln" on the TV show, "Omnibus" (1952-53). But he might possibly be best remembered for his short but stunning portrayal of the mysterious prophet Elijah in John Huston's movie version of "Moby

 Dick" (1956; directed by John Huston, screenplay by Ray Bradbury). After having seen the movie, who could forget Mr. Dano's haunting presence and his doom-filled words? Watch this fine movie and see what I mean. *(Photo, l. Royal Dana as Elijah, the prophet, in* Moby Dick*).*

Royal Dano also appeared in the following movies: "Reign of Terror" (1949) with Robert Cummings, "The Red Badge of Courage" (1951) with Audie Murphy, "Bend of the River" (1952) with James Stewart, "The Far Country" (1954) with James Stewart, "The Trouble With Harry (1955) with Edmund Gwenn, "Tension at Table Rock" (1956) with Richard Egan, "Never Steal Anything Small" (1959) with James Cagney, "Hound Dog Man" (1959) with Fabian, "Cimarron" (1960) with Glenn Ford, "King of Kings" (1961) with Jeffrey Hunter, "Savage Sam" (1963) with Tommy Kirk, "Gunpoint" (1966) with Audie Murphy, "Day of the Evil Gun" (1968) with Arthur Kennedy, "The Undefeated" (1969) with John Wayne, "The Culpepper Cattle Co." (1972) with Gary Grimes, "Electra Glide in Blue" (1973) with Robert Blake, "The Outlaw Josey Wales" (1976) with Clint Eastwood, "In Search of Historic Jesus" (1979) with John Anderson, "Something Wicked This Way Comes" (1983) with Jason Robards, "House II: The Second Story" (1987) with Jonathan Stark, "The Dark Half" (1993) with Timothy Hutton.

Some of his TV appearances include: "Lights Out: The Elevator" (1949) with Helen Dumas, "Suspense" (1949-54) with various actors, "Father Knows Best" (1957) with Robert Young, "Wanted: Dead or Alive" (1959) with Steve McQueen, "Alfred Hitchcock Presents" (1957 & 1960), "Have Gun – Will Travel" (1961) with Richard Boone, "The Rifleman" (1959-62) with Chuck Connors, "Wagon Train" (1959 & 1963) with John McIntire," The Fugitive" (1964) with David Janssen, "Rawhide" (1962-65) with Clint Eastwood, "Bonanza" (1962-67) with Lorne Greene, "Daniel Boone" (1966-67) with Fess Parker, "Death Valley Days" (1965-70) with host Stanley Andrews, "Gunsmoke" (13 appearances) with James Arness, "Cannon" (1973) with William Conrad, "How the West Was Won" (1977; mini-series) with James Arness, "Quincy M. E." (1977 & 1979) with Jack Klugman, "Amazing Stories" (1986) with Mark Hamill, "Twin Peaks" (1990) with Kyle MacLachlan.

He married Peggy Ranck and they remained together until his death. They had two children: actor Rick Dano and Royal E. Dano, Jr.

Sadly, Mr. Dano died of a heart attack after a car collision on May 15, 1994 in Los Angeles. He was buried at the Los Angeles National Cemetery in Los Angeles, California

DARREN, JAMES
1936-

This actor had appeared in teenage oriented films in the 50s and gained much popularity as a teen singer in the 60s with such hits as "Her Royal Majesty" and "Goodbye Cruel World" (for Colpix Records). He was born James William Ercolani on June 8, 1936 in Philadelphia, Pennsylvania. His name was changed to Darren by Columbia Pictures when he was signed with them in 1956. The choice of "Darren" was inspired by the Kaiser-Darrin sports car popular in the 1950s.

Jimmy became a big star in the "Gidget" movies series as Moondoggie, a character he played three times. He stated that he hated "Gidget Goes to Rome" and was afraid of being typed in the character he was playing in those films. But Jimmy did enjoy doing movies like "Diamond Head" and "The Guns of Navarone."

But Jimmy is probably best remember for his starring role in the Irwin Allen, science fiction TV classic, "The Time Tunnel," which aired two seasons from 1966-67. This series didn't last long (30 episodes) but had a large following and is well remembered by loyal fans. Star James Darren stated that it was way ahead of its time for television thanks mainly to producer Irwin Allen who was a futurist and envisioned many of the ideas. It was televised in color. (Rarely remembered, color TV sets were available in the 50s but they were grossly expensive.)

Fans will recall that two brilliant scientists, Doug Phillips and Tony Newman, had invented a method to travel in time. Funded by the federal government in 1968, the installation was called Project Tic-Toc and was buried beneath the desert somewhere in Arizona. Luck being what it is, at the first trial operation of the Time Tunnel, scientists Dr. Tony Newman (played by Jimmy) and Dr. Doug Phillips (played by Robert Colbert whose bio is elsewhere in this book) are hurled back in time and space and find themselves stranded aboard the Titanic on its perilous maiden voyage across the Atlantic. The date: You guessed it. It's April 15, 1912 and the massive ship's fateful collision with an iceberg is only hours away. Fellow scientists Dr. Swain, Dr. MacGregor and project head Lt. Gen. Kirk strive frantically to bring the hapless pair back before they are killed. This pilot episode was called "Rendezvous with Yesterday" and aired September 9, 1966 on ABC.

Some of the films in which Jimmy appeared include: "Rumble on the Docks" (1956) with Robert Blake, "Gidget" (1959) with Sandra Dee, "Gidget Goes Hawaiian" (1961) with Deborah Walley, "Gidget Goes to Rome" (1963) with Cindy Carol, "City Beneath the Sea" (1971) with Stuart Whitman (and Robert Colbert), "The Lives of Jenny Dolan" (1975) with Shirley Jones, "Scruples (1981) with Sean

Allan, "Random Acts" (2001) with Victoria Foyt.

(Photo, l. James Darren as Tony Newman in The Time Tunnel *and wearing the iconic, green turtleneck. He stated that he had no clue whose idea it was that his character had to wear that sweater but that is was made of wool and itched like hell!)*

Some of Jimmy's television appearances include, "The Lineup" (1955) with Warner Anderson, "The Donna Reed Show" (1959 & 1961) with Donna Reed, "Voyage to the Bottom of the Sea" (1966) with Richard Basehart, "Love American Style" (1971) with Stuart Margolin, "Black Sheep Squadron" (1977) with Robert Conrad, "Hawaii Five-0" (1978 & 1979) with James MacArthur, "T. J. Hooker" (1982-1986) with William Shatner,

"Silk Stalkings" (1994) with Charlie Brill, "Star Trek: Deep Space Nine" (1998-99) with Avery Brooks.

Jimmy also directed some TV episodes of "Hunter," "The A-Team," "Melrose Place," and others. Interestingly, he was a close friend of Frank Sinatra and sometimes sang in Mr. Sinatra's style.

He married childhood sweetheart Gloria Terlitsky in 1955, divorced in 1958; they had one son. Jimmy married Miss Denmark of 1958, Evy Norlund, in 1960. They remain together and have two sons.

Jimmy has not appeared in an acting role since 2001.

DAVIS, JOAN
1907-1961

This fine comedic actress was born Madonna Josephine Davis on June 29, 1912 (some sites claim DOB as 1907 but her grave marker says 1912, as does the California Death Index) in Saint Paul, Minnesota to LeRoy Davis and Nina Mae Sinks. She appeared in many B-movie comedies but began her career in vaudeville. Probably her best remembered role is as Joan Stevens, wife of Judge Bradley Stevens on NBC's sitcom, "I Married Joan." It aired from 1952-55 and starred Jim Backus as the judge. Actress Hope Emerson (whose biography appears elsewhere in this book) appeared in the pilot episode. Joan's TV younger sister was played by Beverly Wills, her real-life daughter.

Joan had been a performer since childhood; she also appeared in vaudeville in 1931 with her husband, Si Wills—they were billed as Wills and Davis. But Hollywood stardom was not far off. Tall (5'5") and lanky, with a comically flat speaking voice, Joan soon became one of the few female physical clowns of her time. Her first film was a short subject called "Way Up Thar" (1935) with a then unknown actor named Roy Rogers (still billed with his real name, Leonard Slye). Probably Joan's best comedic role in a movie was as Camille Brewster in Universal Pictures' "Hold That Ghost" (1941) with Bud Abbott and Lou Costello, Evelyn Ankers, Richard Carlson and some fine period numbers by the Andrews Sisters and Ted Lewis.

Joan was also a radio personality as a regular on "The Rudy Vallee Show" from 1941-45. Her contract with the United Drug. Co. in 1941 earned her $1,000,000 a year for four years. Other fine radio shows followed but probably not as lucrative as that one. Still, her earnings from that contract enabled Joan to set up her own production company, Joan Davis Enterprises, later on. The company produced television shows.

(Photo, l. Here's Joan Davis about to do one of her famous screams in Hold That Ghost)

In 1931, Joan married actor Serenus M. "Si Wills" Williams; they had one daughter, Beverly, and were divorced in 1948.

Some of Joan's roles in the movies include, "The Holy Terror" (1937) with Jane Withers, "Sing and Be Happy" (1937) with Tony Martin, "Just Around the Corner" (1938) with Shirley Temple, "Too Busy to Work" (1939) with Spring Byington, "Two Latins From Manhattan" (1941) with Jinx Falkenburg, "Show Business" (1944) with Eddie Cantor, "George White's Scandals" (1945) with Jack Haley, "If You Knew Susie" (1948) with Eddie Cantor, "The Groom Wore Spurs" (1951) with Ginger Rogers, "Harem Girl" (1952) with Peggy Castle.

(Photo, l. Joan in a photo still from The Joan Davis Show)

Joan was awarded two Stars on the Hollywood Walk of Fame, one for her contribution to motion pictures (at 1501 Vine Street) and one for her radio work (in the 1700 block of Vine Street).

Sadly, Joan died of a sudden heart attack on May 22 (California Death Index says May 23), 1961 at her home in Palm Springs, California. She was interred at the Holy Cross Cemetery mausoleum (block 46 crypt D1) in Culver City, California. (Another blow to her family came on October 24, 1963 when Joan's daughter, Beverly, her mother and two grandchildren died in a house fire in Palm Springs. The fire was caused by Beverly falling asleep while smoking.)

As to her famous countenance, Joan was quoted as saying, "I don't get it. Unless my mirror lies to me, I'm not bad looking. But let me get one look at that face on the screen and I'm sick for a week!"

I thought she looked and did quite well. Thanks for being there, Joanie, and making us all laugh with your talent.

DENVER, JOHN
1943-97

One of the most popular recording artists of the 1970s, John Denver was born as Henry John Deutschendorf Jr. on December 31, 1943 in Roswell, New Mexico to Air Force Lt. Col. Henry John Deutschendorf Sr. and Emma Swope. During his career, John released around 300 songs, about 200 of which he wrote himself.

Being in the military meant that the Denver family had to move around a lot. That made things difficult for the shy young Henry, so often being the new kid on the block. For a time they lived in Tucson, Arizona and young Henry was in the Tucson Boys Chorus for two years. Then they moved to Alabama and later Fort Worth, Texas where he graduated from Arlington Heights High School. Interested in music, at age 11 Henry's grandmother gave him an acoustic guitar. He liked it and learned to play it quite well, good enough that by the time he was in college Henry was performing at local clubs. That's when he adopted the surname "Denver" after the capital of his favorite state, Colorado. Randy Sparks of The New Christy Minstrels suggested he change his name completely and so Henry became John Denver.

In 1963, John dropped out of college and moved to Los Angeles where he sang in clubs that specialized in offering folk singers. John joined The Mitchell Trio in 1965, replacing founder Chad Mitchell. But in 1969 John wisely gave up singing with a band and went solo. He released an album for RCA Records, "Rhymes & Reasons," shortly thereafter. John wrote "Leaving on a Jet Plane," a big hit for Peter, Paul and

Mary and for himself in England. Two more albums followed in 1970: "Take Me to Tomorrow" and "Whose Garden Was This."

The hit, "Take Me Home, Country Roads" followed in 1971 and in 1972 came the big one, "Rocky Mountain High." At this time John adopted a casual style of dress commonly associated with the American West (created by artist Anna Zapp) which included his long, blonde hair and "granny" glasses. John started the seasonal "Rocky Mountain Christmas" and made it a hit show.

(Photo, l. George Burns and John Denver in a scene from Oh, God!*)*

His "An Evening With John Denver" won the 1974-75 Emmy for Outstanding Special, Comedy-Variety or Music.

John began making appearances on "The Muppet Show" which became a regular thing and began a lifelong friendship with Muppet creator, Jim Henson. In 1977 John got into movies by appearing with veteran comedic great, George Burns, in "Oh, God!" which also starred Teri Garr, Donald Pleasance, Ralph Bellamy, and Paul Sorvino.

In 1977 John co-founded The Hunger Project to aid in world hunger. He supported it until his death and was also appointed by Pres. Jimmy Carter to serve on the President's Commission on World Hunger. John created the theme song for it, "I Want to Live."

In the mid-70s John's father taught him to fly a small plane and together, in 1980, they co-hosted a TV special entitled, "The Higher We Fly: the History of Flight." And because of John's interest in flying he became involved with the business of NASA and worked to begin the "Citizens in Space" program. In 1985 John actually passed the rigorous physical exam for space travel and was a finalist for the first citizen's trip on the Space Shuttle in 1986 (luckily, as it turned out, he was not chosen). The following year, after the Space Shuttle Challenger's terrible disaster, John dedicated his song, "Flying for Me," to all astronauts.

In 1994 John published his autobiography, "Take Me Home." In it he candidly speaks of his use of cannabis, LSD, and cocaine, as well as his history of domestic violence.

He was inducted into the Songwriters Hall of Fame in 1996. In 1997 John composed his last song, "Yellowstone, Coming Home" for a TV episode of the "Nature" series.

Some of the films in which John appeared include, "The Christmas Gift" (1986) with Jane Kaczmarek, "Foxfire" (1987) with Jessica Tandy,

"Higher Ground" (1988) with John Rhys-Davies, "Walking Thunder" (1997) with James Read.

Some TV roles include, "Owen Marshall, Counselor at Law: The Camerons Are a Special Clan" (1973) with Arthur Hill, "McCloud: The Colorado Cattle Caper" (1974) with Dennis Weaver, "Walt Disney's Wonderful World of Color: The Leftovers" (1986) with Pamela Adlon, "Magnum, P. I." (1987) with Tom Selleck, "Son in Law" (1993) with Pauly Shore. *(Photo, above. John Denver in concert)*

In 1967 John married Anne Martell; he wrote "Annie's Song" for her. After he wrote "Rocky Mountain High" the couple bought a residence in Aspen, Colorado, where John lived the rest of his life. The couple also adopted two children; they were divorced in 1983. John married Australian actress Cassandra Delaney in 1988; they had one daughter and divorced in 1993.

Because of a number of DUI convictions, in 1995 the FAA decided that John should no longer fly a plane due to his failure to abstain from alcohol.

But John loved flying. In 1974 he had bought a Learjet which he used to fly himself to concerts. He also collected vintage biplanes, two Cessna 210s, as well as other aircraft. Yet fate was not to be denied. Sadly, on October 12, 1997, John was killed when his experimental Adrian Davis Long-EZ plane crashed into Monterey Bay near Pacific Grove, California; John was flying alone. Although his remains were recovered his head and body were so seriously disfigured that normal identification—even with dental records—was impossible. Fingerprints had to be taken to prove that the body was actually that of John Denver.

John was flying illegally because his medical certification to fly from the FAA had been revoked due to alcohol misuse. But the day of the crash no alcohol was found in John's body. The cause of the crash seems to be the inability of the pilot to easily switch fuel tanks in flight, a necessity when the first tank runs out. The designer of the Long-EZ had foolishly placed the switch over and behind the pilot's head, making it necessary for the pilot to turn 90 degrees to reach it. According to the

NTSB accident report, because of that the pilot would have inadvertently moved the control stick to the left and down; that would cause the plane to suddenly yaw left and down. Witnesses who saw the crash said John's plane was only a few hundred feet above the water when it suddenly pitched down. Thus, this is probably what happened and caused the crash. Sadly, if John had refueled before his last flight of the day, he would not have had to switch tanks and the accident would not have occurred.

After funeral services at Faith Presbyterian Church in Aurora, Colorado, Johns remains were cremated and his ashes scattered in the Rocky Mountains of Colorado. In 2007 a plaque commemorating the loss of John Denver to the world was placed near the crash site in Pacific Grove, California.

On October 24, 2014 John was awarded at Star on the Hollywood Walk of Fame at 7065 Hollywood Boulevard.

DEVINE, ANDY
1905-77

Raspy-voiced, comedic actor and cowboy sidekick for decades, Andrew Vabre Devine appeared in hundreds of movie and TV roles. Andy was born October 7, 1905 in Flagstaff, Arizona to railroad employee Thomas Devine Jr. and Amy Ward. Of Irish ancestry, his paternal grandfather was born in County Tipperary, Ireland, in 1842. The family emigrated to the United States in 1852.

Thomas Devine moved his family to Kingman, Arizona in 1906 and purchased the four-story Hotel Beale at 325 E. Front Street; the hotel still exists under that name in the Route 66/downtown area. However, in 1955 Front Street was renamed and dedicated as Andy Devine Avenue in the honor of Kingman's favorite son. The designation was announced on TV during the show, "This Is Your Life," while honoring Andy Devine.

(Photo, l., Guy Madison and Andy acting in TV's "Adventures of Wild Bill Hickok.")

Andy is probably best known for his comic sidekick role as 300-pound Jingles P. Jones on TV's western saga, "Adventures of Wild Bill Hickok" (1951-58, although Guy Madison's daughter, Bridget, says 1951-59). Originally a long-running radio program, both shows starred Guy Madison as Hickok and Andy Devine as Jones. They spent each episode righting wrongs and riding the range on their faithful mounts, Buckshot (Wild Bill) and Joker

(Jingles). Originally the role of Jingles was offered to Burl Ives but reportedly he turned it down. Just as well; Ives was a good actor and singer but didn't have the comedic talent that Andy did.

He attended Northern Arizona University in Flagstaff and played football for Santa Clara University in Santa Clara, California. Later six-foot-tall Andy played semi-pro football under the self-made-up-name of Jeremiah Schwartz (to avoid jeopardizing his amateur standing). That experience got him his first good film role in "The Spirit of Notre Dame" (1931) starring Lew Ayres and Sally Blane.

After college Andy was interested in acting so in 1926 he relocated to Hollywood and worked as a lifeguard at nearby Venice Beach while he waited for his big break in the movies. His football experience got him an uncredited part in "The Spirit of Notre Dame." In 1933 director John Ford picked him for a small part in his film, "Doctor Bull," which starred Will Rogers, Marion Nixon, and Veral Allen.

By the way, his peculiar voice—according to Andy and his son, Tad—was the result of a childhood accident. Andy was running with a, of all things, a *curtain rod* in his mouth, fell, and rammed it through the roof of his mouth. He was unable to speak for a year. When his speech returned he had the odd, duel-tone effect that became his lifelong trade mark.

One of my favorite westerns in which Andy appeared was "The Man Who Shot Liberty Valance" (1962) starring John Wayne, James Stewart, Vera Miles, Lee Marvin, Edmond O'Brien, and Woody Strode. In this horse opera Andy plays Marshall Link Appleyard who never can quite get up the courage or the gumption to do his job but always has room for another meal at the local restaurant—"on the cuff," of course!

(Photo, r., Andy starring on his TV children's show, Andy's Gang)

In 1962 (season 3) Rod Serling cast him as veteran bender and stretcher of the truth, Somerset Frisby. In the classic episode of "Hocus-Pocus and Frisby," Andy's character has perhaps fibbed once too often and no one in town will believe that he was abducted by actual invading aliens from space and taken aboard their flying saucer. He has to outwit them and escape, frightening the aliens away and saving the Earth in the process. What was that admonition about crying wolf once too often? Still, Andy's performance was a treasure to behold.

A few of the 400 film roles Andy had include, "That's My Daddy" (1928) with Reginald Denny, "Man Wanted" (1932) with Kay Francis, "Wake Up and Dream" (1934) with Russ Columbo, "The Farmer Takes A Wife" (1935) with Henry Fonda, "A Star is Born" (1937) with Janet Gaynor, "Stagecoach" (1939) with John Wayne, "Buck Benny Rides Again" (1940) with Jack Benny, "North to the Klondike" (1942) with Broderick Crawford, "Ali Baba and the Forty Thieves" (1944) with Jon Hall, "Canyon Passage" (1946) with Dana Andrews (Andy's two, small sons also appeared in this one), "Grand Canyon Trail" (1948) with Roy Rogers, "Island in the Sky" (1953) with John Wayne, "Around the World in Eighty Days" (1956) with David Niven, "Two Rode Together" (1961) with James Stewart, "The Over-the-Hill Gang" (1969) with Walter Brennan, "Myra Breckinridge" (1970) with Mae West, "A Whale of a Tale" (1977) with William Shatner.

Some of Andy's TV roles include, "Andy's Gang" (1955-60; his own show), "Wagon Train" (1959) with Robert Horton, "Burke's Law" (1964) with Gene Barry, "Flipper" (1964-65) with Luke Halpin, "Gunsmoke" (1969) with James Arness, "Walt Disney's Wonderful World of Color: Ride a Northbound Horse" (1969) with Carroll O'Connor, "Alias Smith and Jones" (1972) with Ben Murphy.

Andy married Dorothy House in 1933; they remained together until his death and had two sons, Tad and Denny. He was awarded two Stars on the Hollywood Walk of Fame at 6258 and 6366 Hollywood Boulevard.

Sadly, Andy developed leukemia and died on February 18, 1977 in Orange, California. He was cremated and his ashes given to family.

DIAMOND, BOBBY
1943-

This child actor was born Robert LeRoy Diamond on August 23, 1943 in Los Angeles, California. He is probably best remembered for his TV role as Joey Clark Newton on the children's show, "Fury." That fine western drama ran 1955 to 1960 and also starred Peter Graves, William Fawcett, Jimmy Baird (brother of former Mouseketeer Sharon Baird), and, of course, Fury (played by Beauty). Bobby's character, Joey, had gotten in trouble with the law but had been adopted by Jim Newton, owner of the Broken Wheel Ranch. Joey makes friends with a wild, black stallion and names him, Fury. Bobby said he very much enjoyed doing the show. "Working outside all summer and getting to ride a horse? What's not to like!"

(Photo, below. Cast of Fury: *Peter Graves, Beauty, Bobby Diamond, and William Fawcett)*

Bobby almost was cast as Robbie on "My Three Sons" but, because of the convenience of getting to the set, he chose to do the "Nanette Fabray Show" instead; unfortunately, it only ran for one season as opposed to "Sons" going 12 years. But he did land the job as Dunky Gillis on CBS's "The Many Loves of Dobie Gillis" (1959-63) with Dwayne Hickman and Bob Denver.

His only starring role in a film was in "Airborne" (1962) which also starred Carolyn Byrd. It was not well received by critics who found the story line contrived and predictable. Two more of his film roles were in the musical "Billie" (1965) with Patty Duke and the slasher movie "Scream" (1981) with Pepper Martin and Hank Worden (Hank's bio is elsewhere in this book).

Other film roles for Bobby include, "The Greatest Show on Earth" (1952) with James Stewart, "Untamed" (1955) with Tyrone Power, "To Hell and Back" (1955) with Audie Murphy, "This Could Be the Night" (1957) with Jean Simmons, "The Silent Gun" (1969) with Lloyd Bridges.

Some of Bobby's TV roles include, "Father Knows Best: No Partiality" (1955) with Robert Young, "Code 3: The Search" (1957) with Richard Travis, "The Rebel: Paperback Hero" (1961) with Nick Adams, "Pete and Gladys: Love Go Away" (1961) with Harry Morgan, "The Twilight Zone: In Praise of Pip" (1963) with Jack Klugman, "Wagon Train" (1960 & 1964) with Ward Bond and John McIntire, "Mister Ed: Don't Skin That Bear" (1965) with Alan Young, "The Fugitive: The Savage Street" (1967) with David Janssen, "My Three Sons" (1964-70) with Fred MacMurray, "Emergency +4" (1974) with Peter Haas, "Midnight Caller: Kid Salinas" (1990) with Gary Cole.

In 1964 Bobby graduated from Ulysses S. Grant High School in Van Nuys, California. He got his BA from the California State University in Northridge and in 1970 his Juris Doctor degree from the San Fernando Valley College of Law in Woodland Hills, California. In 1972 Bobby was admitted to the California bar and soon commenced the practice of law in Los Angeles and still does.

In 1986 Bobby married Tara Parker; they have one son, Robby.

DOMINO, FATS
1928-

This rotund man of R & B musical fame was the most popular black, rock and roll star of the 1950s. It was sheer joy to watch and listen to Fats' laid back, piano boogie-woogie style. Fats was born Antoine Domino Jr. on February 28, 1928 in New Orleans, Louisiana (the jazz capital of the world) to French Creole parents; his father, Antoine Sr., was an accomplished violinist. It was his father who inspired Fats to take up music and his uncle, jazz guitarist Harrison Verrett, taught him even more.

In 1947, a well-known New Orleans bandleader named Billy Diamond heard a young pianist performing at a backyard barbeque. Diamond was impressed enough by Fats that he asked him to play with his band, the Solid Senders, at the Hideaway Club. It was Diamond who nicknamed young Antoine "Fats" because Billy was reminded of famous pianists Fats Waller and Fats Pichon when he heard Antoine play.

His first big hit, "The Fat Man," was released by Imperial Records in 1950; by 1953 it had sold one-million copies. Fats hit the pop charts in 1955 with "Ain't That a Shame," which made it to the Top Ten. In 1956, Imperial released Fats' first album, "Rock and Rollin' with Fats Domino." It made No. 17 on the "Pop Albums" chart.

Fats did an old (1940) favorite, "Blueberry Hill," in 1956. It zoomed up to No. 2 in the Top 40, and on to No. 1 on the R&B charts for 11 weeks. "Blueberry Hill" sold more than 5 million copies in 1956-57. "I'm Walkin'" made No. 4 in 1957.

Then Hollywood called and Fats appeared in two musical comedies: "Shake, Rattle and Rock" (1956) with Mike "Touch" Connors and Lisa Gaye; and "The Girl Can't Help It" (also 1956) with Jayne Mansfield and Edmond O'Brien. Always good for Fats' career, Imperial Records released "Walkin' to New Orleans" in 1960 and it went to No. 6. But then Fats moved to ABC-Paramount Records in 1963. Maybe he thought that would be a career boost for him but, unfortunately as it turned out, ABC required Fats to move to and record in Nashville with a whole new team of moguls. The new team changed Fats' vocal style to a more country-western sound and his popularity dropped almost immediately. His release of "Red Sails in the Sunset" in 1963 went into the Top 40 but most of his other songs went downhill. The British Invasion in 1964 didn't help Fats' career as the youthful public's record tastes changed drastically.

Fats continued to record through the 70s and appeared in one film in 1980 ("Any Which Way You Can" with Clint Eastwood) and sang the Country Chart hit, "Whiskey Heaven," in it. In the 1980s Fats decided he would stay put in New Orleans no matter what. He has a mansion there and claims he can't get any good food anywhere else. Fats has been inducted into the Rock and Roll Hall of Fame (1986) and received the Grammy Lifetime Achievement Award (1987). He was awarded the National Medal of Arts in 1998 and has a star on the Hollywood Walk of Fame at 6616 Hollywood Boulevard in Hollywood, California.

When Hurricane Katrina blasted New Orleans in August 2005 no one heard from Fats and the general public thought he had been killed by the fierce storm. But on September 1, CNN reported that Fats and his family had been rescued by a Coast Guard helicopter and taken to safety. Fats stated that "We've lost everything." However, his home was later rebuilt but in the meantime they lived in Harvey, Louisiana.

Fats went back to work on stage on May 19, 2007 at Tipitina's in New Orleans; a full house greeted his return. In 2012 he appeared on TV on "Treme" with Rob Brown.

Fats was in one other film: "Jamboree!" (1957) with Jerry Lee Lewis and Frankie Avalon.

In 1948 Fats married Rosemary Hall and were together until her death in 2008; they had eight children.

To say that Fats was an important influence on the music of the 50s, 60s, and 70s is an understatement and his music was and is just plain good fun to listen to. Way to go, Fats!

DOUGLAS, DONNA
1933-2015

Update: Sadly, I have to report that Donna died January 1, 2015 of pancreatic cancer. She still had been traveling to personal appearances, gardening at home, spending time with friends and family, and answering her fan mail. Donna died at the Baton Rouge General Hospital in Baton Rouge, Louisiana. She was interred in the Bluff Creek Cemetery in East Feliciana Parish, Louisiana.

DOW, TONY
1945-

This former TV actor and later a film producer, director, writer, and sculptor was probably best known for portraying Wally Cleaver, the older straight man to his younger brother and little rascal, Theodore "Beaver" Cleaver on the TV sitcom "Leave It to Beaver." This classic show ran on CBS from 1957-58 and then moved over to ABC from 1958-63. The show starred Jerry Mathers as the Beaver and Hugh Beaumont and Barbara Billingsley as the boys' parents.

(Photo, below. Here's the cast of Leave It to Beaver, *1957-63, l-r: Tony Dow, Barbara Billingsley, Hugh Beaumont, and Jerry Mathers in the lower right corner)*

Tony was born Tony Lee Dow on April 13, 1945 in Hollywood, California to designer John Stevens and stunt woman and former Mack Sennett bathing beauty Muriel Virginia Montrose Dow. At one point young Tony was a Junior Olympics diving champion. When acting entered his life as it does almost everyone living in Hollywood, Tony got the part of Wally Cleaver in a casting call with almost no previous acting experience.

In 1965 Tony joined the National Guard. During the 70s he attended journalism school while simultaneously working in construction.

In 1969 Tony married Carol Marlow; they had one child and divorced in 1980. Tony married Lauren Shulkind in 1980; they have one child.

(Photo, below. The cast of The New Leave It to Beaver *show. Barbara Billingsley seated, center with Jerry Mathers in the rear, 2nd from the left and Tony Dow in the rear, standing, on the right)*

For a time from the late 70s to the early 80s, Tony teamed up with his former TV co-star, Jerry Mathers, and performed in dinner theaters. Today Tony is involved in building luxury condominiums. In 1983 Tony and Jerry and most of the old cast (except Hugh Beaumont who had died the year before) appeared in the reunion movie "Still the Beaver." It was followed up in 1984 with a "Still the Beaver" TV show on the Disney Channel. That ran until 1985 and the following year TBS picked it up where it aired until 1989.

Some of Tony's film roles include, "A Great American Tragedy" (1972) with George Kennedy, "Death Scream" (1975) with Raul Julia, "Still the Beaver" (1983) with Jerry Mathers, "Back to the Beach" (1987) with Annette Funicello, "Playing Patti" (1998) with Richard Beymer, "Dickie Robert: Former Child Star" (2003) with David Spade.

Some of the TV roles in which Tony appeared include, "Dr. Kildare: Four Feet in the Morning" (1963) with Richard Chamberlain, "My Three Sons: Guest in the House" (1964) with Fred MacMurray, "Mr. Novak" (1963-65) with James Franciscus, "Lassie: Hanford's Point" (1968) with Jon Provost, "Mod Squad: The Sands of Anger" (1971) with Michael Cole, "The Hardy Boys/Nancy Drew Mysteries: The Creatures Who Came on Sunday" (1977) with Shaun Cassidy, "Quincy, M. E.: Suffer the Little Children" (1983) with Jack Klugman, "Murder, She Wrote: Crossed Up" (1987) with Angela Lansbury, "Suspense: The Dead Man" (2015) with Rich Federman.

Tony is also a modern art sculptor working in bronze. He is represented by the Karen Lynne Gallery in Beverly Hills. One of his sculptures was on display in the back yard of former "Beaver" co-star and longtime friend, Barbara Billingsley but since she passed away in 2010 I'm not sure if it's still there.

Driscoll, Bobby
1937-68

Fine child actor and once the highest paid performer for the Disney Studios, was born Robert Cletus Driscoll on March 3, 1937 in Cedar Rapids, IA to Cletus Driscoll, an insulation salesman, and Isabelle Kratz, a former schoolteacher. His most famous role was probably as the youthful but capable Jim Hawkins in Walt Disney's classic pirate adventure film, "Treasure Island" (1950) starring Robert Newton, Basil Sydney, and Finlay Currie. This fine action movie (from the Robert Louis Stevenson classic book of the sane title) had previously been done by MGM in 1934 and starred Wallace Beery and Jackie Cooper. However, that had been filmed in black and white; Disney was the first to release it in color.

In 1943, due to the father's health problems, the family moved to Los Angeles, California. Mr. Driscoll was urged by his barber to try to get the cute Bobby into movies. An audition at MGM got Bobby a bit part in "Lost Angel," a 1943 drama starring the relatively new child actress Margaret O'Brien, James Craig, Marsha Hunt, and Keenan Wynn.

He next appeared as Al Sullivan, the youngest of the famed World War II Sullivan brothers family in 20th-Century Fox's "The Fighting Sullivans" (1944) with Thomas Mitchell and Anne Baxter. Bobby did remarkably well and was beginning to be considered a *Wonder Child* with natural acting ability.

Bobby went to the Disney Studios in 1946 and became the first actor to be put under contract there in "Song of the South," also starring Luana Patten and James Baskett as Uncle Remus. Also for Disney, Bob became the voice of the animated children's classic, "Peter Pan" (1953).

In March of 1953, Walt Disney dropped Bob's contract, the reason later given as a severe case of acne in the pubescent teenager. Bob's $1750 weekly salary had made him the highest paid Disney actor during that time. Considered by other studios as "Disney's kid actor," he found it hard to get serious roles in movies and went to television.

Bob's parents took him out of the Hollywood Professional School and enrolled him in the University High School in Westwood. But, he later said, the former Disney child star was not accepted as "one of the gang" and was ridiculed by his fellow students. He became depressed, his grades dropped drastically, and Bob began to experiment with drugs. After getting into fights and "being afraid all the time," he asked his parents to return him to the Professional School, which they did. *(Photo, below, l., Bobby with Robert Newton as Long John Silver in Disney's* Treasure Island, *1950)*

Unfortunately, his heroin drug use continued. In 1956 Bob was arrested for marijuana possession but the charge was dropped. Acting roles became fewer and fewer.

In December 1956 he married Marilyn Jean Rush (yes, that's the right date; they eloped to Mexico to do it); they had three children; later separated and divorced in 1960.

In 1961 Bob was sentenced as a drug addict and incarcerated at the Narcotic Rehabilitation Center of the California Institution for Men in Chino, California; he left early in 1962.

Some of the films in which Bob appeared include, "Sunday Dinner For a Soldier" (1944), with Anne Baxter, "If You Knew Susie" (1948) with Eddie Cantor, "The Window" (1949; Bobby received an Oscar for this one) with Arthur Kennedy, "The Happy Time" (1952) with Charles Boyer, "The Scarlet Coat" (1955) with Cornel Wilde, "The Party Crashers" (1958) with Connie Stevens.

TV appearances include, "The Walt Disney Christmas Show" (1951) with Kathryn Beaumont, "Dragnet" (1953) with Jack Webb, "The Loretta Young Show" (1954) with Chick Chandler, "Crusader" {1956} with Brian Keith, "TV Reader's Digest" (1955-56) with Dabbs Greer, "The Millionaire: The Norman Conover Story" (1958) with Marvin Miller, "Rawhide" (1959-60) with Clint Eastwood, "Dirt" (a short underground film, 1965) with Andy Warhol—this was Bobby's last film.

After Bob's release from the Rehabilitation Center in 1962, he was unable to find acting work and soon became embittered. He told friends:

"I have found that memories are not very useful. I was carried on a silver platter . . . and then dumped into the garbage."

He went to New York City to try to act there but his reputation as a wash-up child actor and part-time druggie preceded him and he found little to no work there. After Warhol, Bobby disappeared into the worst kind of depressed life of the great city. On March 30, 1968. two kids playing in an abandoned Greenwich Village (Manhattan) tenement near Tompkin's Park found a man's dead body. The remains could not be identified and were buried as a "John Doe" in a pauper's mass grave on Hart Island (Potter's Field). About a year later, due to the efforts of Bob's concerned mother, he was identified by his fingerprints in October 1969. His parents, living in Oceanside, California, put up a headstone for him in Eternal Hills Memorial Park with a death date of March 30, 1968 but the actual date of his death is unknown and neither is Bob's precise burial location. At 1200 burials a year on Hart Island in trenches three bodies deep, it's no wonder nobody knows where he is precisely buried. His autopsy revealed that he had died of occlusive coronary arteriosclerosis (basically, a heart attack due to liver failure).

Bob was awarded a Star on the Hollywood Walk of Fame for his fine work as an actor; it is located at 1560 Vine Street. But his body remains buried in a pauper's grave—one of the saddest of sad cases ever to come out of Hollywood.

DUNNE, DOMINIQUE
1959-1982

This petit (5'1") actress is probably best remembered for her role as Dana Freeling in the hit supernatural thriller, "Poltergeist" (1981) with JoBeth Williams, Craig T. Nelson, and Heather O'Rourke (see Heather's bio in this book).

She was born Dominique Ellen Dunne on November 23, 1959 in Santa Monica, California to producer Dominick Dunne and Ellen Beatriz. Dominique spent most of her early life in Beverly Hills, California. She studied acting at the University of Colorado for one year then quit to begin her short-lived career. Dominique was one of those unlucky performers to have been caught up in the "Poltergeist curse," so called. A number of people who worked in that movie died mysteriously (?). Not really. Unfortunate things do happen.

She began working in show business in 1979 and was progressing well. Then Fate stepped in and she met the worst person she could have for her, one John Thomas Sweeney, at a party. They weren't together long before poor Dominique learned that Sweeney was bad tempered and physically abusive toward her. In fact, when she appeared on the set of "Hill Street Blues" in 1981 to do a scene in which she was to play a woman who had been beaten, the studio didn't have to use any make up because her lunatic of a boy friend had already taken care of that—for real. Dominique ended their relationship on October 30, 1982. That same night a maniacal Sweeney went to her house where she was rehearsing a scene for "V: The Final Battle" with actor David Packer, dragged Dominique outside, and strangled her. Sadly, the attack left her brain dead and the young actress (just 22) died November 4, 1982 at Cedars-Sinai Medical Center in Los Angeles, California.

Some of the movies in which Dominique appeared are, "Diary of a Teenage Hitchhiker" (1979) with Dick Van Patten, "The Day the Loving Stopped" (1981) with Dennis Weaver, "The Shadow Riders" (1982) with Sam Elliott.

TV roles included, "Lou Grant" (1979-80) with Ed Asner, "Breaking Away" (1980-81) with Barbara Barrie, "CHiPs" (1982) with Erik Estrada, "The Quest" (1982) with Perry King, "Hill Street Blues" (1982) with Daniel J. Travanti.

Sweeney, 26, was tried for assault and unintentional manslaughter and sentenced to just six years (can you believe it?). Worse, he was released from prison in Susanville, California after serving only three years and just under eight months. For murder. What a lousy justice system we have when a verbose defense attorney can sway a jury from a rightful murder conviction and have a killer back on the streets in hardly any time at all. The judge who presided at Sweeney's trial stated: "He's a murderer; he's murdered and I think he will do it again."

(This, of course, has happened many times in our society. See my book, "Sociopaths: America's Psycho Killers" for more details as to the real-life demons who lurk among us.)

Dominique is interred at Westwood Memorial Park, Section D, plot #189, Los Angeles, California.

EMERSON, HOPE
1897-1960

This scene-stealing, 6'2", 230 lb. actress who said (in "The Guns of Fort Petticoat") that she was better than "any three men," was born October 29, 1897 in Hawarden, Iowa. After graduating high school in Des Moines in 1916, Hope went to New York City and got into vaudeville singing and playing the piano; she released six recordings on the General label. Hope made her Broadway début in 1930 in "Lysistrata" where the aspiring actress played Lamputo; she was also in "Smiling Faces" in 1932.

Hope became well known in the 1940s for her radio voiceover as Elsie the Cow for Borden Milk commercials; later she also did Elsie for television commercials. But her destiny lay in the tradition of Marjorie-Main-type roles that identified with the pioneer-spirited women of the 19th century. Tough, strong-willed, character portrayals gave Hope many lasting and memorable performances.

In 1949 Hope played a circus strongwoman in "Adam's Rib" where she lifted star Spencer Tracey into the air. She played the female backbone for star Robert Taylor and a bevy of wagon-train ladies in "Westward the Women" (1952). And who could forget her tough-lady role as

"Sgt." Hannah fighting the Indians with Audie Murphy in "The Guns of Fort Petticoat" (1957). But probably her most famous movie role was as the sadistic prison matron Evelyn Harper in "Caged" (1950; photo, p. 90) with Eleanor Parker and Agnes Moorehead. Hope earned an Academy Award nomination for Best Supporting Actress for that part.

After Hope made it to TV one of her fine roles was as nightclub-owner, Mother, where she sometimes sang and played the piano for Craig Stevens' character, "Peter Gunn" (1958-59). She received an Emmy nomination for that role.

Some of Hope's movie roles included, "Cry of the City" (1948) with Victor Mature, "Roseanna McCoy" (1949) with Raymond Massey, "Copper Canyon" (1950) with Ray Milland, "Double Crossbones" (1951) with Donald O'Connor, "A Perilous Journey" (1953) with Vera Ralston, "Untamed" (1955) with Tyrone Power, "All Mine to Give" (1957) with Glynis Johns, "Rock-a-Bye Baby" (1958) with Jerry Lewis. *(Photo, above, l. Hope driving a wagon in* Westward the Women*).*

A few of Hope's TV roles included, "I Married Joan" (1952) with Joan Davis, "Private Secretary" (1953) with Ann Sothern, "Make Room for Daddy" (1955) with Danny Thomas, "Medic" (1956) with Richard Boone, "It's a Great Life" (1956) with James Dunn, "The Bob Cummings Show" (1956) with Bob Cummings, "The Red Skelton Hour" (1958) with Red Skelton, "Death Valley Days" (1958) with host Stanley Andrews, "The Dennis O'Keefe Show" (1958-60) with Dennis O'Keefe.

Hope never married and passed away from liver disease on April 25, 1960 in Hollywood, California. She is buried at Grace Hill Cemetery in Hawarden, Iowa.

FIELDS, BONNIE LYNN 1944-2012

(This photo of Bonnie, l., was taken in 2006)

Former Mouseketeer, dancer, and singer born Bonita Lynn Fields on July 18, 1944 in Walterboro, South Carolina to Woodrow W. Fields and Beverly M. Sherrow. Lynn (as she preferred to be called) took dancing lessons early in life at the age of two in Richmond, Indiana after the family moved there. Woodrow and Beverly again moved the family, this time to Granada Hills, California, in 1953 where she continued her dancing lessons and also took singing lessons. Lynn acquired some exposure in local television performances and—according to George Grant of the Original Mickey Mouse Club site—danced for charities and the USO (United Service Organizations; they provide shows for the troops overseas).

When the Disney Studios announced auditions for the third season of the Mickey Mouse Club (on ABC 1955-58; producer Bill Walsh), Lynn went to Burbank to try out to be a Talent Round-Up Winner. However, the judges were so impressed by her talent they immediately cast her as a Mouseketeer (1957).

All of us Mickey Mouse Club fans will remember Lynn's costume shirt with the name "Bonnie" on it. So how did her name get changed? Why not "Bonita" or "Lynn?" Well, the story goes that Walt Disney himself had asked Lynn to use the name "Bonnie" because they already had a boy on the show named "Lynn" (Lynn Ready) and he felt that "Bonita," with three syllables, sounded too long and suggested "Bonnie" for her.

As no changes had been made to the Red Team, Bonnie was placed in the Blue Team, which meant that she did not appear in the Roll Call (beginning of show introduction of the Red Team Mice) or the Alma Mater (end of show sign-off song). Bonnie was not used very much in the skits, not due to a lack of talent but because she was taller than other Mouseketeer boys of her age and thus became difficult to place together in routines. And losing time on the show to a bout with tonsillitis didn't help her career, either.

(l., Bonnie and Lonnie Burr dancing for the Disneyland 4th *Anniversary Show, c. 1957)*

Lynn had a lot of dancing talent and sang quite well, too. Former Mouseketeer Lonnie Burr once told me that Bonnie was his favorite dancing partner—not on the Mickey Mouse Club show as the studio didn't pair them much—but later on in their careers. Still, there were fans aplenty of the original show; so much so, in fact, that the Disney Studios brought out a televised Mouseketeer Reunion on November 23, 1980 and reunion shows at Disneyland from 1981-85, giving Bonnie and Lonnie a chance to reunite and once again demonstrate their dancing skills together.

After the show finished filming late in 1957, putting most of the Mice out of work, Lynn went on to dance that Christmas with the New York City Ballet's touring production of "The Nutcracker." She also sang and danced in "The Great Waltz" at the Los Angeles Civic Light Opera (1965). Broadway called, too, and Lynn appeared in "Kelly" and "Half a Sixpence."

Some films in which Lynn appeared include, "The Five Pennies" (1959) with Danny Kaye, "Funny Girl" (1968) with Barbra Streisand, "Sweet Charity" (1969) with Shirley MacLaine (Lynn worked with Lonnie Burr again in this one), "Angel in My Pocket" (1969) with Andy Griffith.

TV productions in which Lynn appeared were, "Bachelor Father" (1958) with John Forsythe, "Walt Disney Presents: Annette" (1958) with

Annette Funicello, "The Courtship of Eddie's Father" (1969) with Bill Bixby, "Marcus Welby, M. D." (1971) with Robert Young.

Lynn married Thomas D. Clement in February 1960; divorced January 1975.

In 1981 Lynn was living with her retired fireman husband (later divorced), Rick Elder, on a boat in the Marina del Rey harbor. She got the idea to have a Toys For Tots boat parade and talked Lonnie Burr and some of the other former Mice—including Doreen Tracey, Tommy Cole, and Sharon Baird—to be in it with her.

Lynn went on to teach tap dancing at her own schools in Santa Monica and Gardena, California. A few years ago she went back to Winchester, Indiana to be with her aged mother. Still keeping busy, Lynn opened the Academy of Tap there. Sadly, she died from throat cancer in Richmond on November 17, 2012 and was buried at Webster Cemetery in Webster, Indiana.

FULLER, ROBERT
1933-

This former actor and now a horse rancher is probably best remembered for his role as Cooper Smith on the action western TV series "Wagon Train" that ran on NBC from 1957-62 and on ABC from 1962-65. The series starred first with Ward Bond and Robert Horton then later with John McIntire and Robert Fuller as well as Frank McGrath, Terry Wilson, Scott Miller and Michael Burns. He also had a good role as Jess Harper (his personal favorite) on the fine western TV series "Laramie" which aired on NBC from 1959 to 1963 and starred John Smith, Hoagy Carmichael, and Robert L. Crawford Jr.

Of course, we can't forget that other fine, non-western series he was on "Emergency!" where he played Dr. Kelly Brackett. This TV show ran on NBC from 1972 to 1977 and co-starred Randolph Mantooth, Julie London, Bobby Troup, and Kevin Tighe.

Bobby was born Leonard Leroy Lee Jr. on July 29, 1933 in Troy, New York. Prior to his birth, dance instructor mother Betty married Naval Academy officer Robert Simpson. Nicknamed Buddy in his youth, the family moved to Key West, Florida where he took the name Robert Simpson Jr.

Bobby's early life consisted of acting and dancing and went to the Miami Military Academy for the fifth and sixth grades. He attended the Key West High School to the ninth grade but dropped out in 1948. In 1950 the family moved to Hollywood, California and Bobby got a job as a stunt man. He decided to go into acting and joined the Screen Actors Guild, changing his name to Robert Fuller.

His first screen role was in the war film "Above and Beyond" (1952) with Robert Taylor and Eleanor Parker. The next year Bobby got a part in "Gentlemen Prefer Blondes" with Marilyn Monroe and Jane

Russell and got to dance with Marilyn (wow!). Then his career stalled while he went to work for Uncle Sam in the U. S. Army. He served in Korea and mustered out in 1955. He enrolled in Richard Boone's acting classes and later attended the Neighborhood Playhouse in New York City. That led to his getting a role in the film "Friendly Persuasion" (1956) which starred Gary Cooper, Dorothy McGuire, and Anthony Perkins.

(Photo, l. Here's a shot of Bobby as Cooper Smith on Wagon Train*)*

Bobby got his first starring role in a film in 1957 called "Teenage Thunder," which—according to him—was a big break; it starred Chuck Courtney. In the 1950s and 60s he got many parts on TV shows. He almost got the part of Little Joe on "Bonanza" but lost out to a relatively-unknown actor at the time, Michael Landon. But he did get the role on "Laramie" and that was a good thing for him as well. When "Laramie" lost its run in 1963, Bobby moved right into "Wagon Train" as a scout for wagon boss John McIntire, another western role that he enjoyed doing.

Producer Jack Webb decided that he wanted Bobby to co-star in his new series "Emergency!" after seeing him in the film "The Hard Ride" (1971). The show was a big hit and ran until 1979. In the early 70s Bobby did commercials for Budweiser Malt Liquor.

Bobby has largely retired from acting and since 1990 has been on the celebrity panels of the annual Festival of the West where fans question him about his roles in westerns and acting in general. In 2014 my wife, Carol, and I were fortunate to meet and talk with Bobby at the annual Western Legends Roundup at Kanab, Utah. Great event and Bobby and the rest of the western stars who were there were a joy to meet and talk to. Lots of old west stuff to see and well worth the trip.

Bobby married Patricia Lyon in 1962; they had three children and divorced in 1984. In 2001 he married Jennifer Savidge.

Some of the films in which Bobby appeared include, "Come Back, Little Sheba" (1952) with Burt Lancaster, "Calamity Jane" (1953) with Doris Day, "The Harder They Fall" (1956) with Humphrey Bogart, "The

Brain From Planet Arous" (1957) with John Agar, "Spartacus" (1960) with Kirk Douglas, "Return of the Magnificent Seven" (1966) with Yul Brynner, "Whatever Happened to Aunt Alice?" (1969) with Ruth Gordon, "The Gatling Gun" (1971) with Guy Stockwell, "Donner Pass: The Road to Survival" (1978) with Andrew Prine, "Megaforce" (1982) with Barry Bostwick, "Bonanza: The Next Generation" (1988) with John Ireland, "Repossessed" (1990) with Leslie Nielsen, "Maverick" (1994) with Mel Gibson. *(Photo, below. Cast of* Laramie, *l. to r.: John Smith, Robert L. Crawford Jr., Hoagy Carmichael, and Robert Fuller)*

Some of Bobby's TV roles include, "Man Against Crime: Where's Mom?" (1954) with Ralph Bellamy, "The Gray Ghost: Point of Honor" (1957) with Tod Andrews, "The Californians: Pipeline" (1958) with Richard Coogan, "M Squad: The Trap" (1958) with Lee Marvin, "The Adventures of Rin Tin Tin: The Epidemic" (1958) with Lee Aaker, "The Restless Gun: Shadow of a Gunfighter" (1959) with John Payne, "Lawman: The Souvenir" (1959) with John Russell, "The Big Valley: A Flock of Trouble" (1967) with Barbara Stanwyck, "The Virginian: Flight From Memory" (1971) with best friend James Drury, "Hec Ramsey: The Mystery of Chalk Hill" (1973) with Richard Boone, "Fantasy Island: The Ghost's Story" (1982) with Ricardo Montalban, "Matt Houston: New Orleans' Nightmare" (1985) with Lee Horsley, "Murder, She Wrote: The Body Politic" (1988) with Angela Lansbury, "Alaska Kid" (1993) with Mark Pillow, "Diagnosis Murder: Malibu Fire" (1997) with Dick Van Dyke, "Walker, Texas Ranger: The Final Showdown" (Bobby's last role; 2001) with Chuck Norris.

Retired from acting, in 2004 Bobby and his wife moved from Los Angeles to start a horse ranch in Cooke County in northern Texas.

Bobby was awarded a Star on the Hollywood Walk of Fame for his work in TV. It's located at 6608 Hollywood Boulevard. In 1989 he won the Golden Boot Award. In 2007 he was inducted into the National Cowboy and Western Heritage Museum in Oklahoma City, Oklahoma. Also in 2007 Bobby won the Silver Spur Award.

FUNICELLO, ANNETTE
1942-2013

Update: Sadly, I have to report that Disney's former Mouseketeer and "America's Sweetheart" died from complications associated with multiple sclerosis on April 8, 2013 at Mercy Southwest Hospital in Bakersfield, California. She had suffered from MS since 1987. Annette had been holding her own for some time but in the past six years had gotten much worse. I won't say too much about that; her husband, Glen Holt, had a video made of Annette at their home that explicitly shows and tells far more and much better than I could. Glen did so wishing to let all of Annette's fans know what was happening to her. The video can be seen by going to Annette's website at AnnetteConnection.com. She was buried in northern California.

My wife and I will always keep this talented, sweet lady in our hearts and we express our deepest sympathies to her family.

GARVER, KATHY
1945-

Actress best known for her role as Cissy on "Family Affair." She was born Kathleen Marie Garver on December 13, 1945 in Long Beach, California to Hayes and Rosemary Garver. Kathy got into acting in film at age nine with an uncredited role in "I'll Cry Tomorrow" (1955) with Susan Hayward. She also played a slave in Cecil B. DeMille's epic "The Ten Commandments" (1956) with Charlton Heston. After moving to San Bernardino in 1960 Kathy graduated from Pacific Arts High School in 1964, going on to graduate from UCLA in 1968. As if she wasn't working hard enough, while at college in 1966 Kathy auditioned for and won the part of Cissy on "Family Affair," which also starred Brian Keith, Sebastian Cabot, Johnny Whitaker, and Anissa Jones (see Anissa's bio in this book). The show lasted until 1971. Years later Kathy was honored by being awarded the Former Child Star Lifetime Achievement Award for her role as Cissy. Kathy was also a Hollywood Deb Star for 1967.

Some of Kathy's movie appearances include, "The Night of the Hunter" (1955) with Robert Mitchum, "The Bad Seed" (1956) with Patty McCormack, "Kiss Me, Stupid" (1964) with Dean Martin, "The Siege at Ruby Ridge" (1996) with Randy Quaid, "Closer Than the Boy Next Door" (1998) with Erik Bennett, "The Trial of Old Drum" (2000) with Bobby Edner, "Race You to the Bottom" (2005) with Ruben Dario, "Hercules Saves Christmas" (2012) with Anthony Robinson.

TV appearances include, "Dave and Charley" (1953) with Charley Weaver, "Our Miss Brooks" (1953) with Eve Arden, "Crusader" (1956) with Brian Keith, "Fury" (1956) with Bobby Diamond, "Father Knows Best" (1957) with Robert Young, "The Rifleman" (1961) with Chuck Connors, "Daniel Boone" (1965) with Fess Parker, "The Big Valley" (1969) with Barbara Stanwyck, "The Ghost Busters" (1975) with Forrest Tucker, "The Fonz and the Happy Days Gang" (1980, voice) with Henry Winkler, "Chuck Norris: Karate Kommandos" (1986) with Chuck Norris, "Simon & Simon" (1983 & 1988) with Gerald McRaney,

Besides her various acting roles, petit 5'1" Kathy also has produced, narrated, and written the music for quite a number of fine children's audiotapes such as "Beatrix Potter" and "Mother Goose." She also wrote her best-selling book, "The Family Affair Cookbook"

Kathy lives in Hillsborough, California, with her husband David Travis (married 1981); they have a son, Reid.

GILLESPIE, DARLENE
1941-

Update: I'm pleased to write that Darlene has received the Disney Legend Award at the D23 Expo. This honor was bestowed upon her July 18, 2015 for the talented work she provided during the four-year production (1955-59) of TV's Mickey Mouse Club. She joins other former Disney celebrities such as Annette Funicello, Tommy Kirk, and Kevin Corcoran. Congratulations, Darlene!

GRABOWSKI, NORM
1933-2012

Update: Sadly, I have to report that since the release of my last Celebrities book, Norman David "Woo Woo" Grabowski passed away October 12, 2012. Norm was born February 5, 1933 to Anthony and Mary Grabowski in Irvington, New Jersey. Both his parents were born in Poland. Norm was very proud of his Polish ancestry and often referred to himself as "The Big Polocko."

Norm had been suffering from a form of throat and esophageal cancer for some time. About last April (2012) this award-winning hot rod designer, professional wood carver, and former actor (mostly retired since 1981) was diagnosed with a squamous cell carcinoma that formed a lump at the base of his tongue and throat. He had been in and out of the hospital, was supposed to have surgery but refused it, and was in a very weak state, which explains why my emails to him sometimes didn't get answered for weeks. Always a funny guy (see the YouTube in his name), if you met him Norm treated you like he had known you forever. Norm died from cancer in Cassville, Missouri. He had been living in Lead Hill, Arkansas.

GRADY, DON
1944-2012

(Photo, l., Don in his dressing room at Disneyland, 1985. Courtesy of Diane Burr and used with permission.)

Update: I learned today (July 1, 2012) from actor Lonnie Burr that his good friend, Don Grady, had passed away on June 27 after a terrible, four-year struggle with brain cancer. All our prayers are now with his wife, Ginny, and children, Tessa and Joey. As a fan, I will miss him along with millions of others. He was buried at Pierce Brothers Valley Oaks Memorial Park in Westlake Village, Los Angeles County, California.

HAGGERTY, DAN
1941-2016

Television's and filmdom's ruggedly (6'1") good looking outdoorsman was born Daniel Francis Haggerty on November 19, 1941 in Hollywood, Los Angeles, California to Don Haggerty. In the early 60s Dan was a bodybuilder and part of the Muscle Beach crowd. That led to his first role as muscleman Biff in Frankie Avalon's second beach movie, "Muscle Beach Party" (1964) starring Annette Funicello, Don Rickles and Buddy Hackett. An avid motorcyclist, motorcycle restorer, and stuntman got him an uncredited role in the smash hit "Easy Rider" (1969) with Peter Fonda, William Hopper, and Jack Nicholson.

Dan had also worked as an animal handler in film. That got him work in the CBS "Tarzan" TV series (1966-68) with Ron Ely, "When the

North Wind Blows" (1974) with Henry Brandon, and in "My Side of the Mountain" (1969) with Ted Eccles. He also handled animals for the Walt Disney Studio.

Deservedly, Dan won "The People's Choice Award" for most popular actor in 1980; a Star on Hollywood Boulevard (in front of Grauman's Chinese Theatre) in 1994, and a Star in Kanab, Utah— "Hollywood of the West"—in 2009. My wife and I had the opportunity to meet and chat with Dan in Kanab during the Western Legends Roundup in August 2014 and found him to be witty, charming, and friendly; in all, a wonderful experience. *(Photo, above. Dan Haggerty and Bozo the bear as Ben, 1977)*

Probably Dan's best known performance was of James Adams (whose real name was John Capen Adams) in the hit Schick Sunn Classic Pictures 1974 film, "The Life and Times of Grizzly Adams." The film also starred Denver Pyle and Don Shanks; Ben the bear was played by Bozo but the cub was played by Bart the bear. In 1977 NBC aired the TV version which ran for two seasons.

Some of Dan's film appearances include, "Girl Happy" (1965) with Elvis Presley, "Angels Die Hard" (1970) with William Smith, "Bury Me an Angel" (1972) with Dixie Peabody, "When the North Wind Blows" (1974) with Henry Brandon, "The Adventures of Frontier Fremont" (1976) with Denver Pyle, "Terror Out of the Sky" (1978) with Efrem Zimbalist Jr., "King of the Mountain" (1981) with Harry Hamlin, "The Capture of Grizzly Adams" (1982) with Kim Darby, "Abducted" (1986) with Roberta Weiss, "The Chilling" (1989) with Linda Blair, "Spirit of the Eagle" (1991) with William Smith, "Cheyenne Warrior" (1994) with Kelly Preston, "Grizzly Mountain" (1997) with son Dylan Haggerty, "Escape to Grizzly Mountain" (2000) with Miko Hughes, "Big Stan" (2007) with David Carradine, "The Untold Story" (2016) with Miko Hughes.

And some of Dan's TV roles include, "CHiPs" (1979) with Erik Estrada, "Charlie's Angels" (1981) with Cheryl Ladd, "The Love Boat" (1983) with Gavin MacLeod, "Deadly Diamonds" (video 1991) with Troy Donohue. He was also visited by Mike Wolfe and Frank Fritz at Dan's home to buy collectibles on an episode of "American Pickers" which aired February 25, 2013.

In 1959 Dan married Diane Rooker; they had two daughters and divorced in 1984. That same year Dan married Samantha Hilton; they had three children. Samantha died in a motorcycle accident in 2008.

Dan lived on a small ranch in Malibu Canyon with a number of wild animals he had rescued and took care of. Sadly, Dan died of spinal cancer on January 15, 2016 in Burbank, California.

HAMILTON, MARGARET
1902-85

This talented, prolific though petit (five feet) actress with the high-pitched voice was born Margaret Brainard Hamilton on December 9, 1902 in Cleveland, Ohio to Walter J. Hamilton and Jennie Adams. Of course, she deservedly will forever be best remembered as the greatest villian of all time, the Wicked Witch of the West in loveable Judy Garland's MGM hit "The Wizard of Oz" (1939) which also starred Ray Bolger, Jack Haley, Bert Lahr, Frank Morgan, Billie Burke, and Charlie Grapewin.

Even though this role eventually made her famous, Maggie was severely burned during the filming of it in December 1938. In the exciting scene in which the Wicked Witch vanishes from Munchkinland, she was supposed to step onto a trap door which would rapidly lower her beneath the set and thus appear that the witch disappeared. To cover Maggie's exit, smoke would envelope her and at the same time fire would belch from below. However, during one take the very real fire came too early and Maggie's costume started to burn. She was out of the movie for more than a month recuperating. Maggie returned to finish the picture but vowed "no more fire work!"

She first entered acting in children's theater as a member of the Junior League of Cleveland in the 1920s and later in the Wheelock Family Theater in Boston. But before she chose acting as her life's work, Maggie was a kindergarten teacher—a profession she enjoyed very much as she loved children. During that time she taught future actors William Windom and Jim Backus. Her father was against her aspiring to become an actress but the strong-willed, independent young woman went ahead. Maggie first appeared in film in a billed role as Helen Hallam in "Another Language" (1933) with Helen Hayes.

Maggie married Paul Meserve in 1931; divorced in 1938. They had one son, Hamilton Wadsworth Meserve.

(Photo, below, r. Here's Margaret Hamilton as the Wicked Witch menacing co-star Judy Garland as Dorothy Gale in The Wizard of Oz, *1939)*

Though she uttered that memorably cruel line in "Wizard of Oz," "—and your little dog, too!" Maggie liked animals and was an active promoter of animal rights. She personally owned a cat and a dachshund.

In addition to appearing in many dozens of films and on TV, for many years Maggie did a commercial for Maxwell House coffee. She played a feisty storekeeper who states that, "It's the only brand I sell!"

Again as a witch, she did a memorable scene with Lou Costello in the Abbott and Costello film, "Comin' Round the Mountain" (1951).

Some of the movies in which Maggie appeared include, "The Farmer Takes a Wife" (1935) with Henry Fonda, "You Only Live Once" (1937) with Sylvia Sydney, "The Adventures of Tom Sawyer" (1938) with Tommy Kelly, "The Angels Wash Their Faces" (1939) with Ann Sheridan, "Babes in Arms" (1939) with Judy Garland, "My Little Chickadee" (1940) with Mae West, "The Invisible Woman" (1940) with Virginia Bruce, "The Ox-Bow Incident" (1943) with Henry Fonda, "Janie Gets Married" (1946) with Joan Leslie, "State of the Union" (1948) with Spencer Tracy, "The Beautiful Blonde From Bashful Bend" (1949) with Betty Grable, "The Devil's Disciple" (1955) with Ralph Bellamy, "On Borrowed Time" (1957) with Ed Wynn, "13 Ghosts"

(1960) with Charles Herbert, "Angel in My Pocket" (1969) with Andy Griffith, "The Night Strangler" (1973) with Darren McGavin, "Letters From Frank" (1979) with Lew Ayres.

Some of Maggie's TV roles include, "The Stu Erwin Show: Problem Party" (1950) with Stu Erwin, "My Hero: Lady Mortician" (1952) with Robert Cummings, "The Phil Silvers Show: Bilko's Merry Widow" (1957) with Phil Silvers, "Ichabod and Me: The Purple Cow" (1961) with George Chandler, "Make Room for Daddy: Bunny, the Brownie Leader" (1962) with Danny Thomas, "Car 54, Where Are You?: Here Comes Charlie" (1963) with Fred Gwynne, "The Addams Family: Happy Birthday, Grandma Frump" (1966) with John Astin, "The Partridge Family: Reuben Kincaid Lives" (1973) with Shirley Jones, "Mister Rogers' Neighborhood" (1975-76) with Fred Rogers, "Here's Boomer: Jailbreak" (1980) with Michael Alldredge & Johnny the dog, "Lou Grant: Review" (1979 & 1982) with Ed Asner.

She appeared in a stage musical in San Francisco with star Jean Simmons entitled "A Little Night Music" (c. 1975).

In 1976 Maggie made a special appearance as the Wicked Witch on an episode of Sesame Street and reportedly scared the children of the TV audience so much that they never again ran it. No footage of that show is known to exist.

Sadly, Maggie died in her sleep following a heart attack on May 16, 1985 in a nursing home in Salisbury, Connecticut. Her remains were cremated and her ashes scattered on her Amenia, New York estate.

HOGAN, PAUL
1939-

Former bridge painter and now legendary actor, producer, and writer, Paul Hogan was born October 8, 1939 in Lightning Ridge (Walkabout Creek?), New South Wales, Australia. He grew up in Granville, a suburb of Sydney, the state capital of New South Wales and lying on the east coast of Australia. He began acting on Australia's GTV-9 on a program called "A Current Affair." Paul did a comic social commentary and did quite well. Later he got his own program, "The Paul Hogan Show," a comedy piece which aired from 1973-84. On his program, Paul did a series of comedic sketches similar to Red Skelton on his show in the 1960s. Paul also co-produced and co-wrote the show.

During the 70s Paul appeared in commercials advertising Australia's *Winfield* cigarettes. In the 80s he did the internationally popular ads for the Australian tourism industry and practically made the down-under greeting "g'day" an Americanism as well. He also advertised *Foster's Lager* beer and Subaru's Outback car.

In 1985 Paul appeared in the critically-acclaimed mini-series, "Anzacs" with Jon Blake and Andrew Clarke.

But what propelled Paul to fame was the motion picture he wrote and starred in, "Crocodile Dundee" (1986) with Linda Kozlowski, John Meillon, Steve Rackman, Gerry Skilton, David Gulpilil, and Mark Blum. The film popularized catch phrases like "g'day, mate" and—in one scene where Paul's character is confronted by a teenage thug who pulls a folding knife and Crocodile Dundee pulls his own monstrous blade—"That's not a knife— THIS is a knife!" The film and the capable character who purposely didn't kill everybody in sight to achieve what he wanted and help people besides became immensely popular. For the movie Paul received a Golden Globe for Best Actor and an Oscar nomination for Best Screenplay.

Paul married Noelene Edwards in 1958, divorced 1981; they had five children, one of which is actor Brett Hogan. The pair remarried in 1982 but again divorced (1989). In 1990 Paul married his co-star of "Crocodile Dundee," Linda Kozlowski, divorced 2014; they had one child, Chance Hogan. The couple still shares the house in which they had been living in Venice, California as of this writing. *(Photo, above, l. Co-stars Linda Kozlowski and Paul Hogan in* Crocodile Dundee*)*

He earned the award Australian of the Year in 1985 and a Member of the Order of Australia in 1989.

This lanky, 5'9" star appeared in various films, some of which include, "Crocodile Dundee II" (1988) with Linda Kozlowski, "Almost An Angel" (1990) with Elias Koteas, "Lightning Jack" (1994) with Cuba Gooding Jr., "Flipper" (1996) with Elijah Wood, "Floating Away" (1998) with Rosanna Arquette, "Crocodile Dundee in Los Angeles" (2001) with wife Linda Kozlowski, "Strange Bedfellows" (2004) with Michael Caton, "Charlie & Boots" (2009) with Morgan Griffin.

Paul is well known for stating: "I enjoy being part of the entertainment industry, although I'm the laziest person that I've met yet in this business." I say he needs to go on being "lazy" as by doing so he had created some of the best character performances.

HOLLOWAY, STERLING 1905-92

Popular character actor and voice-over genius was born Sterling Price Holloway Jr. on January 4, 1905 in Cedartown, Georgia to grocer Sterling Price Holloway Sr. and Rebecca Boothby. He made his acting debut in silent movies but is probably best remembered for his voice-over role as Winnie the Pooh in a string of Walt Disney Studios' animated features. Because of his bushy, reddish-blonde hair and his near-falsetto voice, Sterling became a natural for the movies.

After graduating from the Georgia Military Academy at the age of 15, Sterling headed for New York City and enrolled with the American Academy of Dramatic Arts. While on the stage there Sterling worked and was friends with Spencer Tracy. Possessed of a fine tenor voice, Sterling introduced "Manhattan" in 1925 and the following year sang "Mountain Greenery." His first movie role was in a silent picture called "The Battling Kangaroo" (1926) with Lige Conley.

Sterling serving in the U. S. Army in WWII with Special Services. He helped develop a military-themed show called "Hey Rookie" which played in Los Angeles and made money for the Army Relief Fund.

At the Pasadena Playhouse in 1931, Sterling was in a musical comedy called "Hullabaloo." Somebody helpful to his career saw him in the show and that got him a part in "Blonde Venus" (1932) with Marlene Dietrich and Cary Grant. In the 1940s, Sterling sang and acted in five of Gene Autry's westerns.

It's said that Sterling turned down a contract offer with Louis B. Mayer at MGM because he didn't want to be a star. Of his career, he said, "I came to Hollywood at a bad time. The movies were in a state of turmoil. Sound was coming in and silents were going out. Nobody thought I was suitable for talkies." Can you imagine anyone telling that to such a fine voice-over actor? One who made over 100 films and appeared in over 40 television shows?

Sterling acted in many radio shows, including "The Railroad Hour," "Suspense," "Lux Radio Theater" and "Fibber McGee and Molly." He also narrated many children's records, such as "Uncle Remus Stories" for Decca, "Walt Disney Presents Rudyard Kipling's Just So Stories" for Disneyland Records, and "Peter and the Wolf" for RCA Victor.

He also did a lot of voice work for TV commercials and the Purina

Puppy Chow dog food commercial, Sterling sang their familiar jingle.

(Photo, l. William Bendix and Sterling Holloway from The Life of Riley, 1957)

He almost began his voice-over career for Walt Disney as Sleepy in "Snow White and the Seven Dwarfs" in 1937 but was beat out by Pinto Colvig. But he returned in 1941 to do the voice of Mr. Stork in "Dumbo" and the following year as the adult Flower (the skunk) in "Bambi."

Sterling narrated in "The Three Caballeros" in 1944 and in "Peter and the Wolf" in 1946. Still for Walt Disney he did the Cheshire Cat in "Alice and Wonderland" (1951) and Kaa the snake in "Jungle Book" (1967). In fact, he did so much work for Disney and was so good at it that the Studio made him a Disney Legend in 1991, the first to ever receive that award in the Voice category. He stopped doing the voice for Winnie the Pooh in 1981 and was replaced by Hal Smith.

Sterling never married but he did adopt a son, Richard Holloway.

Some of Sterling's film roles include, "Hell Below" (1933) with Robert Montgomery, "Down to Their Last Yacht" (1934) with Mary Boland, "Palm Springs" (1936) with Frances Langford, "Nick Carter, Master Detective" (1939) with Walter Pidgeon, "Meet John Doe" (1941) with Gary Cooper, "A Walk in the Sun" (1945) with Dana Andrews, "Death Valley" (1946) with Robert Lowery, "Robin Hood of Texas" (1947) with Gene Autry, "The Beautiful Blonde From Bashful Bend" (1949) with Betty Grable, "Kentucky Rifle" (1955) with Chill Wills, "The Adventures of Huckleberry Finn (1960) with Tony Randall, "It's a Mad, Mad, Mad, Mad World" (1963) with Spencer Tracy, "Live a Little, Love a Little" (1968) with Elvis Presley, "The AristoCats" (animated voice, 1970), "Thunder and Lightning" (1977) with David Carradine, "We Think the World is Round" (1984) with Cesar Romero.

(Photo, below. Here's Sterling in an episode of The Twilight Zone *called*

What's in the Box, *1964)*

Some of Sterling's TV credits include, "Your Show Time: A Capture" (1949) with Arthur Shields, "The Adventures of Ozzie and Harriet: Pancake Mix" (1953) with Ozzie Nelson, "Adventures of Superman" (1953-55) with George Reeves, "The Life of Riley" (1953-56) with William Bendix, "Climax!: Night of a Rebel" (1957) with Eduardo Ciannelli, "Disneyland: Ben and Me" (animated voice over 1957), "The Adventures of Rin Tin Tin (1956-58) with Lee Aaker, "Peter Gunn: The Best Laid Plans" (1960) with Craig Stevens, "Margie: False Alarm" (1962) with Cynthia Pepper, "The Twilight Zone: What's in the Box?" (1964) with host Rod Serling, "The Bailey's of Balboa" (1964-65) with Paul Ford, "F Troop: Wilton, the Kid" (1966) with Forrest Tucker, "Family Affair: Fancy Free" (1967) with Brian Keith, "Daktari: Judy and the Jailbirds" (1967) with Marshall Thompson, "It Takes a Thief: Rock-Bye, Bye Baby" (1969) with Robert Wagner, "Love, American Style" (1973) with Stuart Margolin, "Tony the Pony" (1976) with Scott K. Ratner.

Sadly, Sterling died of cardiac arrest on November 22, 1992 in Los Angeles, California. His body was cremated and his ashes scattered over the Pacific Ocean.

HUNNICUTT, ARTHUR
1910-79

This master of the laconic backwoodsman persona with a gravelly voice was born in—are you ready for this?—*Gravelly,* Arkansas. Yes, that's right. On February 17, 1910. Lanky, six foot tall Arthur went to Arkansas State Teachers College but had to drop out in his third year due to a lack of funds. After acting in a theatre company in Martha's Vineyard, Massachusetts he went to New York to act on Broadway and on tour. He was in many stage plays and gained the lead role in "Tobacco Road," a perfect role for Arthur. He appeared in a few films in the early 40s then returned to stage work.

In 1949 Arthur went back to Hollywood to become a well-known and well-respected supporting actor. His wonderful role as Zeb Calloway in "The Big Sky" (1952) opposite Kirk Douglas won him an Oscar nomination for Supporting Actor. It was in the early 50s that Arthur adopted his growth of facial hair.

Some of the films in which Arthur appeared include, "Pardon My Gun" (1942) with Charles Starrett, "Murder, He Says" (1945) with Fred

112

MacMurray, "Border Incident" (1949) with Ricardo Montalban, "Broken Arrow" (1950) with James Stewart, "The Red Badge of Courage" (1951) with Audie Murphy, "The Last Command" (1955) with Sterling Hayden, "The Kettles in the Ozarks" (1956) with Marjorie Main, "Born Reckless" (1958) with Mamie Van Doren, "A Tiger Walks" (1964) with Brian Keith, "Cat Ballou" (1965) with Lee Marvin, "El Dorado" (1966) with John Wayne, "Shoot Out" (1971) with Gregory Peck, "Climb an Angry Mountain" (1972) with Fess Parker, "Harry and Tonto" (1974) with Art Carney, "Winterhawk" (1975) with Leif Erickson.

Some of his TV appearances include, "Cheyenne" (1956) with Clint Walker, "Sugarfoot" (1957) with Will Hutchins, "Wanted: Dead or Alive" (1959) with Steve McQueen, "The Andy Griffith Show" (1960) with Andy Griffith, "Twilight Zone: The Hunt" (1962) with Jeanette Nolan, "The Outer Limits: Cry of Silence" (1964) with Eddie Albert, "Wagon Train" (1965) with John McIntire, "Daniel Boone" (1966) with Fess Parker, "Bonanza" (1959-69) with Lorne Greene, "Gunsmoke" (1971) with James Arness, "My Three Sons" (1961 & 1971) with Fred MacMurray.

Arthur married Pauline Lilc (date unknown). He served as the Honorary Mayor of Northridge, California.

Sadly, Arthur was stricken with mouth cancer and died in Woodland Hills, California on September 26, 1979. He is buried in the Coop Prairie Cemetery in Mansfield, Arkansas.

JAMES, SHEILA
1941-

This former child actress and now a politician was born Sheila Ann Kuehl on February 9, 1941 in Tulsa, Oklahoma. She was in many roles but is probably best known for pony-tailed Zelda Gilroy, nose wrinkling at her one-sided, teenage love interest, Dobie Gillis (played by Dwayne Hickman) on "The Many Loves of Dobie Gillis" which aired on CBS from 1959-63. This sitcom also starred Bob Denver, Frank Faylen, Florida Friebus, Steve Franken, Doris Packer, and sometimes Tuesday Weld as one of Dobie's paramours.

As a child, Sheila's parents noticed that she liked to try to play the piano and sing but she lacked any training to be good at it. So they signed her up at the Meglin Studios for classes in tap dancing, ballet, singing, and acting. At one weekly recital, Sheila played an assistant who sat under a table listening for clues to help the main character, a detective. To show that she was deeply listening, Sheila made faces which only made the audience laugh. The skit was ruined but the drama teacher was impressed anyway, thinking that the little girl was naturally comedic. The teacher got Sheila an interview for a radio play, she read for the part and got it—the show changing her name to Sheila James.

The NBC radio show was "The Penny Williamson Show" and starred such radio and film veterans as Bea Benaderet, Jim Backus, Gale Gordon, and Penny Singleton as the main character, Penny Williamson. In 1950 Sheila interviewed for the part of Stu Erwin's tomboy daughter on "The Stu Erwin Show" on television and got it. This ABC show ran from 1950-55. After the show ended, Sheila continued to work as an actress while going to school. She had been such a good student she skipped grades and at age 16 was attending the University of California in Los Angeles.

When Sheila tried out for the part of Zelda Gilroy for "The Many Loves of Dobie Gillis" TV show, it is said that one of the reasons she got the part (besides her obvious comedic talent) was because she was the same height (four foot ten) as the writer director of the show, Max Schulman! Sheila also continued to go to college and earned a bachelor's degree in English from the University of California.

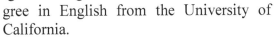

(Photo, l. Here's Sheila James with Dwayne Hickman (center) in The Many Loves of Dobie Gillis*)*

In 1961 Sheila did a pilot for a spin-off series from "Dobie Gillis" to be entitled "Zelda" but CBS president Jim Aubrey rejected it, saying that he thought that "Zelda" and Sheila were both "a little too butch" for him.

Some of the movies in which Sheila appeared include, "Those Redheads From Seattle" (1953) with Rhonda Fleming, "Seven Brides for Seven Brothers" (1954) with Howard Keel, "Teenage Rebel" (1956) with Ginger Rogers, "Daddy-O" (1961) with Don DeFore, "Zelda" (1962) with Joe Flynn, "The Feminist and the Fuzz" (1971) with Barbara Eden, "Bring Me the Head of Dobie Gillis" (1988) with Dwayne Hickman.

Some of Sheila's TV roles include, "Mayor of the Town" (1954) with Thomas Mitchell, "My Little Margie" (1952-54) with Gale Storm, "The Bob Cummings Show" (1955-59) with Bob Cummings, "The Millionaire: Millionaire Susan Johnson" (1960) with Marvin Miller, "National Velvet: The Beauty Contest" (1961) with Lori Martin, "McHale's Navy: The Happy Sleepwalker" (1963) with Ernest Borgnine, "Petticoat Junction: The Ladybugs" (1964) with Edgar Buchanan, "The Beverly Hillbillies" (1964-67) with Buddy Ebsen, "Marcus Welby, M. D.: The Girl From Rainbow Beach" (1970) with Robert Young, "Emergency!" (1976) with Robert Fuller.

She continued to act in the 60s but things were starting to drop off for her. To save money, Sheila moved in with her girlfriend/paramour, Kathy. They had been a lesbian item since college days and that seemed to be the only way for Sheila to go. They stayed together for 12 years before breaking up in the early 70s.

Acting roles pretty much dried up for Sheila in the 1970s (she felt it might have been do to rumors about her lesbian sexuality), she became an adviser to students in campus activist groups at the University of California, and eventually became an associate dean of students. In 1975 Sheila entered the Harvard Law School. While there she became only the second woman to win Harvard's prestigious Ames Moot Court Competition and one of the nation's top five law students.

After graduating, Sheila became an associate at a law firm in Los Angeles and later a firm in Beverly Hills practicing family, anti-discrimination, and civil rights law. In the 1980s, Sheila became an adjunct law professor at University of Southern California and later an associate professor at Loyola Law School.

Sheila was elected to the California State Assembly in 1994, becoming the first openly gay person elected to the California legislature. In the 1997-98 legislative session, she served as Speaker pro tempore—the first woman in California history to hold that position.

In 2000, Sheila was elected to the California State Senate; she was re-elected in 2004. After serving in the Senate, Sheila became a member of the California Integrated Waste Management Board. She then started Kuehl Consulting (she long since had dropped using surname "James").

Sheila was elected as the Los Angeles County Supervisor for District 3 in 2014 and is currently serving in that position (as of July 2016).

When asked if she missed acting, Sheila responded by saying that the comraderie in public service mirrored her favorite aspect of acting. She said, "...and then (sic) I'm termed out, I'll be, you know, fairly elderly but still able to do things, and then I guess my ambition would be to be Betty White for a couple of years."

JEAN, GLORIA
1926-

This cute child actress of the 1930s and 40s was born Gloria Jean Schoonover on April 14, 1926 in Buffalo, New York. Before long her family moved to Scranton, Pennsylvania. Her father owned a music store there; Gloria's mother had formerly been a bareback rider in the circus. Gloria had always been a good singer and while quite young was singing in the Scranton area; she sang on the radio with Paul Whiteman's band. When she was 12, Gloria was taken to an audition by Universal director Joe Pasternak, who was looking for a new face to replace Deanna Durbin. She beat out hundreds of girls and in 1939 appeared in her first film, "The Under-Pup" which also starred Bob Cummings. She was a big hit and a string of movies followed. Gloria did rather well into the 1940s until she took some bad advice from her agent,

chose not to renew her contract with Universal, and went on tour. The tour didn't work out so well and when she returned to Hollywood in 1947, virtually nobody wanted her.

Groucho Marx gave Gloria a small role in his film, "Copacabana" (1947) with the rest of the Marx Brothers. A few roles in movies followed but nothing like her earlier career. A few singing TV roles came up next in the 1950s but her acting career was practically finished. Gloria married Franco Cellini in 1962 and had a son; they divorced in 1966. She left the screen in 1963 and worked for Redken, a cosmetics firm, until her retirement in 1993.

Some of Gloria's movies include, " If I Had My Way" (1940) with Bing Crosby, "Never Give a Sucker an Even Break" (1941) with W. C. Fields, "When Johnny Comes Marching Home" (1942) with Allan Jones, "Follow the Boys" (1944) with George Raft, "Ghost Catchers" (1944) with Ole Olsen & Chic Johnson, "I Surrender Dear" (1948) with David Street, "Wonder Valley" (1953) with Jeffrey Stone, "John Paul Jones" (1954) with Sarah Churchill, "Air Strike" (1955) with Richard Denning, "Laffing Time" (1959) with Edward Finney, "The Ladies Man" (1961) with Jerry Lewis.

(Photo, below. Gloria Jean and Richard Avonde on a Death Valley Days, *episode entitled,* Lotta Crabtree, *1954)*

Some TV roles for Gloria include, "Rebound" (1952) with Richard Erdman, "Death Valley Days" (1954) with host Stanley Andrews, "Annie Oakley" (1955) with Gail Davis, "Lock Up" (1961) with Macdonald Carey, "The Dick Powell Theatre: The Legend" (1962) with Sammy Davis Jr., "Saints and Sinners: The Man on the Rim" (1962) with Nick Adams.

In 1991 Gloria was honored by the Young Artist Foundation with its Former Child Star "Lifetime Achievement" Award.

With the help of her sister, Bonnie, Gloria began selling copies of her movies and signed pics of herself to fans via Ebay. That has been consistently working well—sort of a resurgence of her former popularity. She also does autograph shows where her fans get to meet her. Gloria published her autobiography, "Gloria Jean: A Little Bit of Heaven" in 2005 through iUniverse, Inc. With her permission, there is a website that highlights her career and offers memorabilia for sale.

Gloria now lives happily with her son and his family in Hawaii.

JOLSON, AL
1886-50

"You Ain't Heard Nothin' Yet!"—Al Jolson in "The Jazz Singer," 1927

Known for 40 years as "The World's Greatest Entertainer." Big Al—nicknamed Jolie—sang, danced, joked, wrote songs, toured in vaudeville, starred in motion pictures and a multitude of Broadway stage productions, led the way for sound in talking movies, and entertained the troops overseas—pleasing millions decade after decade. And by their own admission he was an inspiration to other celebrities such as Elvis Presley, Bing Crosby, Judy Garland, and Fred Astaire. Jolie was the first entertainer to sell over 10 million records. His powerful, baritone voice (without a microphone he could bounce his songs off the far wall of any theater) and energetic, tear jerking delivery became synonymous of the Roaring Twenties, the depression-era recovering public, and the entertainment-starved and appreciative GIs of World War Two. Called by Al his favorite audiences, he sang for the troops even when he had malaria and pneumonia—though it weakened him severely and eventually led to his death.

Of Jewish descent, Jolie was born Asa Yoelson on May 26, 1886 in Srednik in the Russian Empire (now Seredžius in Lithuania), the fifth and youngest child of Rabbi Moses Reuben Yoelson and

Naomi Yoelson. Rabbi Yoelson immigrated to New York City, New York in 1891. By 1894 he had obtained work at the Talmud Torah Synagogue in Washington, D. C. and could afford to bring his wife and children to America. Sadly, mother Naomi died later that year leaving little Asa heartbroken.

In 1895, entertainer Al Reeves heard Asa sing and talked him into singing in show business. Asa and older brother, Hirsch, became enthralled with performing before appreciative audiences. By 1897, using the names Al and Harry, the pair were entertaining on local street corners. Al began periodically singing in his trademark blackface (common with singers at the time and was not meant to be a put-down of black people) at the suggestion of veteran blackface comedian James Francis Dooley at Keeney's Theatre Brooklyn, New York. He was soon booked on the vaudeville Orpheum Circuit and appeared with Walter L. Main's Circus (1902), with the Dainty Duchess Burlesquers (1903), and partnered with his brother, Harry Yoelson while working for the William Morris Agency.

For awhile the pair partnered with performer Joe Palmer, but Harry didn't get along with Palmer and split from the team in 1905. Jolie returned to blackface singing at a Brooklyn theater in 1904, much to the delight of the audiences who saw him. Unfortunately, Palmer and Jolie were not very popular together and separated in 1906. On his own, he moved to San Francisco, California, and became popular there as a vaudeville singer.

Al married dancer Henrietta Keller in 1907; divorced in 1920. In 1908 the newly-married pair journeyed to New York City. The following year the singing talent of this 5'8" bundle of energy caught producer Lew Dockstader's attention and he signed Al with Dockstader's popular minstrel show—a definite step up for the young entertainer.

But never anywhere long, Al's talent so impressed theater owner/producer Jacob J. Shubert, that he booked Jolie for one of Shubert's shows at his famous Winter Garden Theater in New York City on March 20, 1911. He sang in blackface and the rest is history. After that he starred in a string of smash hits such as "Vera Violetta" (1911), "Robinson Crusoe, Jr." (1916), and "Sinbad" (1918) in which he first sang George Gershwin's hit, "Swanee" and later added his trademark song, "My Mammy." Jolie was hugely popular on Broadway until he retired from the stage in 1926.

In 1922, Al married Broadway actress Ethel Delmar (born Alma Osbourne); they were divorced in 1926 (another source says 1928). In the summer of 1928, Al met and became enamored with dancer/actress Ruby Keeler (1910-93). Running into her at Texas Guinan's night club, Al spontaneously danced with her. A few weeks later he went to see her at her show, "Show Girl," and rose from the audience to join her singing "Liza." They were married in September 1928. In 1935 the pair adopted a son whom they named Al Jolson Jr. They appeared together in the popular musical "Go Into Your Dance" in 1935. Al and Ruby divorced in December 1940 (another source says 1939).

Jolie died of a heart attack on October 23, 1950 and is buried in an impressive, waterfall monument at the Hillside Memorial Park in Culver City, California *(photo, l.)*.

JONES, ANISSA
1958-76

Child actress primarily known for her role as Buffy (before there were vampire slayers) on TV's sitcom "Family Affair." Mary Anissa Jones was born March 11, 1958 in West Lafayette, Indiana. Her unusual middle name is Arabic (Anissa's maternal grandparents were Lebanese) and means "little friend." The family moved to Playa del Rey, California and, at age two, little Mary was enrolled in dance classes. At six she appeared in a breakfast food commercial on TV.

In 1966 she was cast as Elizabeth "Buffy" Patterson Davis on the CBS sitcom "Family Affair," opposite Brian Keith, Johnny Whitaker, Sebastian Cabot, and Kathy Garver (see Kathy's bio in this book). The show proved to be a big hit and ran until 1971.

After "Family Affair" Anissa believed she had been typecasted as Buffy and couldn't find the kind of roles she wanted. Her parents had divorced in 1965. After a long custody battle, she and her brother, Paul, lived with their father until his death in 1973. Paul went to live with their mother but Anissa moved in with a friend. It was reported that Anissa skipped school and was arrested for shoplifting, was sent to a juvenile hall, and spent some time in state custody. Afterward she moved in with her mother and later began taking illegal drugs with her new boy friend, Allan Kovan; she dropped out of high school.

When Anissa turned 18 in 1976 she gained control of her trust fund—earnings from her work in "Family Affair," a tidy sum that amounted to $180,000. Anissa and her brother, Paul, rented an apartment together and, apparently, began doing a lot of partying. On August 28,

1976, Anissa partied all night with friends in Oceanside, California, doing drugs, and, sadly, was found the following morning dead of an accidental overdose. The coroner who did her autopsy said she was loaded with cocaine, PCP, Quaaludes, and Seconal, one of the most severe drug overdoses he had ever seen.

Anissa's acting career was short but memorable. She appeared on TV in "Family Affair" from 1966-71 with Brian Keith and in "To Rome With Love" (1970) with John Forsythe. Anissa also appeared in the movie "The Trouble With Girls" (1969) with Elvis Presley.

Anissa was cremated at Eternal Hill Memorial Park in Oceanside and her ashes scattered over the Pacific Ocean near her home.

KEITH, BRIAN
1921-97

Ruggedly good looking film, TV, and stage actor Brian Keith was born Robert Alba Keith (another source says he was born as Robert Keith Richey Jr.) on November 14, 1921 in Bayonne, New Jersey to actor Robert Keith and stage actress Helena Shipman. At the age of two his parents divorced and single parent and child moved to Hollywood. He was in the silent film "Pied Piper Malone" (with Thomas Meighan) in 1924 when only three years old. Seems, though, he moved back and forth between Hollywood and Long Island, New York. For two years (1927-29) Brian's stepmother was Peg Entwistle, a well-known Broadway actress who became famous by committing suicide by leaping from the "H" of the famous Hollywood sign in 1932.

Brian graduated East Rockaway High School, Rockaway, New York in 1939. He joined the Marines and served from 1942-45. During WWII he was an tail gunner on a two-man Douglas SBD Dauntless dive bomber and earned an air medal.

After the war Brian became a stage actor, then moved into films and television. He had an uncredited role in "Knute Rockne All American" (1940) with Pat O'Brien and Ronald Reagan. By 1951 he was also appearing on TV in the spy series "Shadow of the Cloak" with Helmut Dantine and in 1952 on the sci fi series "Tales of Tomorrow" with Leslie Nielsen. In film he also worked for Walt Disney in some enjoyable family entertainment, such as "Ten Who Dared" (1960) with James Drury, "The Parent Trap" (1961) with Hayley Mills and Maureen O'Hara, "Savage Sam" (1963) with Tommy Kirk and Jeff York, and "A Tiger Walks" (1964) with Vera Miles and Pamela Franklin.

(Photo, below. Cast of Family Affair. *First row, l-r: Kathy Garver & Anissa Jones; 2nd row: Johnny Whitaker & Brian Keith; and top Sebastian Cabot)*

He became well known for the acclaimed TV sitcom, "Family Affair," which aired on CBS from 1966 to 1971. It co-starred Sebastian Cabot, Kathy Garver (see Kathy's bio elsewhere in this book), Johnny Whitaker, and Anissa Jones (see Anissa's bio elsewhere in this book); it also starred Nancy Walker of McMillan and Wife fame and former Mouseketeer Sherry Alberoni. Brian's performance here earned him three Emmy Award nominations for Best Actor in a Comedy Series.

For awhile Brian had his own series where he played a pediatrician in a free clinic on the NBC sitcom "The Brian Keith Show." The show was filmed in Hawaii and ran two seasons (1972-74). It also starred "The Donna Reed Show" favorite, Shelley Fabares, Nancy Kulp of "The Beverly Hillbillies," and Michael Gray.

Brian had another hit TV show with the crime/action show "Hardcastle and McCormick." It ran on ABC from 1983 to 1986 and co-starred Daniel Hugh Kelly, Mary Jackson, and John Hancock. Brian played retired judge Milton C. Hardcastle who can't quite give up catching the bad guys and Daniel plays soon-to-be close friend Mark "Skid" McCormick, a former race-car driver who bought some time in prison and was paroled into Judge Hardcastle's care. Daniel gets to drive a fast sports car called a Coyote X that is given to his character, Mark. Great car! The pair work together to bring in the hoodlums.

Some of the other films in which Brian appeared include, "Fourteen Hours" (1951) with Richard Basehart, "Arrowhead" (1953) with Charlton Heston, "Jivaro" (1954) with Rhonda Fleming, "Nightfall" (1957) with Aldo Ray, "Fort Dobbs" (1958) with Clint Walker, "The Deadly Companions" (1961) with Maureen O'Hara, "Moon Pilot" (1962) with Tom Tryon, "Those Calloways" (1965) with Vera Miles, "The Rare Breed" (1966) with James Stewart, "Krakatoa: East of Java" (1968) with Maximilian Schell, "The McKenzie Break" (1970) with Helmut Griem,

"The Wind and the Lion" (1975) with Sean Connery, "Hooper" (1978) with Burt Reynolds, "Meteor" (1979) with Sean Connery, "The Mountain Men" (1980) with Charlton Heston, "The Alamo: Thirteen Days to Glory" (1987) with James Arness, "Lady in the Corner" (1989) with Loretta Young, "The Gambler Returns: The Luck of the Draw" (1991) with Kenny Rogers, "T. V." (1992) with Rutger Hauer, "Entertaining Angels: The Dorothy Day Story" (1996) with Martin Sheen, "Walking Thunder" (narrator 1997) with John Denver (see John's bio elsewhere in this book).

Some of Brian's TV roles include, "Crusader" (1955-56) with Arthur Space, "Climax!: Hurricane Diane" (1957) with William Lundigan, "Rawhide: Incident in No Man's Land" (1959) with Clint Eastwood, "The Westerner" (1960) with Hank Gobble, "The Alfred Hitchcock Hour: Night of the Owl" (1962) with host Alfred Hitchcock, "The Fugitive: Fear in a Desert City" (1963) with David Janssen, "Insight" (1960-68) with Martin Sheen, "The Zoo Gang" (1974) with John Mills, "How the West Was Won" (mini-series 1976-78) with James Arness, "Centennial" (mini-series 1978-79) with Raymond Burr, "Murder, She Wrote: The Murder of Sherlock Holmes" (1984) with Angela Lansbury, "Pursuit of Happiness" (1987-88) with Paul Provenza, "Evening Shade: Chip Off the Old Block" (1991) with Burt Reynolds, "The Marshal: The Bounty Hunter" (1995) with Jeff Fahey, "Walker, Texas Ranger: Ghost Rider" (1996) with Chuck Norris, "Spider-Man" (voice 1995-98) with Ed Asner.

In 1948 Brian married Frances Helm; they divorced in 1954. He married actress Judy Landon in 1954; they had five children and divorced in 1969. In 1970 Brian married Victoria Young; they had two children and were together until his death.

Brian suffered for some years with emphysema and terminal lung cancer due to cigarette smoking though he had quit smoking ten years before in 1986. Two months after his daughter, Daisy Keith, committed suicide by gunshot on June 24, 1997 Brian took his own life by gunshot at his home in Malibu, California. The official verdict was suicide but close friend Maureen O'Hara steadfastly maintains that it was an accidental shooting. She stated that he would not have committed suicide because he was Catholic and because she knew him to be in good spirits. Brian had a large gun collection and, she said, was always cleaning and showing them to people and that he might have been just handling one that day and it accidently went off.

126

After a private funeral Brian's remains were cremated and his ashes were interred next to his daughter, Daisy, at the Westwood Village Memorial Park Cemetery in Los Angeles, California. Posthumously, Brian received a Star for his work on television on the Hollywood Walk of Fame in 2008; it is located at 7021 Hollywood Boulevard.

KENNEDY, GEORGE
1925-2016

This fine actor appeared in more than 200 film and TV roles. He is probably best remembered for his portrayal of the big, chain-gang convict Dragline In "Cool Hand Luke," a 1967 Warner Bros. release that also starred Paul Newman, Strother Martin, Morgan Woodward, J. D. Cannon, and Dennis Hopper. George won a Academy Award for Best Supporting Actor for that part. George also got a Golden Globe nomination for his portrayal of the brusque but competent airline mechanic, Joe Patroni, in "Airport" (1970), the movie which pretty much started the disaster genre in film. This movie also starred Burt Lancaster, Dean Martin, Jacqueline Bisset, and Helen Hayes.

He was born George Harris Kennedy Jr. on February 18, 1925 in New York City, New York to musician George Harris Kennedy Sr. and ballet dancer Helen A. Kieselbach. Little George got into show business at the age of two by appearing on stage in a touring production of "Bringing Up Father." By the time he was seven he was a radio disc jockey in his home town.

For a time George pursued a military career. He enlisted in the Army in 1943 during WWII and served in the infantry under Gen. George S. Patton (in 1978 George got to portray Patton in a film called "Brass Target"). For valor he was awarded two Bronze Stars and four rows of combat and service ribbons. George stayed with it for 16 years, dropping out as a captain only because of a back injury.

(Photo, below, Paul Newman (center, l.) and George Kennedy, (center, r.) in a scene from Cool Hand Luke, *1967)*

George's first film role was in 1961 in "The Little Shepherd of Kingdom Come" with Jimmie Rodgers. He became a first class star when he acted in the aforementioned "Cool Hand Luke." His performance was top shelf as the big (6'4") and vicious, shoot-first-and-ask-questions-later, ex-con and thief, Red Leary, in "Thunderbolt and Lightfoot," (1974). Co-star Clint Eastwood plays a professional thief nicknamed "Thunderbolt" who joins forces with a small-time car thief named "Lightfoot," Red Leary, and Leary's pal, Eddie Goody, played by Clint's longtime friend, Geoffrey Lewis. *(Photo, below. George in a shot from* Airport, *1970)*

George got another brake when he was asked to portray Carter McKay in the popular serial, "Dallas" (1978-91) from 1988 to 1991. The show also starred such first-rate actors as Barbara Bel Geddes, Jim Davis, Patrick Duffy, Larry Hagman, and Linda Gray. He got his own show on NBC from 1971-72 as "Sarge," a San Diego police detective sergeant named Samuel Patrick Cavanaugh but nicknamed Sarge. After Sarge's wife is murdered he decides to quit the force and become a priest but, of course, he can't keep his nose out of crime. The series also starred Ramon Bieri, Henry Wilcoxon, and Dana Elcar (later of "MacGyver" fame).

Some of George's other roles in film include, "Lonely Are the Brave" (1962) with Kirk Douglas, "Strait-Jacket" (1964) with Joan Crawford, "Hush . . . Hush, Sweet Charlotte" (1964) with Bette Davis, "The Sons of Katie Elder" (1965) with John Wayne (read the mystery of John Wayne's death elsewhere in this book), "The Flight of the Phoenix" (1965) with James Stewart, "The Dirty Dozen" (1967) with Lee Marvin, "Guns of the Magnificent Seven" (1969) with James Whitmore, ". . . tick . . . tick . . . tick...." (1970) with Jim Brown, "Fools' Parade" (1971) with James Stewart, "Cahill, U. S. Marshal" (1973) with John Wayne, "A Cry in the Wilderness" (1974) with Joanna Pettet, "Airport 1975" (1974) with Charlton Heston, "Airport '77" (1977) with Jack Lemmon,

"Death on the Nile" (1978) with Peter Ustinov, "The Concorde . . . Airport '79" (1979) with Alain Delon, "Death Ship" (1980) with Richard Crenna, "Rare Breed" (1984) with Forrest Tucker, "The Delta Force" (1986) with Chuck Norris, "Counterforce" (1988) with Simón Andreu, "The Naked Gun: From the Files of Police Squad!" (1988) with Leslie Nielsen, "Distant Justice" (1992) with Bunta Sungawara, "Dallas: J. R. Returns" (1996) with Larry Hagman, "Small Soldiers" (voice 1998) with Kirsten Dunst, "Don't Come Knocking" (2005) with Sam Shepard, "Another Happy Day" (2011) with Ellen Barkin.

(Photo, below, r. George in a scene from The Blue Knight, *1975)*

Appearances on TV include, "The Phil Silvers Show" (1956-59) with Phil Silvers, "Cheyenne: Prisoner of Moon Mesa" (1959) with Clint Walker, "Sugarfoot: Funeral at Forty Mile" (1960) with Will Hutchins, "Surfside 6" (1961) with Troy Donahue, "Tales of Wells Fargo: Assignment in Gloribee" (1962) with Dale Robertson, "The Andy Griffith Show: The Big House" (1963) with Andy Griffith, "McHale's Navy" (1964) with Ernest Borgnine, "Daniel Boone: A Rope for Mingo" (1965) with

Fess Parker, "Gunsmoke" (1960-66) with James Arness, "Gomer Pyle: USMC" (1968) with Jim Nabors, "Ironside: The Priest Killer" (1971) with Raymond Burr, "The Blue Knight" (1975-76) with John Steadman, "Backstairs at the White House" (mini-series 1979) with Louis Gossett Jr., "Fantasy Island: God Child/Curtain Call" (1983) with Ricardo Montalban, "Lonesome Dove: The Series: Judgment Day" (1994) with Scott Bairstow, "The Young and the Restless" (2003-10) with Samantha Bailey.

(Photo, above. George in a shot from The Dirty Dozen, *1967)*

George's final film was as the dying grandfather, Ed, in the 2014 remake of Kenny Rogers' "The Gambler" with Mark Wahlberg, John Goodman, and Jessica Lange.

He was awarded a Star on the Hollywood Walk of Fame at 6352 (another source says it's at 6356) Hollywood Boulevard in Hollywood, California in 1991.

In 1946 George married Dorothy Gillooly; they had one son and divorced in 1959. George married Norma Wurman in 1959; they had two children and divorced in 1971. He then remarried Norma Wurman in 1973 and again divorced in 1978. He married Joan McCarthy in 1978; they adopted three children and were together until her death in 2015.

George was also a fine fiction writer. In 1983 he wrote the mysteries "Murder On Location," and "Murder On High" in 1984. In 2011 he published his autobiography, "Trust Me: A Memoir." George also liked to fly his own plane and owned a Cessna 210 and a Beechcraft Bonanza.

Sadly, George died of a heart ailment on February 28, 2016 at an assisted living facility in Middleton (near Boise), Idaho. He had been living in Eagle, Idaho. He had a history of heart disease and underwent triple heart bypass surgery in 2002. He was interred at the Idaho Veterans Cemetery, Boise, Idaho.

KIRK, TOMMY
1941-

(Here's lucky Tommy getting a smooch from co-star Annette Funicello in Disney's 1964 comedy classic, "The Misadventures of Merlin Jones.")

Update: In my last book, "Hollywood Celebrities: Where Are They Now?," I wrote that Tommy's middle name was Lee; however, it's a common error that, I was told by his manager, was started by the Disney Studios years ago. He was actually born Thomas Harvey Kirk on December 10, 1941 in Louisville, Kentucky. The studio thought that "Lee" sounded better.

In November 2012 Tommy moved from a small town in northern California to Las Vegas, Nevada.

Lee, Mary
1924-96

This petit (4'11") child actress and singer was born Mary Lee Wooters on October 24, 1924 in Centralia, Illinois to Louie Ellis Wooters and Lela Myrtle Telford. She was discovered by bandleader Ted Weems in 1936 and sang with his Orchestra (Perry Como also sang with Ted Weems). Warner Bros. got wind of her and Mary appeared as the pesty but talented sister of Bonita Granville's co-star, Frankie Thomas Jr., in "Nancy Drew, Reporter" (1939) where she very enjoyably sang "Nursery Rhyme Melody."

Mary's first western of many was "South of the Border" (1939).

She married Harry J. Banan in 1943; they remained together until his death in 1990. Long retired from acting, Mary worked as an account teller for Bank of America for 15 years. She died June 6, 1996 and is interred at East Lawn Sierra Hills Cemetery in Sacramento, California.

LEE, RUDY
Ca. 1944-

Update: As my readers might remember from my first book, "Hollywood Celebrities: Where Are They Now?", I still haven't been able to learn what happened to this fine young actor and dancer. He had 68 acting credits between 1950 and 1960, then disappeared—until 2013 when he suddenly turned up as an art director and set decorator for the motion picture "Devil's Deal." Man of mystery, that's for sure. Rudy, if you read this, two of your former co-workers at the Disney Studios, Sharon Baird and Beverly Washburn, would like to know how you're doing, as well as I would.

LIVINGSTON, STANLEY
1950-

Everybody remembers this child actor for playing Chip Douglas on the hit, long-running sitcom, "My Three Sons." It aired on ABC and CBS from 1960 to 1972 and starred Fred MacMurray, William Frawley, William Demarest, Tim Considine, and Don Grady. Later Stanley became a producer and director.

He was born Stanley Bernard Livingston on November 24, 1950 in Los Angeles, California to Hilliard Livingston and Lillian Rochelle.

Stanley stated that he enjoyed working with the cast of "My Three Sons" and especially Fred MacMurray, who he looked up to as a mentor. "Mr. MacMurray worked well with everybody. That was just the way he was." His real-life brother, Barry Livingston, co-starred with him as adopted brother, Ernie Douglas, on "My Three Sons" from 1963 to 1972.

Some of Stanley's film roles include, "The Bonnie Parker Story" (1958) with Dorothy Provine, "Rally 'Round the Flag, Boys!" (1958) with Paul Newman, "Please Don't Eat the Daisies" (1960) with Doris

Day, "X-15" (1961) with Charles Bronson, "How the West Was Won" (1962) with James Stewart, "Private Parts" (1972) with Ayn Ruymen, "Smokey and the Hotwire Gang" (1979) with James Keach, "Bikini Drive-In" (1995) with Ashlie Rhey, "In the Picture" (2012) with Paula Drake. *(Photo, l. Stanley as Chip Douglas)*

Some of Stanley's TV appearances include, "Peck's Bad Girl" (1959) with Patty

McCormack, "The Adventures of Ozzie and Harriet" (1958-63) with the Nelson Family, "Day in Court" (1963) with Howard Beckler, "Sarge: The Badge or the Cross" (1971) with George Kennedy (see George's bio elsewhere in this book), "Room 222: A Hairy Escape" (1973) with Michael Constantine, "Lucas Tanner" (1974) with David Hartman.

Stanley also produced five productions and directed three

He married Sandra Goble in 1968; they had one daughter, Samantha, and divorced in 1974. Stanley married Paula Drake in 2015.

Says Stanley, "The name Chip Douglas is probably going to be on my tombstone. That's neither good nor bad; it's just a fact of life."

LORRE, PETER
1904-64

Austere and often macabre character actor Peter Lorre was born László Löwenstein on June 26, 1904 in Rózsahegy, Austria-Hungary (now Ruzomberok, Slovakia) to bookkeeper Alois (or Alajos) Lówenstein and Elvira Freischberger. Short on stature (5'4") and usually laid back and soft spoken, Peter (nicknamed "Lazzy") could deliver a powerful acting performance. He began stage acting in mundane roles in Vienna in 1922. But Peter gained instant world-wide fame in 1931 in the German film "M." Cast as a raspy-voiced, bug-eyed serial killer who preyed on children by director Fritz Lang, Peter was quite believable and frightening.

Lazzy fled from Nazi Germany in 1933 and moved first to Paris, France and then to London, England where he shortly co-starred in the first production of Alfred Hitchcock's suspense thriller, "The Man Who Knew Too Much" (1934) with Leslie Banks. Though unable to speak English at that time, Peter learned his lines phonetically. That seemed to work well for the movie and the relatively new actor once again received acclaim for his role.

He soon moved to Hollywood, California in America and continued playing roles of killers. Then Peter starred in a series of films for 20th Century Fox as the iconic Japanese detective/spy, Mr. Moto.

At Warner Bros. for some years Peter (now a proud, naturalized American citizen) got a big break in the movie version of Dashiell

Hammett's hit novel, "The Maltese Falcon" (1941) with Humphrey Bogart (and Sydney Greenstreet in his debut film role as "The Fat Man," Kasper Gutman). John Huston directed and "Falcon" received three nominations for Academy Awards; the film remains one of the best of Hollywood's *film noir*. Peter plays an international, gun-toting ne'er-do-well named Joel Cairo, who is one of many attempting to track down the

whereabouts of a priceless work of art—the Maltese Falcon. *(Photo, l. Sydney Greenstreet and Peter Lorre in a shot from* The Maltese Falcon*)*

Another big hit followed with "Casablanca" (1942)—also starring Humphrey Bogart. The film ultimately won three Academy Awards for Best Picture, director, and screenplay. The movie's memorable song, "As Time Goes By," was sung by drummer Dooley Wilson, who was not the first choice for the role and was almost replaced—fortunately not as he sings so well.

Another fine film for Peter was "Arsenic and Old Lace (1944) with Cary Grant and Raymond Massey. A great, Halloween movie that combined sinister cliches with riotous comedy; Mr. Grant and Peter are superb, and Raymond Massey gets to ham it up as a Boris Karloff look-alike.

Unfortunately, Peter's film career slowed after he left Warner Bros. in 1946; he worked in radio and on the stage for awhile. Later he went to Disney Studios and co-starred in "20,000 Leagues Under the Sea" (1954) with Kirk Douglas and James Mason.

In his later years he worked for Roger Corman in several of his genre horror films.

Some of the films in which Peter appeared include, "The White Devil" (1930) with Ivan Mozzhukhin, "F. P. 1 Antwertet Nicht [German for "Doesn't Answer"] (1932) with Hans Albers, "Crime and Punishment" (1935) with Edward Arnold, "Think Fast, Mr. Moto" (1937) with Virginia Field, "Mr. Moto Takes a Vacation" (1939) with Lionel Atwill, "Stranger on the Third Floor" (1940) with John McGuire, "You'll Find Out" (1940) with Boris Karloff, "The Boogie Man Will Get You" (1942) with Boris Karloff, "The Mask of Dimitrios" (1944) with Sydney Greenstreet, "Three Strangers" (1946) with Sydney Greenstreet, "The Beast With Five Fingers" (1946) with Robert Alda, "Quicksand" (1950) with Mickey Rooney, "Beat the Devil" (1953) with Humphrey Bogart, "Around the World in Eighty Days" (1956) with David Niven, "The Story of Mankind" (1957) with Ronald Colman, "The Big Circus" (1959) with Rhonda Fleming, "Voyage to the Bottom of the Sea" (1961) with Walter Pidgeon, " Tales of Terror: The Black Cat" (1961) with Vincent Price, "The Raven" (1963) with Boris Karloff, "Muscle Beach Party" (1964, cameo) with Annette Funicello.

Peter also appeared in quite a number of TV shows. Here are a few: "Lux Video Theatre: The Taste" (1952) with Peter Forster, "Suspense: The Tortured Hand" (1952), "The Best of Broadway: Arsenic and Old Lace" (1955) with Orson Bean, "Climax!" (1954-57) with host William Lundigan, "The Milton Berle Show" (1958) as a guest, "Alfred Hitchcock Presents" (1957 & 1960) with George Peppard, "Wagon Train" (1960) with Ward Bond, "The Red Skelton Hour" (1955-60) guest appearances, "Rawhide" (1960) with Clint Eastwood, "77 Sunset Strip" (1963) with Efrem Zimbalist Jr.

Peter married Celia Lovsky in 1934, divorced 1945. He married Kaaren Verne in 1945, divorced in 1950. Peter married Anne Marie Brenning in 1953, they were together until Peter's death. In his last marriage they had one daughter, Catharine (1953-85). Catharine made headlines after having nearly been abducted and murdered in 1977 by serial killers Kenneth Bianchi and Angelo Buono, the "Hillside Stranglers" (see my book, "Sociopaths 2: America's Psycho Killers"). Oddly, but luckily, Catharine was released after the creeps learned that she was the daughter of Peter Lorre (it pays to have family in remarkable places).

Peter received a Star on the Hollywood Walk of Fame; it's located at 6619 Hollywood Boulevard.

Sadly, Peter suffered for years from gallbladder problems and doctors prescribed morphine for the associated pain. He became addicted to the medication but later was able to overcome it. In his later years Peter put on much weight and suffered a stroke; he died on March 23, 1964 in Hollywood, California. His body was cremated and his ashes interred at the Hollywood Forever Cemetery in Hollywood. Actor Vincent Price gave the eulogy at his funeral.

MAIN, MARJORIE
1890-1975

This raspy-voiced, rawboned, full of vim and vigor actress was born Mary Tomlinson on February 24, 1890 in Acton, Indiana to Samuel J. Tomlinson and Jennie L. McGaughey. Marjorie attended Franklin College in Franklin, Indiana. Later, when she became an actress, she changed her name to Marjorie Main so as not to embarrass her father, a minister. In those days becoming an actor was not considered an honorable profession. Probably her most famous role was as the big boned (5'7"), feisty, child-ridden (15 kids) wife to lazy, laid back, slow drawl husband Pa, Ma Kettle in a series of ten Ma and Pa Kettle films.

Marjorie began her acting career on the stage in vaudeville and on Broadway about 1916. She moved to Hollywood where she first appeared in movies playing wealthy, upper-class dowagers. Her first film was "A House Divided" (1931) with Walter Huston. Marjorie repeated her stage role of a rich gangster's poverty-ridden mother in the crime drama "Dead End" (1937) with Humphrey Bogart, Joel McCrea, Sylvia Sydney, and the Dead End Kids (see a triubte to the Kids in this book).

Marjorie signed with MGM in 1940 and stayed with them until the mid-1950s. She made six films with Wallace Beery including "Barnacle Bill" (1941) and "Bad Bascomb" (1946). Her first appearance as Ma Kettle came in "The Egg and I" in 1947 with Fred MacMurray, Claudette Colbert, and Percy Kilbride as Pa Kettle; Percy played that role until his death in 1955 when he and a friend were struck by a car while walking. Marjorie won an Academy Award for Best Actress in a Supporting Role for that part. In 1956 Marjorie appeared as the Widow

Hudspeth in "Friendly Persuasion" with Gary Cooper and won a Golden Globe nomination. *(Photo, below. Percy Kilbride and Marjorie Main in a photo still as Ma and Pa Kettle)*

In 1958 Marjorie's character casts her romantic interests on the wagon master, Major Adams, on TVs hit western series, "Wagon Train" (1957-65) with Ward Bond and Robert Horton in "The Cassie Tanner Story." Marjorie retired from film that same year.

Some of Marjorie's film roles include, "Stella Dallas" (1937) with Barbara Stanwyck, "Angels Wash Their Faces" (1939) with Ann Sheridan, "The Women" (1939) with Rosalind Russell, "The Wild Man of Borneo" (1941) with Frank Morgan, "The Shepherd of the Hills" (1941) with John Wayne, "Meet Me in St. Louis" (1944) with Judy Garland, "Murder, He Says" (1945) with Fred MacMurray, "The Wistful Widow of Wagon Gap" (1947) with Abbott & Costello, "Feudin', Fussin' and A-Fightin'" (1948) with Donald O'Connor, "Ma and Pa Kettle" (1949) with Percy Kilbride, "Ma and Pa Kettle on Vacation" (1953) with Percy Kilbride, "Ma and Pa Kettle at Home" (1954) with Percy Kilbride, "Ma and Pa Kettle at Waikiki" (1955) with Percy Kilbride, "The Kettles in the Ozarks" (1956) with Arthur Hunnicut, "The

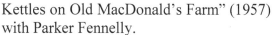

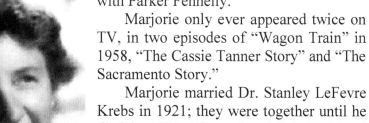

Kettles on Old MacDonald's Farm" (1957) with Parker Fennelly.

Marjorie only ever appeared twice on TV, in two episodes of "Wagon Train" in 1958, "The Cassie Tanner Story" and "The Sacramento Story."

Marjorie married Dr. Stanley LeFevre Krebs in 1921; they were together until he died in 1935. Biographer Michelle Vogel also claims that Marjorie had a long-term lesbian relationship with actress Spring Byington.

It's interesting to note that until Marjorie's death she often had "conversations" with her dead husband, even interrupting a scene while filming a movie, to talk with him. She would let the director know when it was OK to go on, which she did as if nothing had happened.

Sadly, Marjorie died of lung cancer at St. Vincent's Hospital in Los Angeles on April 10, 1975. She is buried in the Forest Lawn Memorial Park Cemetery in Hollywood Hills, California.

MARTINEZ, A
1948-

Veteran actor, writer, and singer born Adolfo Larrue Martinez III on September 27, 1948 in Glendale, California. He was well known for playing Native American parts and deservedly so, for he has Apache heritage on his father's side and Piegan Blackfeet on his mother's (with some Mexican and European stock thrown in as well—melting pot American like most of us). He is probably best remembered for his many western roles and his parts in daytime soap operas.

When he was little his family began calling Adolfo "A" or "Little A" to distinguish him from his father and grandfather; it stuck and later he took A Martinez as his stage name.

A began singing at age 12 at the Hollywood Bowl where he won a talent contest. He graduated from Verdugo Hills High School in Tujunga, Los Angeles, California. A began his passion for acting at UCLA. One of his first acting roles was on TV's popular sitcom, "All in the Family" (1971-79) which starred Carroll O'Connor, Jean Stapleton, Rob Reiner, and Sally Struthers. He appeared with John Wayne in the popular 1972 western, "The Cowboys" as one of the older cowboys named Cimarron. A began his career with soaps by getting a role on "Falcon Crest" in 1982. In "Santa Barbara" as Cruz Castillo he won a Daytime Emmy in 1990 and played the part from 1984-92.

(Photo, below. Here's A Martinez, center, tending to John Wayne's wounds in The Cowboys*)*

He was on "General Hospital" and was awarded three consecutive ALMA Awards.

Some of A's film roles include, "The Young Animals" (1968) with Patty McCormack, "Hunters Are for Killing" (1970) with Burt Reynolds, "Probe" (1972) with Hugh O'Brian, "The Take" (1974) with Eddie Albert, "Exo-Man" (1977) with David Ackroyd, "Roughnecks" (1980) with Cathy Lee Crosby, "She-Devil" (1989) with Meryl Streep, "Not of This World" (1991) with Lisa Hartman, "One Night Stand" (1995) with Ally Sheedy, "The Cherokee Kid" (1996) with James Coburn, "Last Rites" (1999) with Randy Quaid, "Wind River" (2000) with Blake Heron, "Desolation Canyon" (2006) with Stacy Keach, "Fist of the Warrior" (2007) with Peter Greene, "California Winter" (2012) with Michael Ironside, "In Embryo" (2016) with Ross McCall. He is currently working on more films.

A also appeared in many TV roles, some of which include, "Mission: Impossible: The Code" (1969) with Peter Graves, "Bonanza: Gideon the Good" (1970) with Lorne Greene, "Hawaii Five-O: A Bullet for El Diablo" (1973) with Jack Lord, "The Cowboys" (1974) with Moses Gunn, "McCloud: Sharks!" (1975) with Dennis Weaver, "The Streets of San Francisco" (1972-76) with Karl Malden, "Baretta: Por Nada" (1977) with Robert Blake, "Centennial" (mini-series 1979) with Raymond Burr, "CHiPs: A Simple Operation" (1981) with Erik Estrada, "Romance Theatre" (1982) with host Louis Jourdan, "Whiz Kids" (1983-84) with Matthew Labyorteaux, "L. A. Law" (1990-94) with Corbin Bernsen, "Profiler" (1996-97) with Ally Walker, "General Hospital" (2001-02) with Steve Burton, "CSI: Crime Scene Investigation" (2005-07) with Laurence Fishburne, "One Life to Live" (2008-09) with Erika Slezak, "The Bold and the Beautiful" (2011-12) with Susan Flannery, "Days of Our Lives" (2015-2016) with Josh Taylor.

In 1981 A married actress Mare Winningham; they divorced later that year. He married Leslie Bryans in 1982; they have one son and two daughters. A is currently hard at work on TV roles and making movies.

McCLURE, DOUG
1935-95

This fine actor was in the business for four decades and is probably best known for his portrayal of the fun-loving but rowdy cowboy, Trampas, in the long running (1962-71) NBC western series, "The Virginian," which starred James Drury, Lee J. Cobb, John McIntire, Clu Gulager, Roberta Shore, and Randy Boone. "Virginian" was in color and the first TV western to run 90 minutes in length. It placed third for long running TV show after "Gunsmoke" and "Bonanza." Doug became best friends with "Virginian" star James Drury and with the star of "Wagon Train," Robert Fuller.

Doug was born Douglas Osborne McClure on May 11, 1935 in Glendale, California to Donald Reed McClure and Clara Elsie Barker. He attended the University of California in Los Angeles. One of his earliest movie roles was in the war film, "The Enemy Below" (1957) and starring Robert Mitchum and Curt Jurgens.

(Photo, below. The cast of The Virginian: *front, center, Lee J. Cobb; back, l-r: Roberta Shore, Clu Gulager, Doug McClure, Randy Boone, and James Drury)*

The tall (6'1") actor made a lot of action, sci fi movies, one of which was "At the Earth's Core," a fantasy based on the Edgar Rice Burroughs novel of the same name. Made in 1976 it also starred Peter Cushing and Caroline Munro. He did two other sci fi movies based on Burroughs novels: "The Land That Time

Forgot" (1975) with John McEnery and Susan Penhaligon and the sequel, "The People That Time Forgot" (1977) starring Patrick Wayne and Dana Gillespie.

Some of Doug's film roles include, "Friendly Persuasion" (1956) with Gary Cooper, "South Pacific" (1958) with Mitzi Gaynor, "Gidget" (1959) with Sandra Dee, "The Unforgiven" (1960) with Burt Lancaster, "Shenandoah" (1965) with James Stewart, "The Birdmen" (1971) with Richard Basehart, "Death Race" (1973) with Lloyd Bridges, "Satan's Triangle" (1975) with Kim Novack, "Warlords of the Deep" (1978) with Peter Gilmore, "The House Where Evil Dwells" (1982) with Edward Albert, "Cannonball Run II" (1984) with Burt Reynolds, "Omega Syndrome" (1986) with Ken Wahl, "Prime Suspect" (1989) with Don Blakely, "The Gambler Returns: The Luck of the Draw" (1991) with Kenny Rogers, "Maverick" (1994) with Mel Gibson, "Riders in the Storm" (1995) with Bo Hopkins.

Some of Doug's TV appearances include, "Death Valley Days: Fifteen Paces to Fame" (1957) with host Stanley Andrews, "The Adventures of Jim Bowie: Bad Medicine" (1958) with Scott Forbes, "U. S. Marshal: The Threat" (1959) with John Bromfield, "Lawman: The Visitor" (1959) with John Russell, "The Twilight Zone: Mr. Denton on Doomsday" (1959) with host Rod Serling, "Hennesey: Angel Face" (1960) with Jackie Cooper, "Overland Trail" (1960) with William Bendix, "It Takes a Thief: A Thief is a Thief" (1968) with Robert Wagner, "Circle of Fear: Cry of the Cat" (1972) with Sebastian Cabot, "Barbary Coast" (1975-76) with William Shatner, "Roots: Part VI" (1977) with John Amos, "CHiPs: Battle of the Bands" (1982) with Erik Estrada, "Manimal: Night of the Scorpion" (1983) with Simon MacCorkindale, "Hardcastle and McCormick: School for Scandal" (1984) with Brian Keith, "Airwolf: Half-Pint" (1985) with Jan-

Michael Vincent, "Crazy Like a Fox: Fox on the Range" (1986) with Jack Warden, "Murder, She Wrote: Steal Me a Story" (1987) with Angela Lansbury, "Zorro: The Challenge" (1990) with Duncan Regehr, "Out of This World" (1987-91) with Donna Prescow, "In the Heat of the Night: Time's Long Shadow" (1994) with Carroll O'Connor, "Kung Fu: The Legend Continues: Cruise Missiles" (1995) with David Carradine. Doug's last appearance was in "One West Waikiki: Rest in Peace" (1996) with Cheryl Ladd.

Doug married Faye Bush in 1957; they had one child and divorced in 1961. In 1961 he married actress Barbara Luna; they divorced in 1963. He married Helen Crane in 1965 but they divorced in 1968. Doug married Diane Soldani in 1970; they had one child and divorced in 1979. He married Diane Furnberg in 1979; they were together until his death.

In 1994, Doug was awarded a Star on the Hollywood Walk of Fame at 7065 Hollywood Boulevard.

Sadly, Doug died from lung cancer on February 5, 1995 in Sherman Oaks, California. He is interred at the Woodlawn Memorial Cemetery in Santa Monica, California. His gravestone reads, "Forever in Our Hearts—We miss you."

McDANIEL, HATTIE
1895-52

This charming lady of the screen is probably best remembered for her role as Scarlett O'Hara's Mammy in David O. Selznick's 1939 classic hit of "Gone With the Wind." This wonderful epic about the South during the turbulent years of the War Between the States was written by Margaret Mitchell and starred Clark Gable, Vivien Leigh, Leslie Howard, Olivia de Havilland, and Thomas Mitchell. Hattie won the Academy Award for Best Supporting Actress for that role, the first African American to win one.

Hattie was born the youngest of 13 children on June 10, 1895 in Wichita, Kansas to Henry McDaniel, who had fought in the Civil War, and singer Susan Holbert—both former slaves. The family moved to Colorado in 1900, first to Fort Collins and then to Denver. There Hattie

graduated from Denver East High School. *(Photo, l. Here's Hattie trying to* straighten out *Scarlett O'Hara (Vivien Leigh) in* Gone With the Wind*)*

She was a songwriter as part of her brother's minstrel show but after the death of her brother, Otis, in 1916 the troupe began to lose money. Her next big break as a performer came when Hattie appeared with Professor George Morrison's Melody Hounds, a black touring ensemble, from 1920 to 1925. They appeared on radio on station KOA in Denver. Hattie re-

148

corded many of her songs with Okeh Records and Paramount Records in Chicago.

When the stock market crashed in 1929, it basically put Hattie out of the music business. The only work she could find was as a waitress at the Club Madrid in Milwaukee, Wisconsin. But she was not to be held back from once again performing and eventually the club's owner let her sing there and she became a regular performer.

Hattie moved to Los Angeles in 1931 to join her brother, Sam, and two sisters and got some work in movies. Sam was working on KNX radio and got his sister a spot as a bossy maid; the show—called Hi-Hat Hattie—became popular but the money was so bad she had to moonlight as a maid.

Her next big break came when she got a part in the film "The Golden West" (1932) with George O'Brien and the following year worked with Mae West in "I'm No Angel," which also starred Cary Grant and Edward Arnold, in which Hattie played Mae West's maid. In the early 30s Fox Film Corporation put her under contract and Hattie got a role in "The Little Colonel" (1935) with Shirley Temple, Lionel Barrymore, and Bill "Bojangles" Robinson.

Hattie's first major role came in a film with Will Rogers called "Judge Priest" (1934), which also starred Tom Brown and Stepin Fetchit. In this film she does a duet with Will; the pair became close friends.

In 1935 Hattie first played opposite Clark Gable in "China Seas" (for MGM) which also starred Wallace Beery and Jean Harlow. And she got a featured role in Universal Pictures' "Show Boat" (1938) with Allan

Jones and Irene Dunne in which she sings "Can't Help Lovin' Dat Man" with Irene.

(Photo, l. Here's Hattie as Beulah on the TV show, Beulah, *1951)*

During WWII Hattie was the chairman of the Negro Division of the Hollywood Victory Committee, which provided entertainment for soldiers stationed at military bases. She made a lot of personal appearances at military hospitals and performed at USO shows and war bond rallies; Bette Davis and Lena Horne joined her.

Hattie was the first black American to star in her own radio show, "Beulah," which ran on CBS radio from 1945 to 1954; however, Hattie only played the role from 1947 to 1952 when she became ill and had to be replaced by Lillian Randolph and later by Lillian's sister, Amanda Randolph of TV's "Amos 'n' Andy" fame. It later became a TV show on ABC from 1950 to 1952. Hattie played the part of Beulah from 1951 to 1952 when she was replaced by Louise Beavers because she developed breast cancer and was too sick to perform.

Some of Hattie's film roles include, "Merry Wives of Reno" (1934) with Guy Kibbee, "Little Men" (1934) with Ralph Morgan, "Alice Adams" (1935) with Katharine Hepburn, "The Singing Kid" (1936) with Al Jolson, "True Confession" (1937) with Fred MacMurray, "They Died With Their Boots On" (1941) with Errol Flynn, "George Washington Slept Here" (1942) with Jack Benny, "Janie" (1944) with Joyce Reynolds, "Margie" (1946) with Jeanne Crain, "Song of the South" (1946) with Bobby Driscoll, "Mickey" (1948) with Lois Butler, "The Big Wheel" (1949) with Mickey Rooney.

Hattie's only TV role was as Beulah (see above).

Hattie married Howard Hickman in 1911; they were together until his death in 1915. She married George Langford about 1924 but he died of a gunshot wound in 1925. In 1941 she married James Crawford; they divorced in 1945. Hattie married Larry Williams in 1949; they divorced in 1950.

Sadly, Hattie's breast cancer worsened and she died in Woodland Hills, California on October 26, 1952. She was buried at the Angelus-Rosedale Cemetery in Los Angeles, California. Hattie has two Stars on the Hollywood Walk of Fame, one at 6933 Hollywood Boulevard and one at 1719 Vine Street, Hollywood, California.

McDOWALL, RODDY
1928-98

Former child actor who was one of the lucky, talented ones who was able to cross over to adult roles and appeared in over 150 films. He was also a film director, photographer, and voice artist . Roddy was born Roderick Andrew Anthony Jude McDowall on September 17, 1928 in Herne Hill, London, England to Merchant Mariner Thomas McDowall and Winifriede Corcoran. Possibly because his mother always wanted to be a film star but never was, little Roddy was enrolled in elocution courses at age five. By the time he was 10 he was in his first film, "Murder in the Family" (1938) with Jessica Tandy and Glynis Johns. He also appeared in "Scruffy" (1938) with Jack Melford and Billy Merson.

In 1940, because of WWII, his mother brought Roddy and sister, Virginia, to the United States (Roddy became a citizen in 1949 and lived here the rest of his life). Roddy soon got a part in John Ford's tribute to Welsh coal miners, "How Green Was My Valley" (1941) starring Walter Pidgeon, Maureen O'Hara (Roddy became lifelong friends with Maureen), and Donald Crisp. But perhaps his best remembered film as a child actor was in "Lassie Come Home" (1943) with Donald Crisp, Edmund Gwenn, Nigel Bruce, and a young Elizabeth Taylor (another lifelong friend). At 18, Roddy moved to New York and appeared in many stage roles, some of which included Shakespearen parts.

One of his best remembered adult roles was a part in which the audience never got to see him. That's right, when he played the mutated chimpanzee, Cornelius, in the acclaimed sci fi adventure "Planet of the

Apes" (1968) which starred Charlton Heston, Kim Hunter, Maurice Evans, and James Whitmore (all in ape makeup). It became a series of films and a TV show and Roddy got to act in all but one of the original five movies (he wasn't in the first sequel due to the fact that he was directing a film in England).

He went back to Hollywood and did the Robert Louis Stevenson classic adventure "Kidnapped" (1948) for Monogram Pictures. The film starred Sue England and Dan O'Herlihy. Roddy got a small part for his mother in this film, as the innkeeper's wife—the only time she ever acted. Roddy made six more flicks for Monogram and then went back to the stage in New York in 1952; he was also on radio during this time. Eventually he returned to Hollywood to make more movies and do a lot of TV work.

Some of the films in which Roddy appear include, "Man Hunt" (1941) with Walter Pidgeon, "My Friend Flicka" (1943) with Preston Foster, "Thunderhead-Son of Flicka" (1945) with Preston Foster, "Macbeth" (1948) with Orson Welles, "Killer Shark" (1950) with Laurette Luez, "The Steel Fist" (1952) with Harry Lauter, "The Good Fairy" (1956) with Maurice Evans, "The Tempest" (1960) with Richard Burton, "Cleopatra" (1963) with Elizabeth Taylor, "The Greatest Story Ever Told" (1965) with Max von Sydow, "That Darn Cat!" (1965) with Hayley Mills, "Lord Love a Duck" (1966) with Tuesday Weld, "The Adventures of Bullwhip Griffin" (1967) with Karl Malden, "It!" (1967) with Jill Haworth, "Hello Down There" (1969) with Tony Randall, "Pretty Maids All in a Row" (1971) with Rock Hudson, "Escape From the Planet of the Apes" (1971) with Kim Hunter, "Conquest of the Planet of the Apes" (1972) with Don Murray, "The Poseidon Adventure" (1972) with Gene Hackman, "The Legend of Hell House" (1973) with Pamela Franklin, "Battle for the Planet of the Apes" (1973) with Claude Akins, "Funny Lady" (1975) with Barbra Streisand, "The Cat From Outer Space" (1978) with Ken Berry, "Fright Night" (1985) with Chris Sarandon, "The Wind in the Willows" (voice 1987) with Charles Nelson Reilly, "Shakma" (1990) with Christopher Atkins, "The Sands of Time" (1992) with Deborah Raffin, "The Alien Within" (1995) with Alex Hyde-White, "Loss of Faith" (1998) with John Ritter.

Some of Roddy's TV appearances include, "Encounter: Bruno and Sydney" (1954) with Beth Amos, "The Alcoa Hour: He's for Me" (1957)

with Larry Blyden, "The Twilight Zone: People Are Alike All Over" (1960) with host Rod Serling, "Arrest and Trial: Journey Into Darkness" (1963) with John Alderson, "Batman: The Bookworm Turns" (1966) with Adam West, "The Invaders: The Experiment" (1967) with Roy Thinnes, "Night Gallery: Night Gallery" (1969) with host Rod Serling, "Columbo: Short Fuse" (1972) with Peter Falk, "McMillan & Wife: Death of a Monster . . . Birth of a Legend" (1973) with Rock Hudson, "Planet of the Apes" (1974) with Ron Harper, "Ellery Queen: The Adventure of the Black Falcon" (1976) with Jim Hutton, "Mork & Mindy: Dr. Morkenstein" (1979) with Robin Williams, "The Martian Chronicles" (mini-series 1980) with Rock Hudson, "Tales of the Gold Monkey" (1982-83) with Stephen Collins, "Murder, She Wrote: School for Scandal" (1985) with Angela Lansbury, "Around the World in 80 Days" (mini-series 1989) with Pierce Brosnan, "Camp Candy: When It Rains . . . It Snows" (voice 1992) with John Candy, "Quantum Leap: A Leap for Lisa" (1992) with Scott Bakula, "Red Planet" (mini-series 1994) with Mark Hamill, "Gargoyles: The New Olympians" (voice 1996) with Keith David, "The New Batman Adventures: Over the Edge" (1998) with Kevin Conroy.

Relative to when he was a child actor, Roddy said, "I really liked Lassie, but that horse, Flicka, was a nasty animal with a terrible disposition." And as to his role as Cornelius, the chimpanzee, Roddy said that he enjoyed the role but hated the makeup because he was stuck in it all day—couldn't eat, couldn't scratch, and it itched all the time!

Roddy was awarded a Star on the Hollywood Walk of Fame at 6632 Hollywood Boulevard in 1960.

Sadly, Roddy died of lung cancer at his home in Studio City, Los Angeles, California on October 3, 1998. His remains were cremated and his ashes scattered in the Pacific Ocean. It is said of Roddy McDowall that he was a rarity among movie stars in that he seemed to have no enemies, only friends. That, in itself, is a monument to one's life.

McQUEEN, BUTTERFLY 1911-95

This petit (5'1") actress was originally a dancer and first appeared in a film role in the memorable character portrayal of Scarlett O'Hara's maid, Prissy, in "Gone With the Wind" (1939) with Clark Gable, Vivien Leigh, Olivia de Havilland, and Leslie Howard. Butterfly was born Thelma McQueen on January 7, 1911 in Tampa, Florida.

Butterfly graduated from high school in Long Island, New York. She originally planned on becoming a nurse until a high school teacher suggested she try acting. She did and also danced with the Venezuela Jones Negro Youth Group. Butterfly got her nickname when she danced as part of the Butterfly Ballet in a production of "A Midsummer Night's Dream." Somebody tagged her with the nickname "Butterfly" because of her constantly moving hands—a nervous habit that some people have while they talk. She always said that she hated her birth name and later legally changed it to Butterfly.

Her distinctive, high-pitched voice was noted by a critic who described it as "the itsy-little voice fading over the horizon of comprehension." Nevertheless, fans of "Gone With the Wind" and Butterfly McQueen will always fondly remember her famous line in the movie, "Oh, Miss Scarlett—I don't know nothin' 'bout birthin' babies!"

Also in 1939, Butterfly had an uncredited part in the comedy/drama "The Women" which starred Norma Shearer, Rosalind Russell, and Joan Crawford. She appeared on radio on the "Jack Benny Show" and played Eddie "Rochester" Anderson's niece, Butterfly. Butterfly was in several other films but in 1947 she had grown tired of the ethnic stereotypes she had to play and ended her film career.

During WWII Butterfly acted in the Armed Forces Radio broadcast of "Jubilee." She did come back to act on TV from 1950 to 1952 on the sitcom "Beulah;" she had also done the radio version. And just for fun she appeared in an episode of "The Dating Game" in 1969.

Some of Butterfly's film roles include, "Affectionately Yours"  (1941) with Merle Oberon, "I Dood It" (1943) with Red Skelton, "Mildred Pierce" (1945) with Joan Crawford, "Flame of Barbary Coast" (1945) with John Wayne, "Duel in the Sun" (1946) with Jennifer Jones, "Killer Diller" (1948) with Dusty Fletcher, "The Phynx" (1970) with Michael A. Miller, "The Mosquito Coast" (1986) with Harrison Ford. *(Photo, above. Vivien Leigh and Butterfly McQueen in a scene from* Gone With the Wind, *1939)*

Some of her TV roles include, "ABC Weekend Specials: The Seven Wishes of Joanna Peabody" (1978) with Garrett Morris, "Walt Disney's Wonderful World of Color: Polly" (1989) with Keshia Knight Pulliam.

In 1974 Butterfly appeared in the original stage version of "The Wiz" when it debuted in Baltimore, Maryland and later she acted in the Broadway run.

Butterfly decided to take up political study and received a B. A. in political science from City College of New York in 1975. In 1979 she did a part in the "ABC Afterschool Special" episode "Seven Wishes of a Rich Kid." Her glowing performance won her a Daytime Emmy Award for Outstanding Individual Achievement in Children's Programming.

A lifelong atheist, Butterfly always said, "As my ancestor's are free from slavery, I am free from the slavery of religion."

Sadly, Butterfly died from burns she had sustained in her home in trying to light a kerosene heater that malfunctioned and burst into flames. She died at Augusta Regional Medical Center in Augusta, Georgia on December 22, 1995. Butterfly made plans in advance to donate her body to medical science.

MILES, VERA
1929-

This talented, beautiful actress was born Vera June Ralston on August 23, 1929 in Boise City, Oklahoma to Thomas Ralston and Burnice Wyrick. Vera grew up in Pratt, Kansas and later lived in Wichita, Kansas where she worked nights as a Western Union operator. She graduated from Wichita North High School in 1947. Her good looks weren't overlooked as the 5'3" charmer was crowned Miss Kansas in 1948 and was the third runner up in the Miss America.

Vera moved to Los Angeles in 1950 and landed small roles in film and television. One of her first film roles was in "Two Tickets to Broadway," a 1951 musical starring Janet Leigh and Tony Martin. During the 50s she moved from studio to studio so much she said, "I was dropped by the best studios in town!" She chose the stage name Miles after her first husband's last name because there already was an actress named Vera Ralston (that Vera appeared in "Dakota" [1945] with John Wayne).

In 1955 Vera co-starred in the jungle flick, "Tarzan's Hidden Jungle," with Gordon Scott as Tarzan. There was no Jane character in this film but Vera became real-life Jane to Gordon Scott by marrying him in 1956. She worked first with John Wayne in 1956 in "The Searchers" with Jeffrey Hunter and Natalie Wood and, also, in 1962 in "The Man Who Shot Liberty Valance" with James Stewart and Lee Marvin.

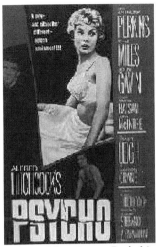

But the role for which she is probably best remembered is as Lila Crane in the Alfred Hitchcock classic horror flick, "Psycho" (1960), the story of a crazed peeping Tom who also murders the ladies he peeks at and anybody else his mother tells him to. The mother, though, is a desiccated corpse that crazed Norman Bates (artistically played by Anthony Perkins) dug up after she was buried, treated her body with chemicals to preserve it, and spends the rest of his life "thinking" that he hears her talking to him. Murder victims, such as Lila's sister, thief Marion Crane (played by Janet Leigh), wind up in a nearby pond to confuse everybody who's looking for them. Great flick. Vera came back to reprise her role as Lila Crane in "Psycho II" (1983) with star Anthony Perkins.

Vera worked in the production of "The Green Berets" as star John Wayne's wife, but—plague of the movie industry—her scenes were edited from the picture.

Vera married Bob Miles in 1948; they had two children and divorced in 1954. In 1956 she married actor Gordon Scott; they had one son and divorced in 1960. Vera married Keith Larsen in 1960; they had one son and divorced in 1971. She married Robert Jones in 1973.

Some of the roles that Vera did in film include, "When Willie Comes Marching Home" (1950) with Dan Dailey, "The Charge at Feather River" (1953) with Guy Madison, "Wichita" (1955) with Joel McCrea, "23 Paces to Baker Street" (1956) with Van Johnson, "The Wrong Man" (1956) with Henry Fonda, "The FBI Story" (1959) with James Stewart, "The Fugitive" (1963) with David Janssen, "A Tiger Walks" (1964) with Brian Keith, "Those Calloways" (1965) with Brian Keith, "Follow Me, Boys!" (1966) with Fred MacMurray, "Gentle Giant" (1967) with Dennis Weaver, "Hellfighters" (1968) with John Wayne, "Cannon" (1971) with William Conrad, "A Howling in the Woods" (1971) with Barbara Eden, "One Little Indian" (1973) with James Garner, "Run for the Roses" (1977) with Stuart Whitman, "Our

Family Business" (1981) with Ted Danson, "BrainWaves" (1983) with Keir Dullea, "The Hijacking of the Achille Lauro" (1989) with Karl Malden, "Separate Lives" (1995) with James Belushi.

Some of Vera's TV roles include, "Strange Stories: Such a Nice Little Girl" (1956) with Robert Armstrong, "Climax!" (1954-58), "Riverboat" (1959) with Darren McGavin, "The Twilight Zone: Mirror Image" (1960) with host Rod Serling, "Checkmate" (1961) with Doug McClure (see Doug's bio in this book), "The Fugitive: Fear in a Desert City" (1963) with David Janssen, "The Outer Limits: The Forms of Things Unknown" (1964) with David McCallum, "Wagon Train: The Silver Lady" (1965) with Robert Fuller (see Bob's bio in this book), "My Three Sons: Brother, Ernie" (1965) with Fred MacMurray,

"Journey to the Unknown: Matakitas Is Coming" (1968) with Leon Lissek, "Gunsmoke: Sam McTavish, M. D." (1970) with James Arness (see Jim's bio in this book), "Alias Smith and Jones: The Posse That Wouldn't Quit" (1971) with Pete Duel, "Columbo: Lovely But Lethal" (1973) with Peter Falk, "The Streets of San Francisco: Men Will Die" (1975) with Karl Malden, "Barnaby Jones: The Reincarnation" (1977) with Buddy Ebsen, "Little House on the Prairie: The Last Summer" (1983) with Michael Landon, "Crazy Like a Fox: Requiem for a Fox" (1985) with Jack Warden, "Simon & Simon: The Richer They Are, the Harder They Fall" (1988) with Gerald McRaney, "Murder, She Wrote: See You in Court, Baby" (1990) with Angela Lansbury.

Vera retired from acting in 1995 and lives in Los Angeles, California. She does not grant interviews nor does she make personal appearances. Vera was awarded a Star on the Hollywood Walk of Fame in 1960; it's located at 1652 Vine St., Hollywood, California. Vera Miles certainly was one of the most beautiful and talented actresses in Hollywood.

MIMIEUX, YVETTE
1942-

Retired movie and TV actress, writer, and producer Yvette Carmen Mimieux was born January 8, 1942 in Hollywood, California to a French father and a Mexican mother—hence the lovely accent she used in many of her acting roles. Yvette was one of four beauty-contest finalists invited by Elvis Presley to try out for a bit role in his current (at the time) movie project, "Jailhouse Rock" (1957). Unfortunately, she wasn't selected. Her first movie role was in a B-teen film entitled "Platinum High School" (1960) which starred Mickey Rooney, Terry Moore, Dan Duryea, and Conway Twitty.

Yvette was a Deb Star of 1959.

But probably her most remembered role was as the beautiful but innocent girl of the far-distant future (802,701 A.D.), Weena, in George Pal's classic sci-fi movie, "The Time Machine" (1960). This fine movie

(Photo, l., Yvette's character, Weena, menaced by a lurid Morlock in "The Time Machine)

(the best version in my opinion) also starred Rod Taylor, Alan Young, Sebastian Cabot, and Whit Bissell. George Pal picked Yvette for the role himself and referred to her as "a cross between a fairy princess and Brigitte Bardot"). Just 18 years old at the time, nevertheless, Yvette showed her talent by doing a fine job as the romantic love interest of co-star and "time traveler," Australian actor Rod Taylor (his first feature film).

Trivia for "The Time Machine": The never-seen actor who did the ominous voice for the almost magical "talking rings" that spoke to time-traveler George and his new Eloi friend, Weena, was done by veteran voice-over genius Paul Frees (Disney's Ludwig Von Drake character and Boris Badenov of "Rocky and Bullwinkle" fame, to name a few of his roles).

That same year (1960) Yvette appeared in the popular comedy beach movie, "Where the Boys Are" starring Connie Francis (who also sang the title hit song), Dolores Hart, George Hamilton, Frank Gorshin, and Jim Hutton. This movie alone probably instituted the annual student pilgrimage to Fort Lauderdale, Florida. She plays shy Melanie Tolman who loses her virginity to aggressive and selfish Yale student Franklin, (played by Rory Harrity), and winds up in the hospital (this is a comedy?).

(Photo, r., Yvette and Rod Taylor during the filming of The Time Machine*)*

Some of the films in which Yvette appeared include, "The Four Horsemen of the Apocalypse" (1962) with Glenn Ford, "Diamond Head" (1963) with Charlton Heston, "Monkeys, Go Home!" (1967) with Dean Jones, "Dark of the Sun" (1968) with Rod Taylor, "The Delta Factor" (1970) with Christopher George, "Sky-jacked" (1972) with Charlton Heston, "Bell, Book and Candle" (1976) with Michael Murphy, "The Black Hole" (1979) with Anthony Perkins, "Forbidden Love:" (1982) with Andrew Stevens, "The Fifth Missile" (1986) with Robert Conrad, "Lady Boss" (1992; her last film) with Kim Delaney.

TV roles included, "Yancy Derringer" (1959) with Jock Mahoney, "One Step Beyond" (1960) with John Newland, "Mr. Lucky" (1960) with John Vivyan, "Dr. Kildare" (1964) with Richard Chamberlain, "The Most Deadly Game" (1970-71) with Ralph Bellamy, "Berrenger's" (1985) with Ben Murphy, "The Love Boat" (1984-86) with Gavin MacLeod.

Yvette married director Stanley Donen in 1972; divorced 1985. She then married Howard F. Ruby in 1986.

This blonde, 5'4" charmer retired from acting in 1992. Currently Yvette is an anthropologist and an accomplished real estate investor.

MINEO, SAL
1939-76

This fine actor who wasn't with us long enough is probably best remembered for his role as the troubled teenager, John "Plato" Crawford, in the classic period piece, "Rebel Without a Cause" (1955) with James Dean, Natalie Wood, Jim Backus, Ann Doran, Dennis Hopper, and Nick Adams. He received a nomination for an Academy Award for Best Supporting Actor for that part. He had real-life background as a tough, street kid for "Rebel" because after Sal was thrown out of parochial school at age eight he became a member of a Bronx street gang; he was also arrested for robbery at age ten.

Sal was born Salvatore Mineo Jr. on January 10, 1939 in The Bronx, New York City, New York to coffins makers Salvatore Mineo Sr. and Josephine Alvisi. His mother enrolled little Sal in dancing and acting school when he was very young. His first stage role was in Tennessee Williams' play, "The Rose Tattoo" in 1951; it starred Eli Wallach and Maureen Stapleton. Sal also played the young prince in the stage musical, "The King and I" starring young actor and TV director Yul Brynner who also did the 1956 film role.

After a few appearances on TV, Sal's first film role was in "Six Bridges to Cross," (1955), beating out Clint Eastwood for the part. The Universal-International movie also starred Tony Curtis and Julie Adams.

161

The big breakthrough for the 5'6" actor was in "Rebel Without a Cause" (see above). The following year he played Angel Obregon II in the hit film," Giant," which also cast James Dean (in his last role before his tragic death in September 1955), Elizabeth Taylor, Rock Hudson, Jane Withers, Rod Taylor, and Dennis Hopper.

In 1958 Sal was again playing a troubled teen, but as a 19th century Sioux this time in the Walt Disney family classic, "Tonka." The film also starred Philip Carey, Rafael Campos, Slim Pickens, and H. M. Wynant.

Sal got a Golden Globe Award and was nominated for an Academy Award as Best Supporting Actor for his part as Dov Landau, a Jewish emigrant in Otto Preminger's "Exodus," a 1960 film which also starred Paul Newman, Eva Marie Saint, Peter Lawford, and Lee J. Cobb.

Unfortunately, by the early 60s Sal's career began to decline because he was getting older and didn't any longer fit his typecast of teen role and possibly his spreading reputation for bisexuality kept him from getting certain parts. Sal was quoted as saying, "One minute it seemed I had more offers than I could handle, the next, no one wanted me." Of course, that's very common in Hollywood with child actors becoming older. But Sal did land a role in the all-star epic religious film, "The Greatest Story Ever Told" (1965); that picture starred Max von Sydow as Jesus, Dorothy McGuire, Charlton Heston, Jose Ferrer, Roddy McDowall, Martin Landau, and Telly Savalas.

In 1969 Sal went back to the stage to direct a Los Angeles production of the gay-interest play, "Fortune and Men's Eyes," which starred the then unknown Don Johnson. The play became a film in 1971.

Sal's last film role was a small part in the sci fi flick, "Escape From the Planet of the Apes" (1971) with Roddy McDowall, Kim Hunter, Bradford Dillman, and Ricardo Montalban. Sal plays a chimpanzee named Dr. Milo.

After "Exodus" Sal dated British actress Jill Haworth and they even became engaged but she broke it off when she found out about Sal's affair with singer/actor

Bobby Sherman; later Sal had a relationship with actor Courtney Burr III, though—in spite of rumors to the contrary—he never had any sexual relations with James Dean or Don Johnson.

Some of Sal's movie roles included, "The Vision of Father Flanagan" (1952) with Dennis Patrick, "The Private War of Major Benson" (1955) with Charlton Heston, "Somebody Up There Likes Me" (1956) with Paul Newman, "Dino" (1957) with Brian Keith (see Brian's bio in this book), "The Gene Krupa Story" (1959) with James Darren (see Jimmy's bio in this book), "The Longest Day" (1962) with John Wayne, "Cheyenne Autumn" (1964) with Richard Widmark, "Who Killed Teddy Bear" (1965) with Juliet Prowse, "The Challengers" (1970) with Darren McGavin, "The Family  Rico" (1972) with Ben Gazzara.

Some of the TV appearances Sal had include, "Janet Dean, Registered Nurse: The Garcia Case" (1954) with Ella Raines, "Climax!: Island in the City" (1956) with Rafael Campos, "The Ann Sothern Show: The Sal Mineo Story" (1959) with Ann Sothern, "Dr. Kildare: Tomorrow is a Fickle Girl" (1964) with Richard Chamberlain, "The Patty Duke Show: Patty Meets a Celebrity" (1965) with Patty Duke, "Combat!" (1964-66) with Vic Morrow, "My Three Sons: The Liberty Bell" (1971) with Fred MacMurray, "Griff: Marked for Murder" (1973) with Lorne Greene, "Hawaii Five-0: Hit Gun for Sale" (1975) with Jack Lord, "Columbo: A Case of Immunity" (1975) with Peter Falk, "Joe Forrester: The Answer" (1976) with Lloyd Bridges.

Sadly, Sal was murdered on February 12, 1976. He was returning to his home at night and was stabbed in the carport behind his apartment building at 8569 Holloway in West Hollywood, California. Contrary to rumors, he was not stabbed repeatedly but only once, though as the knife pierced his heart, that was enough.

163

Former pizza deliveryman but mostly career criminal, Lionel Ray Williams—who confessed to the murder—was sentenced in 1979 to 57 years to life in prison for killing Sal Mineo and for ten robberies in that area where the murder took place. Williams claimed to have no idea who

his victim was, so Sal's sexuality had nothing to do with the murder, as some have erroneously reported. Unfortunately, his killer was paroled in 1990. Whatever happened to *life* being *life?* Eleven years was far too short a sentence for murder.

Sal's remains were interred in the Gate of Heaven Cemetery in Hawthorne, New York.

(Photo, l. The confessed murderer of Sal Mineo, Lionel Ray Williams in prison where they should have kept him)

MONTEZ, MARIA
1912-51

Dominican actress who gained fame in the 1940s as an exotic beauty in a series of action/adventure fantasies filmed in Technicolor. She became so identified with these type of adventure epics that she became known as "The Queen of Technicolor" (I can think of worst things to become known for.). Maria is probably best remembered for her role as Amara, the beautiful love interest of Ali (played by Jon Hall) in an Arabian Nights adventure film, "Ali Baba and the Forty Thieves" (1944) which also starred Andy Devine, Turhan Bey, Kurt Katch, and Frank Puglia. For wrestling fans, watch the movie and look for William "Wee Willie" Davis as the giant Arab (see Willie's bio in the wrestler's section in this book).

Maria was born Maria Antonia Garcia Vidal de Santo Silas on June 6, 1912 in Barahona, Dominican Republic, one of ten children born to the former Spanish consul in the Dominican Republic Ysidoro Garcia and Teresa Montez. Of course, as is so true with some actor's birth records, writer Margarita Vicens del Morales in her book, "Maria Montez, Su Vida," states that she has a photo of a birth certificate proving that Maria's original name was Maria Africa Gracia (not Garcia) Vidal, and that her father's name was Isidoro Gracia (also not Garcia) and her mother's name was Teresa

Vidal. Del Morales claims that Universal Pictures made the changes of record.

In the 1930s, Maria's father was appointed to the Spanish consulship in Belfast, Northern Ireland so the whole family had to pull up stakes and move there.

In 1940 Maria was did modeling work in New York City.

After she made it to Hollywood, she appeared in her first film, the western flick "Boss of Bullion City" (1940 with Johnny Mack Brown and Fuzzy Knight and then a comedy/sci fi, "The Invisible Woman" (1940), which starred Virginia Bruce. Universal also used the 5'7" sultry beauty in six color adventure films co-starring with leading man Jon Hall. Maria also appeared in a western "Pirates of Monterey" (1947) with Rod Cameron and a swashbuckler, "The Exile" (1948) starring Douglas Fairbanks Jr. She got suspended by the studio for awhile for refusing the lead in "Frontier Gal" (1945), so the part went to Yvonne de Carlo. Funny, Alan Curtis was supposed to star in it as well but he refused his part, too—the role going to Sheldon Leonard. Was that movie jinxed or something?

(Photo, below l. This is Maria in a shot from Cobra Woman, *1944)*

Some of Maria's film roles include, "Raiders of the Desert" (1941) with Richard Arlen, "Mystery of Marie Roget" (1942) with Patric Knowles, "White Savage" (1943) with Jon Hall, "Cobra Woman" (1944) with Jon Hall, "Bowery to Broadway" (1944) with Jack Oakie, "Tangier" (1946) with Sabu (see Sabu's bio in this book), "Wicked City" (1949) with Jean-Pierre Aumont, "The Thief of Venice" (1950) with Paul Hubschmid, "Revenge of the Pirates" (1951) with Jean-Pierre Aumont.

Maria never appeared on television.

As the style of films changed in the 50s, Maria's career in the United States began to nosedive. Because of that, she and her husband, French actor Jean-Pierre Aumont, moved to a Paris suburb. Maria appeared in several movies there and took some time to write three books.

In 1932 Maria married banker William G. McFeeters in Ireland at the age of 17; divorced in 1939. In the United States, Maria married

French actor Jean-Pierre Aumont in 1943; they had one daughter and were together until her death.

Sadly, Maria suffered a heart attack and drowned in her bath at her home in Suresnes, Paris, France on September 7, 1951 at the young age of 39. She was buried in the Cimetière du Montparnasse in Paris. In 1996, the city of Barahona where she was born opened the Maria Montez International Airport in her honor.

MURPHY, AUDIE
1924-71

Actor, songwriter, and WW II Medal of Honor winner Audie Leon Murphy was born 20 June 1925 in Kingston, Texas to sharecroppers Emmett Berry Murphy and Josie Bell Killian. He was the sixth of twelve children, which certainly did not help matters when Audie's father ran out on his family in 1936. Young Audie dropped out of school to go to work to help support the family for one dollar per day picking cotton in the area. To supplement the larder he shot small animals for food, becoming a skilled rifleman in the process.

In 1941 his mother died and Audie was forced to put three of his siblings in an orphanage but, true to them, he got them back after returning from World War II. *(Photo, below, l. Audie in a still from his TV show,* Whispering Smith, *1961)*

Having always been interested in joining the military, Audie tried to  enlist after Pearl Harbor (December 7, 1941) but was denied because of his age (not because of his size; he may look short on the screen sometimes but he was 5'8"). Wanting to help him to get into the Army, sister Corinne adjusted the date on his birth certificate so that he appeared to be 18 and able to enlist. (Problems arose in later years because of the falsification of Audie's birth date.) He took boot camp at Camp Wolters, near Mineral Wells, Texas and AIT (Advanced Infantry Training) at Fort Meade, Maryland. During the war he saw action in the Allied invasion of Sicily, the Battle of Anzio, the liberation of Rome, and the invasion of southern France. He was wounded several times and—in spite of his bravery—after the war suffered from combat fatigue, later—after the era of simplicity had died—called posttraumatic stress disorder (PTSD), as did many thousands of combat veterans. Audie mustered out as a first lieutenant with 27 U. S. decorations plus 5 from France and Belgium. For most of his life Audie also suffered from a hair-trigger temper. He was once hassled by a man in a bar; Audie got into a fist fight with him and nearly killed the man. Brought to trial later over the incident, he was acquitted of attempted murder charges over an incident that sounds like self defense to most people as it probably did to the judge trying the case.

The story of Audie's bravery during WWII was read about by actor James Cagney who invited him to Hollywood and got him acting lessons. That eventually led to a string of 44 films in which Audie appeared, mostly westerns which he enjoyed making. One of Audie's best remembered film roles was the autobiography of his life, "To Hell and Back" (1955), in which he played himself and was based on Audie's autobiographical book of the same name (ghostwritten by Audie's friend, David McClure). This fine movie also starred Marshall Thompson, Charles Drake (a good friend who co-starred with Audie in serveral of his movies), Jack Kelly, and David Janssen.

Interesting to note than even though he gained fame as *Audie* Murphy, he actually didn't like his first namc. In his youth, Audie preferred to be called by his middle name, Leon . . . until he was in the Army, that is. There he learned from his buddies that "Leon" was a name synonymous with "rednecks," they said. Thereafter he went back to Audie or his nickname, "Murph."

He made many fine westerns, such as "Sierra" (1950) with Audie's

short-term wife Wanda Hendrix, Dean Jagger, Burl Ives (with some great songs by Burl), Tony Curtis, and James Arness. Another one of Murph's fine westerns was "Walk the Proud Land" (1956), based on the deeds of real-life Indian agent John Clum and starring Anne Bancroft, Charles Drake, Pat Crowley, and Jay Silverheels. *(Photo, l. Audie in* Showdown, *1963)*

Some of Audie's films include, "Texas, Brooklyn & Heaven" (1948) with Guy Madison, "Bad Boy" (1949) with Lloyd

Nolan, "The Red Badge of Courage" (1951) with Andy Devine, "Duel at Silver Creek" (1952) with Stephen McNally, "Destry" (1954) with Mari Blanchard, "The Guns of Fort Petticoat" (1957) with Kathryn Grant, "Night Passage" (1957) with James Stewart, "The Wild and the Innocent" (1959) with Joanne Dru, "Hell Bent for Leather" (1960) with Stephen McNally, "Seven Ways From Sundown" (1960) with Barry Sullivan, "Showdown" (1963) with Kathleen Crowley, "Apache Rifles" (1964) with Michael Dante, "40 Guns to Apache Pass" (1966) with Laraine Stephens, "The Texican" (1966) with Broderick Crawford, "A Time for Dying" (1969) with Anne Randall.

Some of Murph's TV roles include, "Lux Video Theatre: The Bargain" (1952) with James Daly, "Suspicion: The Flight" (1957) with Jack Warden, "Startime: The Man" (1960) with Joseph Campanella, "Whispering Smith" (1961) with Guy Mitchell.

Audie married actress Wanda Hendrix in 1949; they divorced in 1951. He married airline stewardess Pamela Archer in 1951; they had two sons and were together until his death.

He bred quarter horses at the Audie Murphy Ranch in Menifee, California, at the Murphy Ranch in Pima County, Arizona, and one in Texas. Audie raced his horses and invested a lot of money in the hobby. He made some bad investments in oil and other things, losing a lot of money; that caused him to be in trouble with the IRS over unpaid taxes.

In addition to acting and ranching, Audie also wrote songs that were used by such famous singers as Dean Martin, Charlie Pride, Eddie Arnold, and many more.

Murph was awarded a Star on the Hollywood Walk of Fame in 1960; it is located at 1601 Vine St., Hollywood, California.

Sadly, Audie was killed while flying as a passenger with four other people on May 28, 1971; he was on his way to a business meeting. The aircraft was a Aero Commander 680. The pilot was also killed when the plane crashed into the side of a mountain near Catawba, Virginia. Cause of the crash was pilot error accentuated by horrible flying conditions—rain, clouds, fog, and zero visibility; the pilot, incidently, held no instrument rating and really shouldn't have gone up in weather like that. In

1975, a court awarded Pamela Murphy $2.5 million in damages because of the accident.

Audie was buried with full military honors at Arlington National Cemetery in Arlington County, Virginia. His monument remains the second most visited gravesite after that of Pres. John F. Kennedy. Headstones of medal of honor recipients buried at Arlington are normally decorated in gold leaf but prior to his death, Audie had requested that his stone remain plain and inconspicuous like that of an ordinary soldier. He always said, "I never liked being called the "most decorated" soldier. There were so many guys who should have gotten medals and never did—guys who were killed."

Even though his movies, especially the westerns, were very popular and are fondly remembered today, Audie always said about his acting, "I'm working under a great handicap: no talent!"

There is an Audie Murphy National Fan Club and it can be reached at 8313 Snug Hill Lane, Potomac, Maryland 20854-4057 as well as an online website.

NEWMAN, BARRY
1938-

Actor Barry Newman was born on November 7, 1938 in Boston, Massachusetts. This six-foot actor made it big in the 70s as anti-hero Kowalski, a former race-car driver who takes on the task of driving a hopped-up 1970 Dodge Challenger from Denver to San Francisco in the impossible time of just 15 hours. The cult film in question is "Vanishing Point," a 1971 hit that also starred Cleavon Little, Dean Jagger and Gilda Texter as the nude biker (I know they'll be a few who'll want to know that!).

Early on Barry got a college degree in anthropology but decided to go into acting after attending a class at the Actor's Studio. He appeared on the stage in the 60s and had some minor movie roles before making it big in "Vanishing Point" He never made it as big as similar actors Dustin Hoffman and Al Pacino but as a quality actor he continued to work into recent times.

(Photo, r. Barry Newman as Petrocelli)

Barry is probably best remembered on TV for his starring role on the action-based series, "Petrocelli," as Tony Petrocelli, a Harvard-educated lawyer who decides to escape from fast-paced city life to practice in a small town called San Remo in Arizona (filmed in Tucson, Arizona).

172

Keeping a laid back, low profile, Tony and his wife, Maggie, live in a trailer and drive an old pick-up truck. Now, he may be living in a sleepy, backwater town but he runs afoul of plenty of accused murderers to defend, find the truth, and get the innocent party acquitted. The show ran on NBC from September 11, 1974 to March 31, 1976. It was created by Harold Buchman and Sidney J. Furie and directed (mostly) by Irving J. Moore. It was adapted from a movie that Barry Newman starred in called "The Lawyer," a film based (though loosely) on the Sam Shepard murder case. In 1975 Barry was nominated for an Emmy for his role as Petrocelli and the following year nominated for a Golden Globe Award.

Some of Barry's other film roles include, "Pretty Boy Floyd" (1960) with John Ericson, "The Moving Finger" (1963) with Lionel Stander, "Fear is the Key" (1972) with John Vernon, "City on Fire" (1979) with Henry Fonda, "Amy" (1981) with Jenny Agutter, "Fatal Vision" (1984) with Karl Malden, "MacShayne: Winner Takes All" (1994) with Kenny Rogers, "G-Men from Hell" (2000) with William Forsythe, "Manhood" (2003) with John Ritter, "Raise Your Kids on Seltzer" (2015) with Penny Werner.

A few of Barry's many TV roles include, "Naked City" (1963) with Harry Belaver, "Get Smart" (1968) with Don Adams, "Quincy, M. E." (1983) with Jack Klugman, "Nightingales" (1989) with Suzanne Pleshette, "L. A. Law" (1994) with Corbin Bernsen, "Murder, She Wrote" (1988-95) with Angela Lansbury, "NYPD" (1994-98) with Dennis Franz, "The Limey" (1999) with Peter Fonda, "Ghost Whisperer" (2009) with Jennifer Love Hewitt.

Barry still acts and had a role in "Raise Your Kids on Seltzer," a comedy/drama starring Penny Werner, in 2015.

O'BRIEN, CUBBY
1949-

Update: I'm pleased to write that Cubby has received the Disney Legend Award at the D23 Expo. This honor was bestowed upon him July 18, 2015 for the talented work he provided during the four-year production (1955-59) of TV's Mickey Mouse Club. He joins other former Disney celebrities such as Annette Funicello, Tommy Kirk, and Kevin Corcoran. Congratulations, Cubby!

O'CONNOR, DONALD
1925-2003

This accomplished dancer, singer, and actor was one of the finest "hoofers" around in his day, famous for a dance routine that had him doing backflips off the wall! He danced opposite co-star Gene Kelly in the hit musical, "Singin' in the Rain" (1952) which also starred Debbie Reynolds and Cyd Charisse. Don partially gained fame co-starring with established actors like Gloria Jean, Peggy Ryan, and—yes, that's right—Francis the Talking Mule! Don made six comedy films with the obstinate but highly intelligent, talking critter in the 1950s, with voice overs for Francis done by actor/singer Chill Wills (Francis with an "i" was played by a female mule named Molly and trained by Lester Hilton). Don always said his favorite dancing partner was Vera-Ellen; his favorite routine with her was the "It's a Lovely Day Today" number in "Call Me Madam" (1953).

Donald David Dixen Ronald O'Connor was born on August 28, 1925 in Chicago, Illinois to vaudeville entertainer and circus acrobat John Edward O'Connor and circus bareback rider and dancer Effie Irene Crane.

Don's first film was "Melody For Two" (1937) which starred James Melton and Marie Wilson and also had Don's two brothers, Jack and Billy O'Connor; the trio did a dance routine together. In 1938 Don appeared with singing legend Bing Crosby in the Paramount Pictures musical "Sing You Sinners," with Fred MacMurray and Ellen Drew.

175

In 1940 Don went back to vaudeville, but signed with Universal Pictures in 1941. He did seven musicals in a row for Universal, starting with "What's Cookin'" (1942) with The Andrews Sisters and Gloria Jean.

Don was drafted into the Army in 1943, but before he reported for duty in 1944 Universal had him knock out three more films. Then in 1949 Don made his first "Francis" movie, released in 1950; it also starred Patricia Medina, John McIntire, and funny gal Zasu Pitts. Even though his musical career was interrupted once a year to make another Francis movie, Don said he enjoyed making the pictures. "They were fun to make," he said. "Actually they were quite challenging. I had to play straight in order to convince the audience that the mule could talk."

Unfortunately, it was because of another Francis movie that Don missed the opportunity to play opposite Bing Crosby in "White Christmas" (1954). He was supposed to play the part of Phil Davis but Danny Kaye got the role after Don caught an illness from the mule!

Happily, though, Don's masterful dancing part in "Singin' in the Rain" earned him a Golden Globe Award for Best Performance by an Actor in a Comedy or Musical. Don's stamina in that film is legendary: he did the extremely difficult "Make 'Em Laugh" dance number even though he was a chain smoker and smoked four packs a day. After,

though, he was bedridden for three days to recuperate.

Another physically demanding dance number Don did was in the musical classic, Irving Berlin's "There's No Business Like Show Business" (1954) which also starred Dan Dailey, Ethel Merman, Marilyn Monroe, Mitzi Gaynor, and Johnnie Ray. Terrific number and Don said it was the best picture he ever made.

In the 1950s Don appeared on TV quite a lot and, in 1954, got his own series, "The Donald O'Connor Show" on NBC. But he worked and played much too hard and suffered a heart attack in 1971. He overcame his alcoholism after being hospitalized for three months after collapsing in 1978. Then, in 1981, he appeared in film for the first time in 16 years in "Ragtime," which also starred James Cagney and Pat O'Brien.

Some of Don's film roles include, "Tom Sawyer, Detective" (1938) with Billy Cook, "Beau Geste" (1939) with Gary Cooper, "When Johnny Comes Marching Home" (1942) with Gloria Jean (see Gloria's bio elsewhere in this book), "Follow the Boys" (1944) with George Raft, "Are You With It?" (1948) with Olga San Juan, "Francis Goes to The Races" (1951) with Piper Laurie, "Francis Goes to West Point" (1952) with Lori

Nelson, "Francis Covers the Big Town" (1953) with Yvette Duguay, "Francis Joins the WACS" (1954) with Julie Adams, "Francis in the Navy" (1955) with Martha Hyer, "The Buster Keaton Story" (1957) with Rhonda Fleming, "The Wonders of Aladdin" (1961) with Vittorio De Sica, "Li'l Abner" (1971) with Ray Young, "Pandemonium" (1982) with Tom Smothers, "Toys" (1992) with Robin Williams, "Out to Sea" (1997) with Jack Lemmon.

Some of Don's TV roles include, "Playhouse 90: The Jet-Propelled Couch" (1957) with Peter Lorre (see Peter's bio elsewhere in this book), "Vacation Playhouse: The Hoofer" (1966) with Jolene Brand, "Ellery Queen: The Adventure of the Comic Book Crusader" (1975) with Jim Hutton, "The Littlest Hobo: The Clown" (1982) with London, "The Love Boat" (1981-86) with Gavin MacLeod, "Murder, She Wrote: The Big Show of 1965" (1990) with Angela Lansbury, "Tales From the Crypt: Strung Along" (1992) with Patricia Charbonneau, "The Nanny: Freida Needa Man" (1996) with Fran Drescher.

In 1998 Don received a Palm Star on the Palm Springs, California Walk of Stars.

Don married Gwendolyn Carter in 1944; they had a daughter and divorced in 1954. In 1956 he married Gloria Noble; they had three children and remained together until his death.

His health deteriorated quite a lot during the 1990s but he still kept working. Don had quadruple heart bypass surgery in 1990 and nearly died from double pneumonia in 1998. Sadly, Don died from heart failure on September 27, 2003 at the Motion Picture & Television Country House and Hospital in Woodland Hills, California. His remains were cremated and buried at the Forest Lawn Cemetery in Hollywood Hills near Los Angeles, California.

O'ROURKE, HEATHER
1975-88

This little cutie was the child actress who appeared as Carol Anne Freeling in the scary blockbuster, "Poltergeist," a 1982 horror film that starred JoBeth Williams, Craig T. Nelson, Dominique Dunne (see Dominique's bio in this book), Oliver Robins, and Zelda Rubenstein. She was picked by director Steven Spielberg (her older sister, Tammy, was already an actress) to be in the film when he saw her visiting the MGM studios; she beat out Drew Barrymore who was up for the role. In the movie she uttered that memorable line: *"They're heeere!"* She reprised her role in the first and second sequels. In the second film she quips, *"They're baa-aack!"* which became the film's tagline.

Known as Bernie (or Heath), she was born Heather Michele O'Rourke on December 27, 1976 in San Diego, California to construction worker Michael O'Rourke and seamstress Kathleen O'Rourke. She attended Big Bear Elementary School in Big Bear Lake, California while the family was living there; Heather was the president of her fifth-grade class in 1985. She got to keep the goldfish from "Poltergeist" but her main pet was a big, ol' St. Bernard. Believe it or not, mom and dad wouldn't let her watch horror films! Heather's favorite movie was Disney's "Dumbo" (1941); her favorite TV show was "Three's Company" (1977).

For the avid collectors of Barbie toys, Heather appeared on the doll box for Mattel's "My First Barbie" (1980).

After her role in "Poltergeist" Heather appeared in the Walt Disney TV production, "Believe You Can . . . and You Can!" opposite Morey Amsterdam and a host of Disney animated characters. During her short career, Heather appeared in other films and TV shows.

Heather's movie roles were, "Massarati and the Brain" (1982) with Peter Billingsley, "Surviving" (1985) with Ellen Burstyn, "Around the Bend" (1986), "Poltergeist II: The Other Side" (1986) with Craig T. Nelson, "Poltergeist III" (1988) with Tom Skerritt.

(Photo, l. Here's Heather in a shot from Poltergeist, *1982)*

TV roles for Heather were, "Fantasy Island: Elizabeth's Baby" (1981) with Ricardo Montalban, "CHiPs: Fun House" (1983) with Erik Estrada, "Happy Days" (1982-83) with Henry Winkler, "Matt Houston: The Woman in White" (1983) with Lee Horsley, "Webster" (1983) with Alex Karras, "Finder of Lost Loves: Yesterday's Child" (1984) with Anthony Franciosa, "Our House: A Point of View" (1987) with Wilford Brimley, "Rocky Road: Moscow on the Boardwalk" (1987) with Maylo McCaslin, "The New Leave It to Beaver: Material Girl" (1987) with Jerry Mathers.

Heather became ill in 1987 and was misdiagnosed by doctors at Kaiser Permanente Hospital in Oakland, California as having Crohn's disease. Apparently she did get better but on January 31, 1988 Heather became ill again, unable to keep any food in her stomach. Next day she was supposed to go to the hospital but collapsed before the family could take her. Heather's father called the ambulance and on the way to the hospital, Heather suffered a cardiac arrest. After resuscitation she was airlifted to Rady Children's Hospital in San Diego. She was diagnosed as having an acute bowel obstruction caused by congenital stenosis of the intestine complicated by septic shock. Heather was given surgery but, sadly, she died on the operating table. Later reports changed the cause of death to cardiac arrest (i.e., cardiopulmonary arrest) caused by septic shock brought on by intestinal stenosis.

Heather was interred at Westwood Village Memorial Park Cemetery in Los Angeles, California.

About horror movies, Heather had said, "I'm really not afraid of spooky things. When I have to look really frightened, I concentrate on scary things like losing my kittens or something like that."

OSMENT, HALEY JOEL
1988-

The little kid who quietly divulged his secret with the heart-stopping line, "I see dead people," ("The Sixth Sense") started in film as the on-screen, young son of Tom Hanks in "Forrest Gump" (1994) Haley Joel Osment was born April 10, 1988 in Los Angeles, California to actor Michael Eugene Osment and teacher Theresa Seifert. Haley played basketball and football while going to Flintridge Preparatory School in La Cañada, California. He began his acting career at the age of four in a Pizza Hut TV commercial. That started things rolling and later in 1992 he got a part on television in the sitcom "Thunder Alley."

Haley earned an Academy Award for Best Supporting Actor nomination for his role as a youngster that spirits can't seem to do without in M. Night Shyamalan's goosebump-producing film, "The Sixth Sense" (1999) with Bruce Willis. He was exceptional in the tear-jerking role of a child dying from AIDS that he had been born with in "Walker, Texas

Ranger: Lucas" (1997) with Chuck Norris and Mackenzie Phillips. Another of my favorite performances by Haley was as an introverted adolescent who had been dumped off for the summer by his money-hungry mother with two odd, assumed-to-be rich, uncles. Naturally, he is supposed to find out where the wealth is hidden in "Secondhand Lions" (2003) with Robert Duvall and Michael Caine.

Haley was tremendous in the provocative, heart-wrenching film "Pay It Forward" (2000) with Helen Hunt as well as Steven Spielberg's science fiction drama, "Artificial Intelligence: A. I." (2001) with Jude Law. In this one Haley plays David, a child-android who has the unique ability to love. The young actor won critical acclaim for his role and his second Saturn Award for Best Younger Actor, as well (Haley got the first one for his part in "The Sixth Sense).

Haley has done a lot of voice-over work including "The Country Bears" (2002) and "Jungle Book 2" (2003) for the Disney Studios. He's also done voice overs for a number of video games.

On July 20, 2006, Haley was injured in a one-car accident when he lost control of his vehicle and hit a brick mailbox. Fortunately, his injuries were minimal, but—as he had been drinking—Haley was charged and pleaded no contest on October 19; he received three-years' probation and a $1500 fine.

Some of Haley's other film roles include, "Mixed Nuts" (1994) with Steve Martin, "Bogus" (1996) with Whoopi Goldberg, "Last Stand at Saber River" (1997) with Tom Selleck, "The Lake" (1998) with Yasmine Bleeth, "I'll Remember April" (2000) with Pat Morita, "Home of the Giants" (2007) with father Eugene Osment, "Montana Amazon" (2012) with Olympia Dukakis, "Sex Ed" (2014) with Lorenza Izzo.

Currently (April, 2016), Haley is working on a sci-fi film called "Future Man." He plays Dr. Stu Camillo who aids janitor Josh Futterman (played by Josh Hutcherson) to battle an alien invasion.

Some of Haley's TV roles include, "The Jeff Foxworthy Show" (1995-97), "Touched by an Angel: Flights of Angels" (1998) with Roma Downey, "Murphy Brown" (1997-98) with Candice Bergen, "Ally McBeal: Angels and Blimps" (1999) with Callista Flockhart, "Family Guy" (2000-01; voice) with Seth MacFarlane, "The Spoils of Babylon" (2014) with Tobey Maguire.

Unmarried, Haley keeps busy working in show business, playing golf, and collecting geckos (a type of lizard). About his career when he was younger, Haley said: "It makes me feel great when other young actors say they look up to me. I hope I can be a positive role model."

PAL (Animal Actor)
1940-58

(Photo, l., Pal and owner-trainer Rudd Weatherwax, 1955)

One of the finest animal actors in movie and TV history, future Lassie star Pal was born a Rough Collie breed on June 4, 1940 at the Glamis Kennels in North Hollywood, California. His (yes, Lassie was a "he") parents were Red Brucie and Bright Bauble of Glamis. Not thought too much of at the time because of his large eyes and white forehead blaze, Pal was sold as a pet rather than a future actor.

When Pal was eight months old, animal trainer Harold Peck took the mischievous dog to famed Hollywood animal trainer Rudd Weatherwax to cure him of his excessive barking and the nasty, unsafe habit of chasing motorcycles! Mr. Weatherwax gained control of the dog's barking but couldn't convince Pal to give up the thrill of bike chasing. Peck was upset about the result and gave up on the dog, giving him to Rudd. Later, when he learned that MGM was considering making a feature film of the popular new novel, Eric Knight's "Lassie Come Home," Rudd began to train Pal for the role. (In 1957 Rudd would train another dog, Spike, for the classic Disney film, "Old Yeller.")

Hard to believe now, considering that "Lassie" became a classic film, but it was originally planned as a low-budget, black and white children's movie and Pal was only one of 1500 dogs to audition for the part. He didn't even get the starring role. Powers that be didn't like Pal for the role because he was male and because of his aforementioned large eyes and white blaze. (Oh, they of little faith!) Instead, a female, prize-winning show collie trained by Frank Inn was hired and Pal was just kept around as a stunt dog.

However, one scene called for Lassie to dive into a flood-ravaged river (the San Joaquin in central California, although another source says it was the Sacramento River) and swim to the other side but the show dog wouldn't go near the river. Rudd had Pal do the stunt and was so good director Fred M. Wilcox tossed the show dog and hired the stunt dog as the lead, making Pal the first Lassie. In addition, they upgraded the film to a feature and decided to shoot it in Technicolor.

Pal seemed to like his work as an actor and got along well in "Lassie Come Home" (1943) with fellow human actors Roddy McDowall, Elizabeth Taylor, Edmund Gwenn, Donald Crisp, Nigel Bruce, Dame Mae Whitty, Arthur Shields, and J. Pat O'Malley. The movie was hugely popular and ultimately became the classic boy/dog movie.

(Photo, l. Pal as Lassie with Roddy McDowall in a scene from Lassie Come Home, *1943)*

Two years later Pal played Lassie and Laddie, in "Son of Lassie," with Peter Lawford, Donald Crisp, Nigel Bruce, and June Lockhart (Ms. Lockhart became a regular on the Lassie TV show from 1958-64).

Other films that Pal appeared in include, "Courage of Lassie" (1946) with Elizabeth Taylor, "Hills of Home" (1948) with Edmund Gwenn, "Challenge to Lassie" (1949) with Edmund Gwenn, "The Painted Hills" (1951) with Gary Gray.

Pal starred in the two pilots for the "Lassie" TV show in 1954 but the actual television part went to Lassie Jr. as Pal retired at age 14. But Pal was on the set every day behind the scenes and made sure his three-year-old son did a good job. The Lassie role was followed by Pal's grandsons, Spook and Baby.

In 1950 Rudd Weatherwax and John H. Rothwell wrote and published "The Story of Lassie: His Discovery and Training from Puppyhood to Stardom."

Sadly, by 1957 Pal was growing blind, deaf, and full of arthritis. He rarely went to the studio any longer. Pal passed away in June of 1958 at Mr. Weatherwax's home in North Hollywood. Rudd was devastated by the loss and went through several bouts of deep depression. Rudd passed away in 1985, never watching another Lassie film.

But Lassie is still around. Today, owner and trainer Carol Riggins supplies a tenth-generation descendant of Pal to play the part.

PATTERSON, MELODY
1949-2015

This pretty and vivacious five-foot-five actress was best known for her role as "Wrangler" Jane Angelica Thrift in the TV western sitcom, "F Troop" (1965-67) which aired on ABC. The series also starred Forrest Tucker, Larry Storch, Ken Berry, Frank de Kova, Bob Steele, James Hampton, and Don Diamond. Melody was very precocious and that helped her to get the role of Wrangler Jane at the tender age of 15—along with a forged birth certificate that indicated she was 18. By the time the studio found out Melody was underage she was already an established part of the show and couldn't very well be replaced. Wonder how 32-year-old Ken Berry felt about being pawed and smooched during scenes by a pretty girl half his age? Oh, well; that's tough. The show must go on!

Melody was born on April 16, 1949 in Inglewood, California to machinist Pat Patterson and Miss Universe contest official Rosemary Wilson. Her mother had also been a dancer with Warner Bros. Studios and sometimes doubled for Joan Crawford. Before the age of 10, Melody had already been a model and an actress and in her teenage years enrolled and studied at the Hollywood Professional School.

She first appeared in film in an uncredited, walk-in part in "Bye, Bye Birdie," a 1963 musical comedy hit that starred Dick Van Dyke, Ann-Margret, Janet Leigh, and Bobby Rydell. Melody also appeared with Bruce Dern in the 1969 action film entitled, "The Cycle Savages." On stage Melody acted with Barbara Rush and Dirk Benedict in "Butterflies Are Free;" she also played the part of Peggy in "The Front Page" and was directed by her husband, James MacArthur.

(Photo, l. The cast of F Troop: *front row, l.-r.: Ken Berry, Melody Patterson; back, l.-r.: Forrest Tucker, Larry Storck)*

During the Vietnam War, Melody went overseas to entertain the troops with the Johnny Grant Christmas Tour and was a DJ for the Armed Forces Radio Service. In 1965 Melody was voted one of the Deb Stars of 1966. In 1970 Melody married actor James MacArthur; they divorced in 1975. She married Robert Seaton (date unknown) but divorced in 1993. Melody then married Vern Miller in 1998; they were together until her death.

The films in which Melody appeared are, "The Angry Breed" (1968) with James MacArthur, "Blood and Lace" (1971) with Gloria Grahame, "The Harrad Experiment" (1973) with James Whitmore, "The Immortalizer" (1990) with Ron Ray.

Her TV roles are, "Shindig!" (1965), "Wendy and Me: You Can Fight City Hall" (1965) with Connie Stevens, "The Monkees: Hillbilly Honeymoon" (1967) with Davy Jones, "Adam-12: Log 141, The Color TV Bandit" (1968) with Martin Milner, "Green Acres: Eb's Romance" (1968) with Eddie Albert, "Hawaii Five-0" (1969-74) with James MacArthur. During this time Melody was living with her husband, James MacArthur, in Hawaii and appeared in three of his shows.

Melody wrote a column called "Wrapping With Wrangler" for "Wildest Westerns Magazine."

Sadly, Melody died on August 20, 2015 at the Point Lookout Nursing & Rehab in Hollister, Missouri of "multiple organ failure." It seems Melody had been in poor health after breaking her back a few years before.

PELLEGRINI, MARGARET
1923-2013

Actress who co-starred as one of the "Munchkins" in the classic family film, "The Wizard of Oz." She had been one of two of the last surviving Munchkin troupe (the last one is Jerry Maren, 96; Ruth Robinson Duccini—the last female Munchkin—died in 2014). Margaret was born Margaret Williams on September 23, 1923 in Tuscumbia, Alabama. This charming, four-foot tall lady will probably be best remembered for her role as a Sleepyhead and Flowerpot Hat Dancer (at that time she was 3'4"), one of the 124 Munchkins, in "The Wizard of Oz" (1939) which also starred Judy Garland, Ray Bolger, Bert Lahr, Jack Haley Jr., and Margaret Hamilton (see Maggie's bio in this book). Interestingly, Margaret said that she made just $50 and room and board a week while Dorothy's little dog, Toto, made $125 a week, adding "He had a better agent than I did!"

She got her start acting when she was helping a relative tend a booth at the Tennessee State Fair. A group of little people happened by and asked her if she wanted to join their show, Henry Kramer's Midgets—although, at that time, Margaret says, she didn't consider herself a midget.

Margaret married an average-sized, ex-boxer named

Willie Pellegrini about 1940. They stayed together until his death and had two children.

She also appeared in "Johnny Got His Gun" (1971) with Timothy Bottoms, Marsha Hunt, Kathy Fields, Jason Robards, and Donald Sutherland.

On TV she appeared on "Entertainment Tonight" (2005) with Gisele Bündchen, Mickey Carroll, and fellow Munchkin Meinhardt Raabe (1915-2010).

Margaret didn't accrue many film credits but she did appear in a lot of documentaries related to "The Wizard of Oz." Keeping busy, she also went on to do a lot of fan festivals and autograph signings (she appeared May 31, 2012 at the Turning Stone Casino courtesy of the Oneida Indian Nation; but, says Margaret, "There's no place like home!).

There is a Munchkins star on the Hollywood Walk of Fame located at 6915 Hollywood Blvd., Hollywood, California. Sadly, Margaret succumbed to a stroke on August 7, 2013 in Glendale, Arizona. She was cremated and her ashes given to family members.

PENDLETON, KAREN
1946-

Update: I'm pleased to write that Karen has received the Disney Legend Award at the D23 Expo. This honor was bestowed upon her July 18, 2015 for the talented work she provided during the four-year production (1955-59) of TV's Mickey Mouse Club, at Disneyland, and later for the Studio as well. She joins other former Disney celebrities such as Annette Funicello, Tommy Kirk, and Kevin Corcoran. Congratulations, Karen!

PEPPER, CYNTHIA
1940-

Update: Being a fan of Cynthia's work I was excited to learn that she recently released an autobiography through AuthorHouse entitled, "Pigtails, Presley & Pepper." Got it and read it so I can say that it's a very good book and I highly recommend it.

SABU
1924-63

Sabu was primarily a child actor who first began his acting career in India and later in America where he obtained American citizenship. He is probably best known for his role as Mowgli in Zoltán Korda's outdoor classic, "Jungle Book." The movie was taken from Rudyard Kipling's book of the same title and made into a Technicolor film which also starred Joseph Calleia, John Qualen, and Rosemary DeCamp.

Sabu was born Sabu Dastagir on January 27, 1924 in Karapur in the Kingdom of Mysore, British India. He was the son of an Indian *mahout,* an elephant rider—a profession very common in India at that time as in the back country elephants were used as beasts of burden. As to Sabu's name, some sources claim that Sabu Dastagir was his brother's name and his was Selar Shaik Sabu or Sabu Francis; his brother managed Sabu's career. *(Photo, below. Patricia O'Rourke and Sabu in a scene from* Jungle Book, *1942)*

When his father died in 1933, Sabu became a ward of the royal elephant stables. In 1937 Sabu was discovered by documentary film maker Robert Flaherty who put him in the British film "Elephant Boy," based on another one of Kipling's works, "Toomai of the Elephants." Sabu

190

and his guardian older brother moved to England to work in film and were wards of the British government. Sabu quickly learned the English language.

Another great film portrayal for Sabu was as Abu the Thief in the British color, Arabian-fantasy classic, "The Thief of Baghdad" which also starred Conrad Veidt, John Justin, June Duprez, and Rex Ingram as the giant and very loud djinn.

Director George Stevens wanted to borrow Sabu from Alexander Korda to star in the title role of his upcoming production, "Gunga Din" (1939) to star Cary Grant and Douglas Fairbanks Jr. But Korda wouldn't do it so the part went to Sam Jaffe. But Jaffe patterned his role the way he felt Sabu would have played the part. Jaffe said that whenever he was acting the part of Gunga Din he said to himself, "Think Sabu."

After becoming an American citizen in 1944, Sabu joined the United States Army Air Forces and served as a tail gunner and ball turret gunner (two very dangerous places to be on a plane when it's getting shot at). He flew numerous missions in the Pacific during WWII and received the Distinguished Flying Cross. When he returned from the war good parts didn't seem to come to him, perhaps because he was now in his 20s and couldn't get the youth-oriented roles he had before. Through most of the 1950s he starred in mostly unsuccessful European films. In 1952 Sabu starred in the Harringay Circus with an elephant act.

Some of Sabu's film roles include, "Drums" (1938) with Raymond Massey, "Arabian Nights" (1942) with Jon Hall, "White Savage" (1943) with Maria Montez (see Maria's bio elsewhere in this book), "Cobra Woman" (1944) with Jon Hall, "Man-Eater of Kumaon" (1948) with Wendell Corey, "Savage Drums" (1951) with Lita Baron, "Jungle Hell" (1956) with K. T. Stevens, "Sabu and the Magic Ring" (1957) with Daria Massey, "Mistress of the World" (1960) with Martha Hyer, "Rampage" (1963) with Robert Mitchum.

His last film was in the Disney family adventure drama, "A Tiger Walks" (1964) with Brian Keith, Vera Miles, and Pamela Franklin. It was released after his death.

191

Sabu never appeared on television.

In 1948 Sabu married actress Marilyn Cooper; they had two children and were together until his death.

Sadly, Sabu died of a sudden heart attack at his home on December 2, 1963 in Chatsworth, California. He is interred at the Forest Lawn Memorial Park Cemetery in Hollywood Hills, California. He may be gone but his early youthful charm and athletic abilities in film will be long remembered.

SMITH, "BUFFALO" BOB
1917-1998

Bob: *"Say kids, what time is it?"*
Kids: *"It's Howdy Doody Time!"*

"Buffalo" Bob Smith, actor, comedian, radio disk jockey, singer, and co-creator/host of the popular children's program "The Howdy Doody Show," was born Robert Emil Schmidt—the youngest of four—on November 27, 1917 in Buffalo, New York to coal miner Emil H. Schmidt and Emma Kuehn Schmidt.

In 1933 Bob and two of his friends formed a trio, auditioned for, and ultimately was chosen by a local Buffalo brewery who was sponsoring a radio show to appear on that program. They called themselves "The Hi-Hatters." The trio was go good they were hired to regularly appear on the radio show. When Bob was 17 the trio was heard by famous entertainer Kate Smith who liked the boys so much that she took them back to New York City to perform with her on "The Kate Smith Show"; later Bob did vaudeville. Bob's mother was a big fan of his work but lonely because

Bob's father had passed away so the group broke up and he returned to Buffalo. *(Photo, l.: Howdy Doody with Bob Smith, l., and Lew Anderson as Clarabelle the Clown, r.)*

Not to stay out of work for long, Bob—who loved working in radio—was soon hired to be the staff pianist at the WKBW radio station in Buffalo,

193

changing his name to Robert E. "Bob" Smith in the process.

In 1947 Bob was doing a radio show called "The Triple B Ranch" on which he had a puppet character called Elmer (voiced by Bob) who was always saying "howdy doody." Eventually, to the kids who listened, the puppet became known as Howdy Doody. Later that year Bob talked NBC in New York into letting him do an appearance on their children's television show "Puppet Playhouse" on December 27, 1947. He was so popular that a visual Howdy Doody marionette was created and Bob stayed. Later the show's name was changed to "The Howdy Doody Show" because Bob thought that sounded more appealing to kids. The puppet that is best remembered was a marionette (a puppet with strings operated at a distance above by a puppeteer) designed and carved by California puppet maker/puppeteer Velma Dawson (1912-2007) in 1948.

As a side note, there were no daytime television shows in those days so there was a test pattern on all day long until "The Howdy Doody Show" came on NBC at 5:30 ET.

Bob remained with the show for 13 seasons except for about a year (1954-55) following a massive heart attack he had. The show also starred Bob Keeshan (Clarabelle 1947-52; he went on to play Captain Kangaroo on his own show), Nick Nicholson (Clarabelle 1952-54), musician Lew Anderson (Clarabelle 1954-60), singer/dancer Judy Tyler (Princess Summerfallwinterspring; sadly, she died in a car crash in 1957 at the age of 24), and Bill LeCornec (Chief Thunderthud). The show went off the air on September 24, 1960 with the only words ever uttered by the always silent Clarabelle the Clown: "Goodbye, kids."

Bob married childhood friend Mildred Metz in 1940; they had three sons.

After the "Doody" show ended in 1960, Bob and family moved to Maine where he bought three radio stations. In 1970 a student at the University of Pennsylvania invited him to come to the college to put on a show about his career. It was hugely popular and spawned hundreds of other shows at various colleges around the country.

In addition to his many other achievements in show business, Bob also appeared in, "Track of Thunder" (1967) with Tommy Kirk, "Andy's Funhouse" (1979 voice) with Andy Kaufman, "Treasure Island" (1982) with Piers Eady, "Problem Child 2" (1991) with John Ritter.

He also appeared on TV in, "Happy Days" (1975) with Ron Howard, "The New Howdy Doody Show" (1976-77) with Lew Anderson.

In 1990 Bob wrote a book about his experiences on "The Howdy Doody Show" called "Howdy and Me." The Smiths moved to Flat Rock,

North Carolina in 1991 where he spent a lot of time pursuing his favorite hobby, playing golf.

A very informative and enjoyable interview of Bob was made by Michael Rosen on April 30, 1998 and is available online at YouTube.

Sadly, Buffalo Bob Smith died at a hospital in Hendersonville, North Carolina from cancer on July 30, 1998. He was cremated.

STANG, ARNOLD
1918-2009

Small (5'3"), bespectacled, but brash and street smart, funny man Arnold Stang was born on September 18, 1981 in Manhattan, New York City, New York. Fans probably remember him best as the voice of T. C. in the animated TV series "Top Cat" that aired on TV from 1961-62. The show didn't run long but Arnold's rendition of the slick, wise-ass leader of a gang of Brooklynesque alley cats was quite good and popular. He also appeared in a lot of TV commercials, such as the high-pitched voice selling the tasty attributes of Chunky candy ("Chunky . . . what a chunk o' chocolate!")

The little guy with the horn-rimmed glasses started out on radio and also did Broadway, film, and TV. He grew up in Brooklyn and went to New Utrecht High School. In the 1930s Arnold got a role on radio's

"Horn and Hardart's Children's Hour" and "Let's Pretend," a popular children's show that ran for two decades. Arnold also did the squeaky voice of Jughead in the "Archie Andrews" series and played the neighbor Seymour Fingerhood on the Bronx-styled radio classic, "The Goldbergs" with Gertrude Berg.

Arnold also did a radio show called "The Remarkable Miss Tuttle" (1942) with Edna May Oliver and also "That Brewster Boy" in 1943. He also worked in radio with Eddie Cantor and Milton Berle.

During the 1940s Arnold also did some stage work in "Sailor Beware," "All in Favor," and "Same Time Next Week" with Milton Berle. He also got into film in "My Sister Eileen" in 1942 starring Rosalind Russell and Janet Blair; he also did "So This is New York" with Henry Morgan and Rudy Vallee in 1948.

Arnold first appeared on TV way back in the early days on the DuMont Television Network in 1949. The show was called "The School House." It was a vaudeville-inspired, comedy variety show and starred Kenny Delmar as the teacher and his students were played by Arnold, Wally Cox, and Buddy Hackett. Another early show he did was the sci fi show "Captain Video and His Video Rangers," which aired on DuMont from 1949 to 1955 and starred Richard Coogan in the lead role (from 1949-50) and later Al Hodge (from 1950-55).

He also did a lot of voice-over work for animated features and TV shows such as "Top Cat," which was popular but only aired for one season. Creators William Hanna and Joseph Barbera were going to do another offer of the show but couldn't because co-star, Maurice Gosfield—who was the voice of Benny the Ball—died in 1964. He was also the voice of Popeye's pal, Shorty; the voice of Herman the mouse in various Famous Studios cartoons; and the voice of Tubby Tompkins in some of the Little Lulu cartoons.

Arnold married writer JoAnn Taggart in 1949; they had two children and were together until his death.

Some of Arnold movie roles include, "They Got Me Covered" (1943) with Bob Hope, "Laughter in Paris" (1946) with Michael Rosenberg, "Naughty But Mice" (voice 1947) with Carl Meyer, "Two Gals and a Guy" (1951) with Robert Alda, "The Man With the Golden Arm" (1955) with Frank Sinatra, "Frighty Cat" (voice 1958) with Jack Mercer, "Dondi" (1961) with David Janssen, "It's a Mad, Mad, Mad, Mad World" (1963) with Spencer Tracy, "Hello Down There" (1969) with Tony Randall, "The Bureau" (1976) with Henry Gibson, "I Go Pogo" (voice 1980) with Vincent Price, "Norman's Corner" (1987) with Gilbert Gottfried, "Ghost Dad" (1990) with Bill Cosby, "Dennis the Menace" (1993) with Walter Matthau.

And some of Arnold's TV spots include, "Search for Tomorrow" (1951) with Mary Stuart, "Texaco Star Theatre" (1953-56) with Milton

Berle, "December Bride: The Jockey" (1956) with Spring Byington, "Wagon Train: The Ah Chong Story" (1961) with John McIntire, "Broadside" (1965) with Kathleen Nolan, "Batman: The Great Train Robbery" (1968) with Adam West, "Emergency!: Weird Wednesday" (1972) with Robert Fuller, "Chico and the Man: In Your Hat" (1976) with Jack Albertson, "Yogi's Treasure Hunt" (1985-86) with Daws Butler, "The Cosby Show: No Way, Baby" (1989) with Bill Cosby, "The Cosby Mysteries: Home, Street Home" (1994) with Bill Cosby, "Courage the Cowardly Dog" (1999-2002) with Thea White.

Arnold made his last appearance in 2004 in a interview with animator Earl Kress; they talked about the making of "Top Cat."

Sadly, Arnold died of pneumonia on December 20, 2009 in Newton, Massachusetts. His remains were cremated and the ashes interred in Newton's cemetery.

Arnold once described himself as "a frightened chipmunk who's been out in the rain too long!" Fans will remember his off-sided brand of comedy for a long time.

TAYLOR, ROD
1930-2015

Update: Sadly, this fine actor died of a heart attack on January 7, 2015 at home in Beverly Hills, Los Angeles, California. The man and his work will be greatly missed.

(Here's a shot, below, of Rod in a scene from my favorite movie of all others: The Time Machine*)*

TRACEY, DOREEN
1943-

Update: I'm pleased to write that Doreen has received the Disney Legend Award at the D23 Expo. This honor was bestowed upon her July 18, 2015 for the talented work she provided during the four-year production (1955-59) of TV's Mickey Mouse Club. She joins other former Disney celebrities such as Annette Funicello, Tommy Kirk, and Kevin Corcoran. Congratulations, Doreen!

VINCENT, JAN-MICHAEL
1944-

Action actor possibly best remembered for his portrayal of Stringfellow Hawke, pilot of the sophisticated helicopter in the CBS TV series, "Airwolf," that ran from 1984 to 1986 and starred Ernest Borgnine, Alex Cord, and Deborah Pratt. He was born Jan-Michael (sometimes nicknamed Mike) Vincent on July 15, 1944 in Denver, Colorado to Lloyd and Doris Vincent; he also has Cherokee heritage. Early on the family moved to Hanford, California. He graduated from Hanford High School in 1963 and went to Ventura College in Ventura, California.

Just after Mike finished pulling his duty for the California Army National Guard he was spotted by a talent scout that liked his good looks.

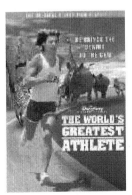

That got him a role in the western movie, "The Bandits," made in 1967 and starring Robert Conrad. Mike's career boosted after he was put under contract with Universal Studios and he appeared on "Dragnet 1967" as a muscular high school student who suffered an attack by a mentally unstable classmate. The episode was called "The Grenade" and starred Jack Webb, Harry Morgan, and Mickey Sholdar.

Some of the roles Mike portrayed in film include, "Journey to Shiloh" (1968) with James Caan, "The Undefeated" (1969) with John Wayne, "The Tribe" (1970) with Darren McGavin, "Going Home" (1971) with Robert Mitchum, "The Mechanic" (1972) with Charles Bronson, "The World's Greatest

Athlete" (1973) with Tim Conway, "Deliver Us from Evil" (1973) with George Kennedy, "White Line Fever" (1975) with Kay Lenz, "Shadow of the Hawk" (1976) with Chief Dan George, "Vigilante Force" (1976) with Kris Kristofferson, "Damnation Alley" (1977) with George Peppard, "Hooper" (1978) with Burt Reynolds, "Defiance" (1980) with Danny Aiello, "Airwolf" (1984) with Ernest Borgnine, "Enemy Territory" (1987) with Gary Frank, "Alienator" (1990) with John Phillip Law, "Raw Nerve" (1991) with Glenn Ford, "Sins of Desire" (1993) with Gail Harris, "Indecent Behavior" (1993) with Shannon Tweed, "Body Count" (1995) with Robert Davi, "Jurassic Women" (1996) with James Phillips, "No Rest for the Wicked" (1998) with Stefan Lysenko, "Escape to Grizzly Mountain" (2000) with Dan Haggerty. Mike's last acting role was in "White Boy" (2002) with Johnny Green. *(Photo, below. Traci Lords)*

Some of Mike's TV roles include, "The Hardy Boys: The Mystery of the Chinese Junk" (1967) with Richard Gates, "Lassie: Hanford's Point" (1968) with Jon Provost, "Bonanza: The Unwanted" (1969) with Lorne Greene, "Dan August: Death Chain" (1971) with Burt Reynolds, "Gunsmoke: The Legend" (1971) with James Arness, "Marcus Welby, M. D.: Catch a Ring That Isn't There" (1973) with Robert Young, "The Winds of War" (mini-series 1983) with Robert

Mitchum, "Hotel: Undercurrents" (1986) with James Brolin, "Renegade: Hard Rider" (1994) with Lorenzo Lamas, "Nash Bridges: Revelations" (1997) with Don Johnson.

In 1991 Mike appeared in the suspense film "Raw Nerve" with former underage porno actress, later turned legitimate actress, Traci Lords.

During the filming of "Airwolf" Mike admitted to having drug and alcohol problems but he kicked the habit after seeking help. In 1983 he was arrested for drunk driving but avoided jail by entering a rehab. In 1996 Mike was driving drunk and had a collision, causing him to nearly be killed with a broken neck; he also sustained a permanent injury to his vocal chords from an emergency medical procedure.

(Photo, l. Jan and his wife, Anna)

Mike married Bonnie Poorman in 1969; they had one daughter and divorced in 1975. In 1986 he married Joanne Robinson and they divorced in 1997. In 1999 Mike married Patricia Ann (couldn't locate her last name).

He's been completely retired from acting since 2009. His wife, Anna, says that Mike has suffered from epilepsy since childhood.

Sadly, Mike contracted peripheral artery disease and as a result of complications from it had to have his right leg amputated just below the knee in 2012. He has a prosthetic limb but sometimes uses a wheelchair. Mike keeps in good spirits and resides with his wife, Anna, on their horse ranch at Eagle Lake in Redwood near Vicksburg, Mississippi.

WALKER, JIMMIE
1947-

This wisecracking, six foot one inch *dyn-o-mite* actor was born James Carter Walker on June 25, 1947 in the Bronx, New York City, New York. Just about all by himself, J. J. symbolized the 1970s American dream of success. Originally, he wanted to get into professional basketball but that didn't pan out for him. Instead he got a degree in radio engineering and announcing. Soon J. J. was hired as an engineer for a small radio station and quickly gained a reputation as a funny guy and a good writer. He made his debut in comedy as an opening act in 1967 as part of a group called "The Last Poets." J. J. ultimately got a shot on TV on Jack Paar's show in 1972. He was successful and that moved him on toward the big time.

J. J. auditioned for and got the part of James "J. J." Evans on "Good Times" (1974) with co-stars BernNadette Stanis, Ralph Carter, Esther Rolle, Ja'net DuBois, and John Amos (look for a biography of John Amos in my first book, "Hollywood Celebrities: Where Are They Now?"). Life in the Chicago projects was never the same after J. J. Evans blew through it! He made his catchphrase *dyn-o-mite* a popular, household word. The series was so popular it lasted six seasons.

He made it into the movies with his appearance in "Let's Do It Again" (1975), a comedy with Sidney Poitier and Bill Cosby.

After "Good Times" ended in 1979, J. J. went back to stand-up comedy on the stage. Today, J. J. tours 25-30 weeks a year to appreciative audiences. In his spare time he writes scripts for television and the movies.

Some of J. J.'s film roles include, "The Greatest Thing That Almost Happened" (1977) with James Earl Jones, "The Concorde . . . Airport '79" (1979) with Robert Wagner, "The Jerk, Too" (1984) with Ray Walston, "Going Bananas" (1987) with Dom DeLuise, "Home Alone 2: Lost in New York" (1992) with Macaulay Culkin, "Open Season" (1995) with Lloyd Adams, "Monster Mash: The Movie" (1995) with Ian Bohen, "Chasing Robert" (2007) with Len Austrevich, "Big Money Rustlas" (2010) with Violant J, "Sweet Lorraine" (2015) with Tatum O'Neal. J. J. is currently working on two movies scheduled to be out in 2016: "Renaissance Man" with Joyce DeWitt and "Hospital Arrest" with Gilbert Gottfried. Also in one scheduled for release in 2017 called "The Comedian" with Robert DeNiro.

Never boastful about his career J. J. says, "I'm no actor. I'm a comic who lucked into a good thing."

Lucky for all his fans.

WASHBURN, BEVERLY
1943-

Update: Glad to let all Beverly's fans (including me) know that she is appearing in three films: "Paranormal Extremes: Text Messages From the Dead" (now completed) and co-starring with Dawna Lee Heising in this horror flick; "Unbelievable!!!" (still filming at this writing but scheduled to be released later this year, 2016) a comedy sci-fi starring Dina Meyer; and "When the World Came to San Francisco (also still filming at this writing but scheduled to be released later this year) a docu-drama starring Beverly.

Also exciting to learn that Beverly released an updated autobiography that contains more about her career and lots more photos. She used the same title as her first book, "Reel Tears: The Beverly Washburn Story." Published by BearManor Media (2013) I found it to be a very informative and interesting book, a fine addition to anyone's collection.

WEISSMULLER, JOHNNY 1904-84

This Olympic swimming champion and actor will probably be best remembered for playing Tarzan in the series of films in the 1930s and 40s and as Jungle Jim in the 1950s. Johnny played Tarzan 12 times and created the distinctive Tarzan yell that was used by other actors later playing the part. And Johnny was one of the best swimmers of the 20th century.

He was born Johann Peter Weissmuller on June 2, 1904 in Freidorf, Austria-Hungary (now Timisoara, Romania), of German ancestry, to Peter Weissmuller and Elisabeth Kersch. The family immigrated to America early in 1905, arriving at Ellis Island. They moved to Windber, Pennsylvania where father Peter worked in the coal mines. The census of 1910 shows they were living in Chicago.

When nine years old Johnny contracted polio and it was suggested by his doctor that he take up swimming to help fight the debilitating disease. He got much better and eventually earned a spot on the YMCA swim team. Johnny attended Lane Technical College Prep High School but dropped out to go to work, including a position as a lifeguard on a Lake Michigan beach. He also worked as a bellboy at the Illinois Athletic Club and it was there that Johnny was seen by swim coach William Bachrach who decided to train him. Bachrach must have done a good job because in 1921 Johnny won the national championships in the 50-yard and 220-yard distances.

In 1922 Johnny earned the world record in the 100-meter freestyle swim in just 58.6 seconds. And he won the gold at the 1924 Summer Olympics. He won a bronze medal on the U. S. water polo team in 1924 and in 1928, Johnny won another gold medal at the Summer Olympics in Amsterdam. About this time he adopted a vegetarian lifestyle.

In all Johnny won five Olympic gold medals and one bronze, 52 U. S. national championships, and set 67 world records. He never lost a race and retired with an unbeaten amateur record. *(Photo, below l. Here's Johnny with an unknown, nude actress in* Glorifying the American Girl, *1929)*

Johnny did some modeling and some radio and made an appearance in a movie playing Adonis in which he wore only a fig leaf! The film was Florenz Ziegfeld's "Glorifying the American Girl" (1929) with Mary Eaton; since it was pre-code, the movie had some nude scenes including Johnny wearing only a fig leaf standing next to a nude actress!

For the most part Johnny began working in film when the 6'3" athlete signed a seven-year contract with MGM to play Tarzan in "Tarzan the Ape Man" (1932) which also starred Maureen O'Sullivan and C. Aubrey Smith. The movie was a huge success as Tarzan had been popular since it first came out as a novel by Edgar Rice Burroughs in 1912. Burroughs liked Johnny Weissmuller played Tarzan but hated the way the studio had Johnny portray his creation as barely articulate. Johnny made six more Tarzan flicks for MGM. In 1942 he went over to RKO to play Tarzan in "Tarzan's New York Adventure" with Maureen O'Sullivan, Johnny Sheffield and to do five more Tarzan movies for them. During this time frame he also did a film for Pine-Thomas Productions called "Swamp Fire" (1946) with Buster Crabbe, Virginia Grey, and Carol Thurston.

After trading in his loin cloth, Johnny went over to Columbia to play a safari-suited good guy named Jungle Jim in a flick of the same name made in 1948 and also starring Virginia Grey and George Reeves (of TVs "Superman" fame). The Jungle Jim character was based on Alex Raymond's comic strip. Altogether Johnny made 16 of these films, although in the last three the character was called Johnny Weissmuller instead of Jungle Jim as the rights to that character name had been sold to Screen Gems.

(Photo, below. Maureen O'Sullivan and Johnny Weissmuller as Jane and Tarzan, ca 1939)

In 1955 Johnny began doing the "Jungle Jim" TV series for Screen Gems. It aired until 1956 with a total of 26 episodes that also starred Martin Huston and Dean Fredericks. After these episodes were completed Johnny retired from acting. He moved back to Chicago and started a swimming pool company. Johnny retired completely in 1965 and moved to Fort Lauderdale, Florida where he became the Founding Chairman of the International Swimming Hall of Fame. He was inducted into the ISHOF the same year.

Some of the films in which Johnny appeared include, "Tarzan and His Mate" (1934) with Maureen O'Sullivan, "Tarzan Finds a Son!" (1939) with Johnny Sheffield, "Tarzan's Secret Treasure" (1941) with

Maureen O'Sullivan, "Tarzan Triumphs" (1943) with Frances Gifford, "Stage Door Canteen" (1943) with Judith Anderson, "Tarzan and the Amazons" (1945) with Brenda Joyce, "Tarzan and the Mermaids" (1948) with Brenda Joyce, "Mark of the Gorilla" (1950) with Trudy Marshall, "Jungle Jim in the Forbidden Land" (1952) with Jean Willes, "Cannibal Attack" (1954) with Judy Walsh, "Devil Goddess" (1955) with Angela Stevens, "The Phynx" (1970) with Maureen O'Sullivan, "The Great Masquerade" (1974) with Kaye Stevens, "Won Ton Ton: The Dog Who Saved Hollywood" (1976) with Dennis Morgan.

Twenty-six episodes of "Jungle Jim" (1955-56) was the only TV spot that Johnny did.

Johnny had for years been interested in health food and in 1969 opened a small chain of health food stores called Johnny Weissmuller's American Natural Foods. He lived in Florida until 1973 when he moved to Las Vegas, Nevada and took a job as a greeter at Caesar's Palace along with former boxer Joe Louis.

In 1931 Johnny married Bobbe Arnst; they divorced in 1933. He married actress Lupe Vélez in 1933; they divorced in 1939. He then married Beryl Scott in 1939; they had thee children including actor Johnny Weissmuller Jr.; they divorced in 1948. In 1948 Johnny married Allene Gates; they divorced in 1962. He married Maria Baumann in 1963; they were together until his death.

In 1974 Johnny broke his leg and hip; while in the hospital he learned that, in spite of his lifelong exercise and proper eating, he had a serious heart condition. In 1977 Johnny had a series of strokes. He and wife Marie moved to Acapulco, Mexico in 1979.

Sadly, Johnny died from pulmonary edema on January 20, 1984. He was buried at the Valley of the Light Cemetery just outside of Acapulco. He was awarded a Star on the Hollywood Walk of Fame at 6541 Hollywood Boulevard; it faces the Star of Maureen O'Sullivan.

WESTERMAN, FLOYD (RED CROW)
1936-2007

Popular actor and country and western singer of Native American heritage. Remembered for, among many roles, playing Uncle Ray to Chuck Norris' character on the TV crime hit, "Walker, Texas Ranger" (1993-2001) during the first and second seasons.

Born Floyd "Kanghi Duta" ("Red Crow") Westerman on August 17, 1936 on the Lake Traverse Indian Reservation located in northeastern South Dakota and southeastern North Dakota. This reservation is the home of the federally-recognized Sesseton Wahpeton Oyate, one of the Eastern Dakota sub-groups (Santee) of the Great Lakota (Sioux) Nation. While only ten years old Floyd was sent to the Wahpeton Boarding School where all the boys were forced to have their traditionally-long hair cut and forbidden to speak their native languages to satisfy a "white" law. This unjust treatment greatly effected Floyd and in later life he would become a Native American activist.

Floyd graduated from Northern State University, Aberdeen, South Dakota after majoring in art and speech & theatre. He served two years in the U. S. Marines.

Perhaps not known to most of his movie and TV fans, Floyd began a career early on as a country and western singer and became quite popular. He also sang with Willie Nelson, Harry Belafonte, Joni Mitchell, and others. One of his best albums is "Custer Died for Your Sins." After years as a singer Floyd became interested in acting and began his film career in "Renegades" (1989), an action crime drama with Lou Diamond Phillips and Kiefer Southerland. He played Red Crow, the Lakota father of Phillips' character, Hank Storm. Floyd was also Chief Ten Bears in the major western hit, "Dances With Wolves" (1990) with Kevin Costner, Mary McDonnell, and Graham Greene.

Some of his other films in which he appeared include, "Son of the Morning Star" (1991) with Gary Cole, "The Doors" (1991) with Val Kilmer, "Rio Shannon" (1993) with Blair Brown, "Jonathan degli orsi" (1994) with Franco Nero, "Lakota Woman: Siege at Wounded Knee" (1994) with Irene Bedard, "Buffalo Girls" (1995) with Angelica Huston, "The Brave" (1997) with Marlon Brando, "Grey Owl" (1999) with Pierce Brosnan, "Graduation Night" (2003) with Adrain R'Mante, "Hidalgo" (2004) with Viggo Mortensen, "The Legend of Tillamook's Gold" (2006) with Brian McNamara, "Swing Vote" (2008) with Kevin Costner.

Some of Floyd's TV appearances include, "MacGyver: Mask of the Wolf" (1988) with Richard Dean Anderson, "Captain Planet and the Planeteers: Tree of Life" (1990) with David Coburn, "L. A. Law: Dances with Sharks" (1991) with Harry Hamlin, "Murder, She Wrote: Night of the Coyote" (1992) with Angela Lansbury, "Roseanne" (1995) with Roseanne Barr, "The Pretender: Mirage" (1997) with Michael T. Weiss, "Baywatch Nights: The Vortex" (1997) with David Hasselhoff, "Poltergeist: The Legacy: Shadow Fall" (1997) with Derek de Lint, "The X-Files" (1995-99) with Gillian Anderson, "Dharma & Greg" (1997-2001) with Jenna Elfman, "Comanche Moon" (2008) with Steve Zahn.

Besides singing and acting, Floyd was an immensely talented artist of Lakota/Dakota-inspired bronze sculptures as well as bronze busts of influential leaders in American Indian history, such as Geronimo, Sitting Bull, and Chief Joseph.

Some sources state that Floyd was married a number of times and the father of five children. At the time of his death he was married to Rosemarie Laaser; they had married in 1989.

Floyd has deservedly received many accolades and awards for his work in promoting his Native American heritage.

Sadly, Floyd Westerman died of complications from leukemia on December 13, 2007 at Cedars Sinai Hospital in Los Angeles, California. He is buried in Saint Mathew's Catholic Cemetery in Veblen, South Dakota.

WICKES, MARY
1910-95

This fine character actress and funny lady was born Mary Isabella Wickenhauser on June 13, 1910 in St. Louis, Missouri to Frank Wickenhauser and Mary Shannon. She is probably best remembered as Miss Cathcart on the "Dennis the Menace" TV show (1954-63) with Jay North and Gloria Henry.

Mary's parents were theater buffs and took little Mary to see stage shows as soon as she was old enough to stay awake. She was an excellent student and skipped two grades in elementary school, graduating from high school at the age of 16. Mary graduated from Washington University in St. Louis in 1930 with a double major in English lit and political science. She planned to go on and study law but a favorite college professor suggested she try acting.

Mary first appeared on Broadway "The Farmer Takes a Wife" in 1934, starring Henry Fonda. She began acting in film in the late 30s; her first significant role was as Nurse Preen in "The Man Who Came to Dinner" (1942) with Bette Davis and Ann Sheridan.

Mary was a tall (5'10"), gangly woman but in spite of her awkward appearance really knew how to deliver her lines and would prove herself to be an adept comedienne. She played the wisecracking nurse who helped Bette Davis' character in "Now, Voyager" (1942). And she was the quintessential funny lady in "Who Done It?" (1942) with funny men

214

Bud Abbott and Lou Costello. Mary was also sensational as the efferves-
cent secretary and lodge owner's assistant, Emma Allen, in the hit musical "White Christmas" (1954) with Bing Crosby and Danny Kaye.

In 1949 Mary went on the new medium
of TV by starring in the title role of a CBS
Westinghouse Studio One version of "Mary
Poppins." She appeared as the caring but
comical maid to Annette Funicello's
character in the Walt Disney "Mickey
Mouse Club" serial, "Annette" in 1958. A
longtime friend of Lucille Ball, Mary made
many appearances on "I Love Lucy," "The
Lucy Show," and "Here's Lucy." In fact,
there's hardly a TV show that Mary wasn't
on.

Some of Mary's film roles include, "Charlie Chan at the Opera"
(1936) with Warner Oland, "Blondie's Blessed Event" (1942) with
Penny Singleton, "June Bride" (1948) with Bette Davis, "On Moonlight
Bay" (1951) with Doris Day, "The Story of Will Rogers" (1952) with
Will Rogers Jr., "Destry" (1954) with Audie Murphy (see Audie's bio in
this book), "Dance With Me, Henry" (1956) with Abbott & Costello,
"The Proud Rebel" (1958) with Alan Ladd, "The Sins of Rachel Cade"
(1961) with Angie Dickinson, "Fate is the Hunter" (1964) with Glenn
Ford, "The Trouble With Angels" (1966) with Hayley Mills, "Where
Angels Go Trouble Follows!" (1968) with Rosalind Russell, "Snowball
Express" (1972) with Dean Jones, "Ma and Pa" (1974) with Arthur
Space, "Willa" (1979) with Deborah Raffin, "The Canterville Ghost"
(1985) with Richard Kiley, "The Christmas Gift" (1986) with John Den-
ver (look for John's bio in this book), "Postcards From the Edge" (1990)
with Meryl Streep, "Sister Act" (1992) with Whoopi Goldberg, "Sister

Act 2: Back in the Habit" (1993) with
Whoopi Goldberg, "The Hunchback
of Notre Dame" (voice 1996) with
Demi Moore.

*(Photo, l. Bing Crosby and Danny
Kaye in* White Christmas, *1954)*

Some of the TV roles Mary appeared in include, "The Halls of Ivy"
(1954-55) with Herbert Butterfield,
"Alfred Hitchcock Presents: Toby" (1956) with host Alfred Hitchcock,

"Make Room for Daddy: Too Good for Words" (1958) with Danny Thomas, "Zorro: The Well of Death" (1958) with Guy Williams, "The Thin Man: Bat McKidderick" (1959) with Peter Lawford, "Shirley Temple's Storybook: Little Men" (1960) with host Shirley Temple, "Our Man Higgins: Love is Dandy" (1963) with Stanley Holloway, "F Troop: Marriage, Fort Courage Style" (1967) with Larry Storch, "I Spy: Shana" (1968) with Robert Culp, "Columbo: Suitable for Framing" (1971) with Peter Falk, "Kolchak: the Night Stalker: They Have Been, They Are, They Will Be . . ." (1974) with Darren McGavin, "M*A*S*H: House Arrest" (1975) with Alan Alda, "The Waltons: The Hostage" (1981) with Jon Walmsley, "Murder, She Wrote: Widow, Weep for Me" (1985) with Angela Lansbury, "Highway to Heaven: Country Doctor" (1988) with Michael Landon, "Life With Louie" (voice 1995-97) with Louie Anderson.

(Photo, below. Mary Wickes as Sister Mary Lazarus in Sister Act, *1992)*

Mary's last film role before she became ill was in "Little Women" (1994) with Winona Ryder and Susan Sarandon. Towards last, Mary suffered from kidney failure and gastrointestinal bleeding, complicated with low blood pressure, anemia, and breast cancer. Sadly, Mary died of complications from surgery on October 22, 1995 in Los Angeles. She was interred at the Shiloh Valley Cemetery in Shiloh, Illinois. Mary was unmarried and without children, but her legacy of a wonderful, caring, and funny lady will long endure. She always said, "I love playing good comedy with a heart, comedy which touches the audience."

WILLIAMS, PAUL
1940-

Actor and songwriter of such timeless classics as "Rainy Days and Mondays," "Just an Old-Fashioned Love Song," "We've Only Just Begun," and "Rainbow Connection." Though small of stature (5'2") but hugely talented, Paul Hamilton Williams, Jr. was born on September 19, 1940 in Bennington, near Omaha, Nebraska to Paul Hamilton Williams, Sr. and Bertha Mae Burnside.

Paul's father was killed in a car accident in 1953, forcing the adolescent to live with his aunt in Long Beach, California. His songwriting career began when Paul co-wrote "Fill Your Heart" with Biff Rose. It was released on Rose's first album "The Thorn in Mrs. Rose's Side." In 1968 it appeared on the B-side of Tiny Tim's single, "Tiptoe Through the Tulips." In the 1970s Paul co-wrote (with Roger Nichols) "An Old-Fashioned Love Song" for Three Dog Night, Helen Reddy's "You and Me Against the World," and the Carpenters "We've Only Just Begun."

Paul auditioned for but was not selected to become a Disney Mouseketeer (1955) and a part on The Monkees TV show (1966). He wrote and sang "Where Do I Go From Here" in the Clint Eastwood hit bad guys/good guys film, "Thunderbolt and Lightfoot" (1974) with George Kennedy and Jeff Bridges.

"Evergreen" (lyrics by Paul, melody by Barbra Streisand) from the movie "A Star is Born" (1976) won an Academy Award for Best Original Song and a Grammy for Song of the Year.

Paul wrote the music for and co-starred as the Satanic character Swan in Brian DePalma's musical horror film "Phantom of the Paradise" (1974) with Jessica Harper.

We can't forget Paul as the memorable genius orangutan Virgil in "Battle for the Planet of the Apes" (1973) with Roddy McDowall and Claude Akins. He also jokingly appeared as Virgil on the Johnny Carson Tonight Show (February 9, 1973) and sang a song. It broke Johnny up.

He appeared on Jim Henson's Muppet Show many times and wrote the music for the hit "The Muppet Movie" (1979) and even had a live cameo in it as the piano player in the nightclub scene where Kermit the Frog first meets Fozzie Bear.

In 1980 Paul was the host of the "Mickey Mouse Club 25th Anniversary Special" with Annette Funicello, Bobby Burgess, Sharon Baird, and many of the original Mouseketeers. Paul didn't make it as a Mouseketeer when he auditioned in 1955, but Annette made him an honorary mouse and gave him his "ears." Great show. If you were a fan of the original show like I was it's well worth getting a DVD copy of the reunion.

In 1971 Paul married Kate Clinton. They have two children, Sarah and Cole, later divorced. In 1993 he married Hilda Keenan Wynn (daughter of actor Keenan Wynn). They were divorced and Paul married Mariana Williams in 2005.

(L. Paul as Little Enos Burdette in Smokey and the Bandit (1977).)

As an actor, Paul began his career in "The Loved One" (1965) with Robert Morse. Others include, "Watermelon Man" (1970) with Godfrey Cambridge, "Smokey and the Bandit" (1977) with Burt Reynolds, "Stone Cold Dead" (1979) with Richard Crenna, "Smokey and the Bandit II" (1980) with Burt Reynolds, "The Night They Saved Christmas" (1984) with Art Carney, "Frog" (1987) with Shelley Duvall, "Headless Body in Topless Bar" (1995) with Raymond J. Barry, "A Muppets Christmas: Letters to Santa" (2008) with Whoopi Goldberg, "The Ghastly Love of Johnny X" (2012) with Will Keenan.

Some of Paul's TV appearances include, "The Odd Couple" (1974) with Jack Klugman, "Baretta" (1975) with Robert Blake, "Hawaii Five-0" (1979) with James MacArthur, "B. J. and the Bear" (1981) with Greg Evigan, "Gimmee a Break!" (1987) with Nell Carter, "She-Wolf of London" (1991) with Neil Dickson, "The Pirates of Dark Water" (1992-93 voice overs) with Jodi Benson, "Walker, Texas Ranger" (1995) with Chuck Norris, "Phantom 2040" (1994-95) with Margot Kidder, "Superman" (1998) with Tim Daly, "The Bold and the Beautiful" (1998) with Katherine Kelly Lang, "Adventure Time" (2015) with Jeremy Shada.

Paul has also appeared on the stage and in 1989 played Truman Capote in the one-man play, "Tru."

Unfortunately, Paul fell victim to drug and alcohol abuse but steadfastly recovered (1989). Because of that he became a licensed drug rehabilitation counselor and works with the Musician's Assistance Programme, a non-profit organization that helps music-industry professionals on their difficult journey away from substance abuse.

He was inducted into the American Songwriters Hall of Fame in 2001 and awarded a Star (1983) on the Hollywood Walk of Fame in Hollywood, California (at 6931 Hollywood Blvd.).

Interesting to note that after Paul wrote his hit "Rainy Days and Mondays" it was offered to The 5th Dimension but they chose not to do it. That was smart.

Thus Paul Williams is very much alive and keeping busy acting, writing, and working with those recovering from substance abuse.

During Paul's acceptance speech after winning his 1977 Oscar for "Evergreen," the man in the crimson sunglasses—on the subject of those who may be giants—was quoted as saying, "I was going to thank all the little people; then I remembered, I am the little people!"

WOOD, NATALIE
1938-81

This adorable, child actress and later a beautiful woman was lucky enough and talented enough to make the transition to adult acting. Natalie created a memorable performance as the little girl who didn't believe in Santa Claus until she met an old, bearded man who claimed to be Kris Kringle in "Miracle on 34th Street (1947) which starred Edmund Gwenn, Maureen O'Hara, and John Payne. One of her unforgettable adult roles was as Alva Starr, the beautiful but petit (5'), somewhat naive older daughter of a greedy, scheming mother who owned a broken-down hotel/saloon in the south during the turbulent days of the Depression in "This Property is Condemned" (1966). This fine movie also starred Robert Redford as the railroad supervisor who came to destroy the town and as Alva's love interest; Kate Reid as Hazel Starr, the greedy mother; Charles Bronson as J. J. Nichols, an ardent suitor; and Mary Badham as Willie Starr, Alva's vibrant younger sister who came crammed with humorous quips like "Okey-doke!" (Mary is the same child actress who, four years before, had played Scout in "To Kill a Mockingbird) Natalie received a Golden Globe nomination for Best Actress in "Condemned."

Natalie was born Natalie Zacharenko on July 20, 1938 in San Francisco, California to Russian immigrant father Nikolai Zacharenko and mother Maria Zudilova. Soon after Natalie's birth the family moved to Santa Rose, California. Her mother had deep-seated ambitions of becoming and actress and often went to the movies, taking young Natalie with her. Sometime during those years the family changed their surname to Gurdin. The family then moved to

Los Angeles and mother Maria pursued an acting career for Natalie. Younger sister Svetlana also later became an actress under the name of Lana Wood.

Natalie had her first film appearance as a big player in "Happy Land" (1943) with Don Ameche. The director, Irving Pichel, liked Natalie's work and kept his eye out for another role for her. It came in 1946 in "Tomorrow is Forever" with Orson Welles and Claudette Colbert. Welles said that Natalie was so professional in the part that "she was terrifying." She went to 20th Century Fox under contract and got the role that zoomed her career: "Miracle on 34th Street." In the movie most of the story line revolves around New York City's Macy's department store; after the film came out and was a big hit, Macy's invited Natalie to appear in their annual Thanksgiving Day Parade.

(Photo, below. Natalie Wood and Edmund Gwenn in Miracle on 34th Street*)*

Following her role in "Miracle" Natalie got increasingly good parts in movies with name stars, such as Fred MacMurray, James Stewart, and Margaret Sullavan. In her teen years, Natalie also got parts on television. She played the teenage daughter in the ABC sitcom "The Pride of the Family" (1953-54) and starring Paul Hartman and Fay Wray (of 1933's "King Kong" fame). But she officially made the transition from child star to *ingenue* in "Rebel Without a Cause" (1955) which starred James Dean and Sal Mineo (see Sal's bio elsewhere in this book). Natalie was nominated for an Academy Award for Best Supporting Actress for that part.

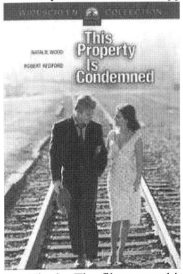

Her next movie wasn't a big part but an important role for Natalie's career for her portrayal of a young girl kidnapped by Indians and kept for a number of years in the classic western film "The Searchers" (1956) with John Wayne, Jeffrey Hunter, Vera Miles (look for Vera's bio in this book), and Ward Bond. She was signed to Warner Bros. in the 50s and they kept her busy in teenage flicks—roles that Natalie felt were unfulfilling.

Natalie's career almost dive-bombed after she appeared in the flop "All the Fine Young Cannibals" (1960) with Robert Wagner and George Hamilton. But her career was salvaged when she was cast in Elia Kazan's "Splendor in the Grass" (1961) with Warren Beatty and Pat Hingle. The film was a hit and Natalie received Best Actress Nominations at the Academy Awards, the Golden Globes, and at the BAFTA Awards.

Around the time after she did "Condemned," Natalie became depressed and went through professional therapy. She took three years off away from acting and then came back in 1969 to do "Bob & Carol & Ted & Alice," a film that starred Robert Culp, Elliott Gould, and Dyan Cannon. In 1970 Natalie went into semi-retirement and only made four more films during the remainder of her life. In 1980 Natalie acted in the TV mini-series, "From Here to Eternity" with Kim Basinger and William Devane. For her part in that she won a Golden Globe Award for Best Actress.

In 1957 Natalie married actor Robert Wagner; they divorced in 1962. She married writer/producer Richard Gregson in 1969; they had one child and divorced in 1972. Natalie then remarried Robert Wagner in 1972; they had one child and were together until her death.

Some of Natalie's film roles include, "The Moon is Down" (1943) with Cedric Hardwicke, "The Ghost and Mrs. Muir" (1947) with Gene Tierney, "Never a Dull Moment" (1950) with Fred MacMurray, "The Star" (1952) with Bette Davis, "One Desire" (1955) with Anne Baxter, "A Cry in the Night" (1956) with Edmond O'Brien, "Cash McCall" (1960) with James Garner, "West Side Story" (1961) with Richard Beymer, "Sex and the Single Girl" (1964) with Lauren Bacall, "Inside Daisy Clover" (1965) with Robert Redford, "The Candidate" (1972) with Robert Redford, "Cat On a Hot Tin Roof" (1976) with Laurence Olivier, "Meteor" (1979) with Brian Keith, "The Last Married Couple in America" (1980) with George Segal.

TV roles in which Natalie appeared include, "Chevron Theatre: Playmates" (1952) with Alan Napier, "Mayor of the Town" (1954) with Thomas Mitchell, "Conflict: Girl on the Subway" (1957) with June Blair, "Switch: The Cruise Ship Murders" (1975) with Robert Wagner, "Hart to Hart" (1979) with Robert Wagner.

(Photo, l. Robert Wagner and Natalie Wood)

Due to the fact that Natalie nearly drowned after she was thrown into the Pacific Ocean by "a mean director" (said Natalie) during the filming of "The Star" in 1952, Natalie was deathly afraid of water for the rest of her life. Odd, then, that husband Robert Wagner bought a yacht and made her go out on it knowing how she felt about deep water.

During 1981, Natalie was filming a science fiction film called "Brainstorm," released in 1983 and starring Christopher Walken and Cliff Robertson. Sadly, Natalie died of drowning after she disappeared from her husband's (Robert Wagner) yacht on November 28, 1981; her body was recovered November 29. She drowned in the Pacific Ocean off Santa Catalina Island. Because of her death, Natalie's part in the movie had to be finished with a stand-in and sound-alike actresses.

A mystery surrounds the actual circumstances of Natalie's death. She had gone for a weekend cruise with her husband, Robert Wagner, her "Brainstorm" co-star Christopher Walken, and boat captain Dennis Davern. They all had been drinking onboard that night and nobody noticed when Natalie disappeared over the side into the water. Wagner stated that when he went to bed Natalie was not there. I can't believe he didn't immediately look for her. Questioned, Wagner stated that he and Natalie "had a fight before she disappeared"; the extent of "the fight" has never been determined. The autopsy report stated that Natalie had bruises on her body and arms as well as an abrasion on her left cheek.

The case of Natalie's death was reopened in 2011 when Captain Dennis Davern came forward and stated that he had lied to police during the initial investigation in 1981. He said that Natalie and Wagner did have a fight that evening and that Wagner was responsible for her death; Davern was given a polygraph test and passed. In 2012 her death certificate was amended from "accidental drowning" to "drowning and other undetermined factors." It also stated that how Natalie got into the water "was not clearly established." In 2013, the Los Angeles County coroner's office also added an addendum to Natalie's autopsy report that stated "the bruises on her body may have been sustained before she went into the water."

Los Angeles police still consider Natalie's drowning as accidental but state that the case is still open; Wagner is not considered a suspect.

Robert Wagner has consistently denied any involvement in Natalie's death.

Natalie was interred at Westwood Village Memorial Park Cemetery in Los Angeles, California. She was posthumously awarded a Star on the Hollywood Walk of Fame in 1986; it is located at 7000 Hollywood Boulevard.

Natalie was quoted as saying, "You get tough in this business, until you get big enough to hire people to get tough for you. Then you can sit back and be a lady."

WORDEN, HANK
1901-92

Hank Worden was a cowboy turned character actor who delighted audiences with his folksy, western charm in over 149 films. Hank was born Norton Earl Worden on July 23, 1901 in Rolfe, Iowa to railroad engineer Norton Albert Worden and Ella Webb and grew up on a cattle ranch near Glendive, Montana. This lanky six foot two inch westerner was educated at Stanford and the University of Nevada as an engineer. He served in the Army as a pilot. Later, Hank was a saddle bronc rider in rodeos for some time and actually broke his neck in a fall in the 1920s. He was sore, yes, but nobody knew he had the break until he got an x-ray in the 40s. When he was doing a rodeo in Madison Square Garden, New York City, Hank was picked along with Tex Ritter to appear in a Broadway play entitled, "Green Grow the Lilacs" (1930). Before Hollywood beckoned he worked as a cab driver in New York and as a guide on The Bright Angel Trail at the Grand Canyon in Arizona.

While working as a wrangler on a dude ranch, Hank met actress Billie Burke. She must have been impressed with him because she recommended him to several film producers. Cecil B. DeMille grabbed him up and Hank appeared as an extra in DeMille's epic, "The Plainsman," (1936) which starred Gary Cooper and Jean Arthur. Tex Ritter had since become a star and, not forgetting his old friend Hank Worden, used him as a comic sidekick in some of Tex's films (sometimes Hank was billed as Heber Snow). He worked for Howard Hawks and soon came to the attention of director John Ford. Ford used him 12 times in film and TV

(Hank worked in 17 of John Wayne's movies). Perhaps Hank's best remember role was that of Mose Harper in "The Searchers," (1956) which starred John Wayne, Ward Bond, Vera Miles, Harry Carey Jr., Jeffrey Hunter, and Natalie Wood.

Hank married Emma Louise Eaton in 1940. They adopted a daughter and were together until she died in 1977.

In 1992, Hank hosted a TV special entitled, "Thank Ya, Thank Ya Kindly." It was a tribute to Hank's career and featured guest stars Clint Eastwood, Paul Hogan, Harry Carey Jr., Ben Johnson, and Frankie Avalon.

(Photo, below. Here's Hank in Red River, *1948)*

Some of the movies in which Hank appeared include, "Barbary Coast" (1935) with Edward G. Robinson, "Ghost Town Riders" (1938) with Bob Baker, "Stagecoach" (1939) with John Wayne, "Deep in the Heart of Texas" (1942) with Tex Ritter, "Lumberjack" (1944) with William Boyd (Hopalong Cassidy), "Abbott and Costello in Hollywood" (1945) with Bud and Lou, "Angel and the Badman" (1947) with John Wayne, "Fort Apache" (1948) with John Wayne, "Red River" (1948) with John Wayne, "Comin' Round the Mountain" (1951) with Abbott and Costello, "Ma and Pa Kettle at Home" (1954) with Marjorie Main, "The Indian Fighter" (1955) with Kirk Douglas, "The Horse Soldiers" (1959) with John Wayne, "The Alamo" (1960) with John Wayne, "True Grit" (1969) with John Wayne, "Big Jake" (1971) with John Wayne, "Smokey and the Bandit" (1977) with Burt Reynolds, "Bronco Billy" (1980) with Clint Eastwood, "UFOria" (1985) with Cindy Williams, "Big Bad John" (1990) with Jimmy Dean, "Almost An Angel" (1990) with Paul Hogan.

Some of Hank's roles in television include, "The Stu Erwin Show" (1951) with Stu Erwin, "Disneyland: Davy Crockett and the River Pirates" (1955) with Fess Parker, "The Lone Ranger" (1949-57) with Clayton Moore, "The Adventures of Jim Bowie" (1957) with Scott Forbes, "Bronco" (1959) with Ty Hardin, "Tales of Wells Fargo" (1957-59) with Dale Robertson, "Rawhide" (1960) with Clint Eastwood, "Bonanza" (1960-66) with Dan Blocker, "Daniel Boone" (1965-67) with Fess

225

Parker, "Iron Horse" (1967) with Dale Robertson, "Petticoat Junction" (1966-68) with Edgar Buchanan, "Night Gallery" (1971) with host Rod Serling, "Gunsmoke" (1974) with James Arness, "Knight Rider" (1986) with David Hasselhoff, "Twin Peaks" (1990-91) with Kyle McLachlan.

Hank enjoyed good health right up until his passing. On December 6, 1992, he went inside his home in the Brentwood section of Los Angeles, California to take a nap and died peaceably of natural causes in his sleep. His remains were cremated and his ashes are interred in the Freedom Mausoleum Columbarium of Victory (niche 32616) at the Forest Lawn Memorial Cemetery in Glendale, California.

ZACHERLEY, JOHN
1918-

This fine comic personality and voice actor was born John Zacherle on September 26, 1918 in Philadelphia, Pennsylvania. He grew up in the Germantown area and went to high school there. John graduated from the University of Pennsylvania with a degree in English literature. During WWII he enlisted in the Army and served in north Africa and in Europe. His first acting role was in a TV western series called "Action in the Afternoon" (1953-54) for WCAU (later bought by CBS) in which he played several characters. John was hired in 1957 to play a role he made famous: as the crypt-living undertaker Roland (pronounced Ro-LAND although I seem to remember him as Dr. Shock and calling himself the Shocky Doc on his show), the host on WCAU's "Shock Theater." He did comedic horror skits during breaks of a horror film.

John was a close friend of Dick Clark and sometimes filled in for Dick on his show, "American Bandstand." It is said that Dick gave John the nickname the six-foot, four-inch Zacherley became famous for as "The Cool Ghoul." In 1958 John released a 45 rpm record of a gag cut called "Dinner with Drac" for Cameo Records; it broke the top ten. He also did a version of Bobby "Boris" Pickett's popular "Monster Mash." In 1963 John hosted a teenage dance show called "Disc-O-Teen" for three years at WNJU-TV in Newark, New Jersey

In 1967 John became a morning radio host for WNEW-FM, moving to WPLJ-FM in 1971 where he stayed for ten years. He made a lot of appearances in costume as Roland/Zacherley in New York and Philadel-

227

phia in the 1980s and 90s. At one Holloween appearance he narrated Edgar Allen Poe's "The Raven." And he is the only horror host to appear on the cover of "Famous Monsters of Filmland" twice.

John starred in a documentary entitled "The Model Craze That Gripped the World" in 2010. It was made by the Witch's Dungeon Classic Movie Museum in Bristol, Connecticut. The film won a Rondo Award.

John continues to make guest appearances at conventions and his collectibles still sell quite well. He lives in an apartment in Manhattan, New York.

Some of the films in which John appeared or did voice overs include, "Key to Murder" (1958) with Lynn Dollar, "Horrible Horror" (1986) with John Agar, "Brain Damage" (1988) with Rick Hearst, "Frankenhooker" (1990) with Janes Lorinz, "The Zacherley Archives" (1998) with Bob Prescott, "Dr. Horror's Erotic House of Idiots" (2004) with Debbie Rochon, "Chiller Theatre: Tarantula" (2008) with John Agar, "Bygone Behemoth" (2010) with David Chaskin.

Some TV appearances include, "The Dick Clark Show" (1958) with Dick Clark, "Play of the Week: Uncle Harry" (1960) with Jeff Donnell.

(*Photo, l., John as* Zacherley, the Cool Ghoul, *on WCAU's* Shock Theater, *1957)*

JOHN WAYNE

Was the government responsible for the death of
John Wayne and for many others?

Boyhood

Actor, producer, director, best-selling recording artist, veteran and all-around American John Wayne was born Marion Robert Morrison on May 26, 1907 in Winterset, Iowa, the son of Clyde Leonard Morrison and Mary Alberta Brown. Early on, due to ill health, Clyde moved the family to the more pristine climate of southern California. Father Wayne and family tried ranching on the Mojave Desert. When the ranch failed they moved to Glendale, California.

229

Humor

It seems that Duke and his close friend, actor Ward Bond, frequently played jokes on each other. Ward Bond bet Duke that they could stand on opposite ends of a newspaper and Duke wouldn't be able to hit him. Ward placed the newspaper on the floor in an open doorway and they each stood at one end. Immediately, Ward slammed the door in Duke's face and cackled that he should now try to hit him. Not one to be up-staged, Duke hauled off and slammed his fist through the door, hitting his friend and knocking him down. The bet was won.

Duke once floored one of Frank Sinatra's body guards and knocked him out with a chair. Sinatra—who Duke hadn't much liked anyway—was having a loud party that was keeping him awake in the hotel they both occupied. After repeated, ignored requests by phone on Duke's part for less noise, he went downstairs to Sinatra's room and was confronted by a surly, threatening body guard. Oh, yeah? Duke went into action and put the man out. The noise level immediately dropped and stayed that way for the remainder of Sinatra's party!

Duke once made a cameo appearance on televisions sitcom, "The Beverly Hillbillies" (1962). When Duke was asked how he wanted to be paid, he said: "Give me a fifth of bourbon—that'll square it!"

The Curse of Genghis Khan

After director Dick Powell threw out a script he considered terrible, John Wayne found it in the director's trash can, read it, and told Powell that he liked it very much and wanted to play the lead, the Mongol chief Temujin (later Emperor Genghis Khan) in, "The Conqueror." (Years later the Duke decided, along with most other people, that the film was the worst picture for entertainment quality that he had ever made and he considered himself badly casted for the part. As it turned out, making "The Conqueror" may have been a much worse decision than Duke realized.)

Escalante Desert

Producer Howard Hughes (at RKO) decided to do location filming on the Escalante Desert near St. George, Utah, a decision he later regretted. As it turned out, the site was 137 miles downwind from the Nevada

Proving Grounds (later the Nevada National Security Site located in Nye County, 65 miles northwest of

(Photo, l. Some of the cast of The Conqueror. *L. Susan Hayward and John Wayne to her right, 1956)*

Las Vegas). Since 1951 it had been used to test (explode) nuclear devices. In 1953 Operation Upshot-Knothole was responsible for eleven detonations of nuclear weapons. It had been previously (early 1950s) proven that St. George, Utah, received the most above-ground testing, radiation fallout from Yucca Flats and the Nevada Proving Grounds in general. Later on, it was found that this heavily increased the incidences of cancer among the local (St. George) population, including (but not limited to) leukemia, thyroid cancer, breast cancer, melanoma, and lymphoma.

(Photo, below. RKO producer Howard Hughes)

Prior to making a decision to use the Escalante site for exterior location filming, Howard Hughes contacted the federal government and was told it was safe to be in that area. But was it? Notwithstanding the obvious discomfort of temperatures well over 100 degrees and super low humidity, the westerly winds continuously carried heavy concentrations of dust onto the set and into the lungs of all those present—dust that had previously been proven to be highly radioactive with strontium 90, cesium 137, plutonium, and radio iodine. As if the natural winds weren't bad enough, giant wind machines were used to make sure there was enough *windy realism* on film.

Yucca Flats and Murphy's Law

Some 220 cast and crew members arrived in St. George, Utah in 1954. They stayed at local accommodations at night but had to be up early to be driven the 50-some miles over rough, dusty roads to the set in

Snow Canyon. It should be noted that on May 19, 1953, the nicknamed "Dirty Harry" bomb—a 32-kiloton monster—had been detonated at the Nevada Proving Grounds and could well have been the one most directly responsible for the radiation contamination of the set of "The Conqueror." It is well known that a pink-orange, radioactive cloud from the explosion hovered over St. George for two hours. The AEC (later the Department of Energy) released only vague public information about the test and dodged questions relative to fallout as much as possible. How much contaminated dust, ash, and gases was really released during that time alone?

Evidence

During 1953, sheep grazing in that area began to sicken and die mysteriously. The AEC wrote it off and side-stepped the many deaths, contributing the cause to *malnutrition!*

In years to come, cancer-related deaths and cancer cases among the cast and crew of "The Conqueror" were three times above normal, according to Dr. Robert Pendleton of the University of Utah. He stated: "With these numbers, this case could qualify as an *epidemic* (my italics)...." No mention is made here as to the number of Native American extras who worked in the film because—at that time--nobody kept any records about *those people.* Several of the cast and crew considered suing the "government" (probably the Atomic Energy Commission) for negligence, feeling that the powers-that-had-been certainly knew more than they had told anyone when they pooh-poohed the radioactivity danger level at the film site in Utah. Meanwhile, the death rate among locals in southwestern Utah from leukemia and cancer far exceeded the normal rate.

It looks as though co-star Pedro Armendariz was the first to sicken, diagnosed with kidney cancer in 1960 (in June 1963 he committed suicide rather than suffer through his terminal disease to the end).

The director of "The Conqueror," Dick Powell, died from lung cancer in January 1963. Prior to that, in 1962, Powell's doctor found malignant growths on his neck and chest.

Susan Hayward contracted brain and lung cancer in 1972, dying from this terrible disorder in 1975. Agnes Moorehead died of uterine cancer in 1974. Skeptics snicker over the fact that Misses Hayward and Moorehead smoked heavily, but—as far as I know—you can't contract uterine or brain cancer from smoking. John Wayne's son, Michael Wayne (who had been in the cast with his brother, Patrick), survived skin cancer (in spite of the fact that nine out of ten people who contract lupus are women, Michael died from that disease on April 5, 2003; lupus, however, is not a form of cancer), as did Patrick Wayne who had a benign mouth tumor removed. *People* magazine stated that 91 of the cast and crew of "The Conqueror" developed some form of cancer, 46 dying.

It is well known that the Duke smoked heavily, my research showing four to six packs a day (depending on the source); also his brother, Robert Wayne, died from lung cancer; and the Duke's father, Clyde, had some form of lung problems. Thus there could have been a genetic propensity to . . . something. But the heavy concentrations of known, cancer-causing radiation from the Nevada Proving Grounds lends a lot of credence to Mr. Wayne's condition and ultimate death.

Sadly, Michael Robert "John Wayne" Morrison died from stomach cancer on June 11, 1979 and was buried at Pacific View Cemetery in Corona del Mar, a community near Newport Beach, California where he had lived.

In 1990, due to Utah's Senator Orrin Hatch and Congressman Wayne Owens, Congress passed the Radiation Exposure Compensation Act that established a trust fund for *some of the injuries.*

Not good enough, you say? Where's the whole truth and admissions of guilt? Still buried in the bureaucratic realm of cover-up?

Should the Atomic Energy Commission/Department of Energy and the former Nevada Proving Grounds be held responsible for the deaths and debilitating terrors of John Wayne and so many others? Perhaps somebody can and will come forward some day soon with all the information it will take to place the blame where it belongs.

Here's a section dedicated to the famous comedy, film group, The Dead End Kids (Warner Bros., 1937-39); also billed as the East Side Kids (Monogram Pictures 1939-45), the Bowery Boys (1946-58), and the Little Tough Guys (Universal 1938-43).

Dell, Gabriel
1919-1988

This Dead End Kid was born Gabriel Del Vecchio on October 8, 1919 in New York City, New York to an Italian immigrant doctor. Early on he sang on a children's radio show and made his stage debut in "Dead End" (1935), later made into a film (1937) with Humphrey Bogart. Then during WWII he served in the Merchant Marine. After the war Gabe made more movies with the Bowery Boys but left the series with Huntz Hall in 1950. Did some Broadway plays and acted in film and on TV. Son Gabriel Dell Jr. is also an actor. Some of his many films include, "Angels With Dirty Faces" (1938) with James Cagney, "Spook Busters" (1946) with Leo Gorcey, "Escape From Terror" (1955) with Jackie Coogan, "The 300 Year Weekend" (1971) with William Devane, "The Escape Artist" (1982) with Raul Julia. Some of Gabe's TV spots include, "The Steve Allen Show" (1957-61), "The Fugitive" (1967) with David Janssen, "I Dream of Jeannie" (1970) with Barbara Eden, "McCloud" (1971) with Dennis Weaver, "A Year at the

Top" (1977) with Greg Evigan. Gabe died from leukemia on July 3, 1988 in North Hollywood, California and was cremated.

Gorcey, David
1921-1984

This Dead Ender was the brother of the customary leader of the gang, Leo Gorcey. David was born on February 6, 1921 in Washington Heights, New York. He was in the original stage play, "Dead End," and got his older brother a part that ultimately made him a star while David only got small roles. Some of his movie roles include, "Little Tough Guy" (1938) with Marjorie Main, "Spooks Run Wild" (1941) with Bela Lugosi, "Smuggler's Cover" (1948) with Leo Gorcey, "Abbott and Costello in the Foreign Legion" (1950) with Bud & Lou, "Dig That Uranium" (1955) with Huntz Hall, "Cole Younger, Gunfighter" (1958) with Frank Lovejoy. His TV appearances were, "The Silent Service" (1957) with Thomas M. Dykers, and "M Squad" (1958) with Lee Marvin. He married Dorothea Jocker; they had one son, David Gorcey Jr. After his film career he became a clergyman and helped those recovering from substance abuse. David died from a diabetic seizure on October 23, 1984 in Van Nuys, California.

Gorcey, Leo
1917-69

This well-known Dead Ender was born Leo Bernard Gorcey on June 3, 1917 in New York City, New York to vaudeville actors Bernard Gorcey and Josephine Condon. His parents were both quite diminutive—father at 4'10" and mother at 4'11" (Leo made it to 5'6"). His acting career began as those of the other Dead Enders; i. e., in the famous stage play, "Dead End." Leo was a plumber at the time that his brother, David (already in the cast) got him a part in the 1935 stage hit, "Dead End," which later on became a movie with Humphrey Bogart. At one time, while making scores of Dead End/Bowery Boys movies, Leo was one of the highest paid actors in Hollywood. He was married five times and had four children. Sadly, after father Bernard was killed in a car accident in 1955, Leo started drinking heavily, perhaps in an attempt to drown his unhappiness. After he threw a drunken fit on the set, the studio refused to pay him the high salary he demanded and Leo quit the Bowery Boys series. He didn't do much acting during the 1960s but had a small part in "It's a Mad, Mad, Mad, Mad World" (1963) with Spencer Tracy and Sid Caesar. Some of his many films include, "Crime School" (1938) with Humphrey Bogart, "Hell's Kitchen" (1939) with Ronald Reagan, "Bowery Blitzkrieg" (1941) with Bobby Jordan, "Ghosts on the Loose" (1943) with Bela Lugosi, "Blonde Dynamite" (1950) with Adele Jergens, "Crashing Las Vegas" (1956) with Huntz Hall, "The Phynx" (1970) with Michael A. Miller. Some of Leo's TV roles include, "The Dick Powell Theatre" (1962) with Mamie Van Doren, "Mr. Smith Goes to Washington" (1962) with Fess Parker. After years of alcoholism, Leo died of liver failure on June 2, 1969 in Oakland, California and is buried in Molinos Cemetery in Los Molinos, California.

Hall, Huntz
1920-99

Henry Richard Hall was born the 14th of 16 children on August 15, 1919 in New York City, New York to Joseph Hall and Mary Ellen Mullen. Henry got the nickname "Huntz" from a brother who said his big nose made him look German (he was actually Irish)! He made his first acting appearance on stage at the age of one in a play called, "Thunder on the Left." In 1932 Huntz appeared on television. That's right! It was an experimental early version of TV (guess that didn't work very well as television didn't really amount to anything until the late 40s). Huntz enlisted in the Army during World War II; after his discharge he went back to Hollywood. In addition to having been in more Bowery Boys films than any other Dead Ender (81), Huntz owned 10% of the pictures. He performed in dinner theater productions until he retired in 1994. Some of Huntz movie roles include, "They Made Me a Criminal" (1939) with John Garfield, "Junior G-Men of the Air" (1942) with Lionel Atwill, "A Walk in the Sun" (1945) with Dana Andrews, "Crazy Over Horses" (1951) with Ted de Corsia, "Second Fiddle to a Steel Guitar" (1965) with Arnold Stang, "Gentle Giant" (1967) with Dennis Weaver, "Herbie Rides Again" (1974) with Ken Berry, "Cyclone" (1987) with Heather Thomas. Some of Huntz's TV roles include, Flipper" (1966) with Brian Kelly, "The Chicago Teddy Bears" (1971) with Dean Jones, "CHiPs" (1978) with Erik Estrada, "Night Heat" (1988) with Scott Hylands, "Daddy Dearest" (1993) with Don Rickles. Huntz died of congestive heart failure on January 30, 1999 in North Hollywood, California and was interred in a niche at All Saints Episcopal Church in Pasadena, California.

Halop, Billy
1920-76

Former Dead Ender was born William Halop on February 11, 1920 in New York City, New York. Billy began in show business on the radio in the 20s, then went on to Broadway where he was in the stage hit, "Dead End." He went on to do the famous film version in 1937. He left the Kids' series in the early 40s but didn't do very well. After serving in WWII, Billy was a Gas House Kid (knock off of the Dead End Kids perpetrated by PRC Studios) and starred with former Alfalfa of the Our Gang comedy series, Carl Switzer, in 1946. In the mid-50s Billy worked as an electric dryer salesman for the Leonard Appliance Co. of Los Angeles, California. His sister, Florence Halop, was an actress (she was on "Night Court" for one season). Because his wife, the former Suzanne Roe, suffered from multiple sclerosis, he became quite proficient at caring for her. Later, Billy became a registered nurse and worked at St. John's Hospital in Santa Monica, California. Some of Billy's films include, "Angels With Dirty Faces" (1938) with James Cagney, "Angels Wash Their Faces" (1939) with Ann Sheridan, "Tom Brown's School Days" (1940) with Freddie Bartholomew, "Challenge of the Range" (1949) with Charles Starrett, "Air Strike" (1955) with Richard Denning, "The Courtship of Eddie's Father" (1963) with Glenn Ford, "Fitzwilly" (1967) with Dick Van Dyke. Some of his TV roles include, "Racket Squad" (1952) with Reed Hadley, "The Cisco Kid" (1953) with Duncan Renaldo, "Richard Diamond, Private Detective" (1959) with David Janssen, "Wagon Train" (1962) with John McIntire, "Glynis" (1963) with Glynis Johns, "The Fugitive" (1963) with David Janssen, "Gunsmoke" (1966-67) with James Arness, "All in the Family" (1971-76) with Carroll O'Connor. Billy died from a heart attack on November 9, 1976 in Brentwood, California and was buried at Mount Sinai Memorial Park Cemetery in Los Angeles, California.

Morrison, Sunshine Sammy 1912-89

East Side Kid Sunshine Sammy was also one of the Little Rascals kids from 1921-24. Sammy (his stage name) was born Frederick Ernest Morrison on December 20, 1912 in New Orleans, Louisiana. He made his film debut as an infant and worked with such famous silent film actors as Harold Lloyd and Snub Pollard. Said Sammy: "I was the first black movie personality to be featured in fan magazines." Sammy went into vaudeville for the next 16 years and appeared on the same bills with Abbott and Costello and Jack Benny. Producer Sam Katzman remembered Sammy from years before and hired him for the East Side Kids movies. He left the series when he was drafted during WWII and never returned to it, even though he was asked to return. Sammy did some film roles then left show business and took a job in an aircraft assembly plant where he spent the next 30 years. Some of Sammy's film roles include, "Grab the Ghost" (1920) with Snub Pollard, "Fire Fighters" (1922) with Allen "Farina" Hoskins, "It's a Bear" (1924) with Jackie Condon, "Pride of the Bowery" (1940) with Leo Gorcey, "Ghosts on the Loose" (1943) with Huntz Hall, "Greenwich Village" (1944) with Don Ameche—Sammy appeared in this musical as one of the Four Step Brothers dancing group. He only appeared on one TV show, "Good Times" (1974) with Jimmie Walker. Sammy died of cancer on July 24, 1989 in Lynwood, California and is interred at Inglewood Park Cemetery in Inglewood, California.

PUNSLEY, BERNARD
1923-2004

Only with the Dead End series for a short time, he is, nevertheless, well remembered for his roles as Milt and Ape. He was born Bernard Punsly (his last name is usually misspelled in film credits as "Punsley") on July 11, 1923 in New York City, New York. He never aspired to be an actor, and got a part in the stage version of "Dead End" in 1935 because he thought it might be fun. He was also in the film version in 1937 where he played the part of Milt; later as Ape. He played one of the Kids only until he went into the Army. There Bernard received medical training and continued with it after he got out. He entered medical college at the University of Georgia and got a medical degree. After graduation Bernard set up a medical practice in Torrance, California. He never went back to show business and was the last surviving Dead End Kid after Huntz Hall died in 1999. In 1950 he married Lynne (last name unknown); they had one child and were together until his death. Sadly, he died of cancer on January 20, 2004 in Torrance, California.

JORDAN, BOBBY
1923-65

A talented youngster, at age six Bobby could already sing, tap dance, and play the saxophone. He was born Robert Jordan on April 1, 1923 in Harrison, New York. Bobby was the youngest of the Dead End Kids and first played the role of Angel in "Dead End" (1937) with Humphrey Bogart and Joel McCrea; he also appeared with the East

Side Kids and the Bowery Boys. In 1943 he entered the Army and was in the infantry. In later years he worked as a bartender and a roughneck for an oil driller. He married Lee (last name unknown) in 1946; they divorced in 1957. An alcoholic for years, in 1965 Bobby entered the Veterans Hospital in Sawtelle, Los Angeles, California for treatment of Cirrhosis of the liver. Sadly, he died there on September 10, 1965. He was interred at the Los Angeles National Cemetery in Los Angeles, California.

PERFORMERS FROM "GODSPELL" MUSICAL

The legendary gospel musical, stage and screen, with music and lyrics by Stephen Schwartz (except for "By My Side;" that was done by Peggy Gordon), wowed fans like me with awesome performances, dance, and inspirational songs rendered by talented singers. The 1973 movie was filmed on location in Manhattan, New York for an estimated budget of $1.3 million. Let's see where the actors are now:

Victor Garber—1949-

Victor Jay Garber was born on March 16, 1949 in London, Ontario, Canada. In "Godspell" he sang "Save the People." During his long acting career Victor has earned two Screen Actors Guild Award nominations for Outstanding Motion Picture Cast and an Emmy nomination for "Life with Judy Garland: Me and My Shadows." Besides film, he is also an accomplished stage actor. In 2015 he married Rainer Andreeson. Interestingly, Victor played Jesus in "Godspell" and the Devil in "Damn Yankees" (on the stage). Currently he finished the documentary "The Gettysburg Address," and the films "Rebel in the Rye" (with Zoey Deutsch) scheduled to be out in 2017 and "Kill the Poet" (with Anita Briem), also scheduled to be out in 2017.

Katie Hanley— 1949-

Katie was born on January 17, 1949 in Evanston, Illinois. Besides singing "By My Side" in "Godspell" and doing a great job, she appeared in "The Chisholm's" TV mini-series in 1979 with Ben Murphy. Her last movie role was in "Xanadu" (1980) with Olivia Newton-John and Gene Kelly. Katie's last TV appearance was on "Charlie's Angels: To See an Angel Die" (1980) with Tanya Roberts. She's is currently retired from acting.

Robin   Lamont— 1950-

Robin was born on June 2, 1950 in Boston, Massachusetts. Besides singing "Day By Day" and "Light of the World" in "Godspell" and doing a great job, Robin appeared in the TV series "Ryan's Hope" (1979-80) with Michael Levin. She was also in the film "He Knows You're Alone" (1980) with Don Scardino and Tom Hanks. She is retired from acting. Robin attended Carnegie-Mellon University and was admitted to the New York State Bar in 1996. She was an Assistant District Attorney in Worcester County, New York for many years and is an award-winning novelist.

Joanne Jonas—1951-

Joanne was born May 31, 1951 in the Bronx, New York City, New York. In "Godspell" she sang "Turn Back, O Man" and "All For the Best." Besides singing in the movie, Joanne was an assistant choreographer and before the film was in the stage productions. After "Godspell" she continued her work acting, singing, and dancing on Broadway; she was in "Candide" and "Death of a Salesman" with George C. Scott. She also made hundreds of TV commercials and appeared in the movie "You're Gonna Love It Here" (1977) with Austin Pendleton. Eventually, Joanne moved to Northern California with her boyfriend and helped form HearthMath, a training and technology organization. She is still married and works as a graphic artist at HearthMath.

David Michael Haskill—1948-2000

David was born on June 4, 1948 in Stockton, California. In "Godspell" he sang "Prepare Ye the Way of the Lord" and appeared as both John the Baptist and Judas Iscariot. Some movies in which he appeared include, "The Ordeal of Patty Hearst" (1979) with Dennis Weaver, "Seems Like Old Times" (1980) with Goldie Hawn, "Missing Pieces" (1983) with Elizabeth Montgomery, "Body Double" (1984) with Craig Wasson, "K-9" (1989) with James Belushi. Some TV appearances for David include, "Lou Grant: Scoop" (1977) with Ed Asner, "Mork and Mindy: The Mork Syndrome" (1979) with Robin Williams, "Knight Rider: Just My Bill" (1982) with David Hasselhoff, "Santa Barbara" (1985-86) with A Martinez (see his biography elsewhere in this book), "Highway to Heaven: Heavy Date" (1987) with Michael Landon, "Dallas: Pillow Talk" (1988) with Larry Hagman, "Matlock: The Brothers" (1990) with Andy Griffith, "Home Improvement: All's Fair Lady" (1998) with Tim Allen.

Sadly, David died of brain cancer August 30, 2000 in Woodland Hills, Los Angeles, California.

Merrell Jackson—1952-91

Merrell was born on April 26, 1952 in Chicago, Illinois. In "Godspell" he sang "All Good Gifts." After the movie Merrell joined the Chicago stage cast of "Godspell" in November 1972. Later, he joined Nell Carter in the Chicago cast of the musical "Don't Bother Me, I Can't Cope." While living in New York he performed with dance companies and in Broadway musicals. Merrell also did TV commercials for 7 Up. Sadly, Merrell died on February 23, 1991.

Jerry Sroka—1946-

Jerry was born on January 30, 1946. In "Godspell" he sang "Light of the World." Some of the movies in which Jerry appeared include, "Nocturna" (1979) with John Carradine (see John's biography elsewhere in this book), "The Berenstain Bear's Comic Valentine" (voice over 1982) with Ron McLarty, "That's Adequate" (1989) with Tony Randall, "Antz" (voice over 1998) with Gene Hackman, "Connecting Dots" (2003) with Nikolai Kinski. Some of his TV roles include, "Sisters: Dear Georgie" (1993) with Swoosie Kurtz, "Murphy Brown: Specific Overtures" (1995) with Candice Bergen, "Murder One: Diary of a Serial Killer" (mini series 1997) with D. B. Woodside, "Ally McBeal: The Playing Field" (1998) with Calista Flockhart, "All Grown Up!: Separate But Equal" (voice over 2007) with Elizabeth Daily, "The Comeback Kids" (2014-2015) with Joe Cipriano.

In 2005 Jerry married actress Mariette Hartley. He is still active in acting.

Gilmer McCormick— 1947-

Gilmer was born on March 13, 1947 in Louisville, Ken-

tucky. In "Godspell" she sings "Light of the World." Gilmer graduated from the Moravian Academy in Bethlehem, Pennsylvania in 1965. She attended the Carnegie-Mellon University in Pittsburgh and became involved with a stage production of "Godspell" with some of her classmates. Gilmer was also part of the original off-Broadway cast. Some of Gilmer's film roles include, "Squares" (1972) with Andrew Prine, "Slaughterhouse-Five" (1972) with Ron Leibman, "Starting Over" (1979) with Burt Reynolds, "The Burning Bed" (1984) with Farrah Fawcett, "Silent Night, Bloody Night" (1984) with Lilyan Chauvin. Some of her TV roles include, "The Adams Chronicles" (mini series 1976) with Tom Bair, "Hill Street Blues: Double Jeopardy" (1981) with Daniel J. Travanti, "Crisis Counselor: Agraphobia" (1982) with Thom Thompson, "I Had Three Wives: You and I Know" (1985) with "Godspell" co-star Victor Garber.

Gilmer married the associate musical supervisor for "Days of Our Lives," Stephen Reinhardt in 1972; they have two children. She is currently Associate Director of the Young Actors Space in Sherman Oaks, California where she started in 2003. Gilmer and family moved to Louisville, Kentucky in 2010 and she has done some stage work there.

Jeffrey Mylett— 1949-86

Jeffrey Martin Mylett was born June 8, 1949 in North Canton, Ohio. Jeff studied theater at the Carnegie-Mellon University in Pittsburg, Pennsylvania. He was in both the stage and film cast and was also a songwriter. Jeff was in the off-Broadway musical "Thoughts" (1973) and the Broadway musical "The Magic Show" (1974). Besides "Godspell," Jeff appeared in "Money Talks" (1972), an Allen Funt "Candid Camera" flick with Muhammad Ali, "Brewster's Millions" (1985) with Richard Pryor, and "My Man Adam" (1985) with Raphael Sbarge.

Sadly, Jeffrey died on May 7, 1986 in Los Angeles, California from complications arising from AIDS.

Lynne Thigpen— 1948-2003

Lynne was born Cherlynne Theresa Thigpen on December 22, 1948 in Joliet, Illinois. In "Godspell" she sang "O Bless the Lord My Soul." Lynne was an actress as well as a fine singer and is probably best known for her role as The Chief in the various "Carmen Sandiego" TV series'. She was nominated for six Daytime

Emmy Awards and won a Tony in 1997 for her role as Dr. Judith Kaufman on "An American Daughter" (1997) with Hal Holbrook. Lynne previously taught high school English before studying theater and dance at the University of Illinois. She moved to New York City in 1971 to pursue her career as a stage actress. Lynne did well and was in many plays.

Lynne was in many roles; some film parts include, "The Warriors" (1979) with Michael Beck, "Streets of Fire" (1984) with Michael Paré, "Sweet Liberty" (1986) with Alan Alda, "Lean on Me" (1989) with Morgan Freeman, "Article 99" (1992) with Kiefer Sutherland, "Just Cause" (1995) with Sean Connery, "A Mother's Instinct" (1996) with Lindsay Wagner, "Night Ride Home" (1999) with Keith Carradine, "Anger Management" (2003) with Jack Nicholson.

Some of her TV roles include, "Lou Grant: Double-Cross" (1981) with Ed Asner, "Gimme a Break!" (1985-86) with Nell Carter, "The Equalizer: Blood & Wine" (1987) with Edward Woodward, "Roseanne: The Slice of Life" (1989) with Roseanne Barr, "Hunter: Where Echoes End" (1990) with Fred Dryer, "L. A. Law" (1991-92) with Corbin Bernsen, "Where in the World is Carmen Sandiego?" (1991-95) with Greg Lee, "Where in Time is Carmen Sandiego?" (1996) with Kevin Shinick, "All My Children" (1983-2000) with Cameron Mathison.

Sadly, Lynne died of a cerebral hemorrhage on March 12, 2003 in her home in Marina del Ray, California. She was buried at Elmhurst Cemetery in Joliet, Illinois.

WRESTLERS

Here are some of the quintessential wrestlers from the past, some famous, some less well known, some are my favorites.

Abdullah the Butcher—b. Jan. 11, 1941 as Lawrence Shreeve in Windsor, Ontario, Canada; 6'3"; 360 lbs. Wrestled from 1958-still active.

Alaskan Bear, The—see Jay S. York

Andre the Giant—André Roussimoff; b. Jun 19, 1946; d. Jan. 27, 1993 in Paris, France; billed height 7'4" but closer to 7'0"; billed weight 475-540 lbs. Another wrestler who had the disfiguring disease, acromegaly. Wrestled from 1963-92. In 1986 he co-starred in "The Princess Bride" with Cary Elwes and Mandy Patinkin as Fezzik, his favorite role.

Argentina Apollo—b. circa 1938 as Vincente Denigris, d. Aug. 2, 1984; 5'10"; 175 lbs. Started wrestling in 1960.

Baron Mikel Scicluna—b. 1929 on the island of Malta in the Mediterranean Sea; wrestled during 60s and 70s; 6'3"; 256 lbs.; famous for hidden roll of coins and size 16 feet; retired 1984.

Big John Studd—b. Feb. 19, 1948 as John Mintonin in Butler, Pennsylvania; d. March 20, 1995 in Burke, VA; 6'7"; 320 lbs.

Bobby "The Brain" Heenan (wrestling manager)—b. Nov. 1, 1944 as Raymond Louis Heenan in Chicago, Illinois; managed Andre the Giant, Big John Studd, King Kong Bundy, Rick Rude. In wrestling from 1960 until he retired in 2000. Wrestled for awhile but mostly managed.

Bobo Brazil—b. Jul. 10, 1923 as Houston Harris in Little Rock, Arkansas; d. Jan. 20, 1998 in St. Joseph, Michigan; 6'6"; 270 lbs. Wrestled 1951-93.

Bronko Nagurski—b. Nov. 3, 1908 as Bronislau Nagurski, d. Jan. 7, 1990; wrestler and football player (Chicago Bears); 6'2"; 226 lbs.

Bomber Kulky—b. Aug. 11, 1911 as Henry Kulkovich (one source says it was spelled Kulakowich) in Hastings-on-Hudson, New York; d. Feb. 12, 1965 in Oceanside, California; wrestler and actor (in the TV series' "Life of Riley" (1953-58) with William Bendix and "Voyage to the Bottom of the Sea" (1964-65) with Richard Basehart; 5'11"; appeared in "Mighty Joe Young" (1949) with Ben Johnson. During WWII he served in the US Navy.

Bruno Sammartino—b. Oct. 6, 1935 in Pizzoferrato, Italy; 6'1"; 250 lbs.; he set world record in 1959 for bench pressing 565 lbs.; retired 1981. One of the all-time clean, well-respected professional wrestlers.

Captain Lou Albano—b. Jul. 29, 1933 as Louis Vincent Albano in Rome, Italy; d. Oct. 14, 2009 in Westchester County, New York; 5'10"; 250 lbs. Wrestler (1953-69), manager (1969-95), and actor. He acquired the moniker "Captain" from when he was captain of his White Plains, NY, high school football team. In 1986 he appeared in the movie "Wise Guys" with Danny DeVito.

Chief Jay Strongbow—b. Oct. 4, 1928 in Philadelphia as Luke Joseph Scarpa (The Professional Wrestling Hall of Fame and Museum gives his name as Joseph Luke Scarpa); d. Apr. 3, 2012, the result of a fall at his home in Griffin, Georgia; 6'0" (one source, and one only, has his height as 6'6"); 265 lbs.; Italian, not Indian. Wrestled from 1947-85, but wrestled from time to time until 1994.

Chief Thundercloud—b. January 31, 1934 as Jesus Mario Lopez in Nashville, Tennessee; wrestled in the 60s and 70s. According to several sources, Lopez is currently (as of this writing) serving 22 years in the Three Rivers Federal prison in Three Rivers, Texas on drug-related (large cocaine bust) charges.

Dick "Bulldog" Brower—b. Mar. 28, 1934 as Richard Gland, d. Sep. 15, 1997; famous for his trademark "hearing bells" and generally acting crazy; 5'8"; 270 lbs.

Dick the Bruiser—b. Jun. 27, 1929 as Richard (some sources say William Fritz) Afflis in Delphi, Indiana; d. Nov. 10, 1991 in Tampa, FL. Football player (Green Bay Packers, early 50s) and wrestler (1954-85). 6'1"; 261 lbs.

Dory Funk Sr.—b. May 4, 1919 in Hammond, Indiana; d. Jun. 3, 1973 in Amarillo, Texas; 5'11"; 230 lbs. Father of wrestlers Dory Jr. and Terry Funk

Dory Funk Jr.—b. Feb. 3, 1941 in Hammond, Indiana; 6'3", 240 lbs.; wrestled from 1963-2008.

Fabulous Moolah—b. July 22, 1923 as Mary Lillian Ellison in Tookiedoo, Kershaw County, South Carolina; d. Nov. 2, 2007 in Columbia, South Carolina; 5'4", 138 lbs. Wrestled 1949-06. Well known for the so-called "Bra and Panties Match" against Victoria (Lisa Marie Varon) where Moolah stripped Victoria of her top! (Sort of a "coming out?" Sorry, couldn't find any pictures.)

French Angel, The—b. Maurice Tillet, Oct. 23, 1903 in the Ural Mountains in Russia; d. Sep. 4, 1954 in France of heart disease. He is buried at the Lithuanian National Cemetery in Justice, Ill.

Fritz von Erich—b. Aug. 16, 1929 as Jack Barton Adkisson in Jewett, Texas; d. Sep. 10, 1997 in Dallas, Texas; 6'6"; 260 lbs. Wrestled from 1958-82.

George "The Animal" Steele—b. Apr. 16, 1937 as William James Myers in Detroit, Michigan; 6'2". Wrestler (1962-89) and actor (played Tor Johnson in Tim Burton's "Ed Wood," 1994).

Gorgeous George—b. Mar. 24, 1915 as George Raymond Wagner in Butte, Nebraska; d. Dec. 26, 1963 in Van Nuys, California; 5'9"; 215 lbs. Wrestled 1932-62. Gimmick: wig and cape.

Gorilla Monsoon—b. Jun. 4, 1937 as Robert James Marella in NYC, New York; d. Oct. 6, 1999 in Willingboro, New Jersey; 6'5"; 401 lbs. Wrestled 1959-81. Also ring announcer and booker.

Hacksaw Jim Duggan—b. Jan. 14, 1954 as James Duggan; 6'3"; carried a 2x4 and/or an American flag into the ring with him

258

Happy Humphrey—b. Jul. 16, 1926 as William Cobb, d. Mar. 14, 1989; 6'1"; 750+ lbs.

Haystacks Calhoun—b. Aug. 3, 1934 as William Dee Calhoun in McKinney, Texas; d. Dec. 7, 1989; 6'1"; 601-800 lbs. (varied). As a one-time actor he made a brief appearance in Rod Serling's "Requiem For a Heavyweight" (1962) with Anthony Quinn.

Hulk Hogan—b. Aug. 11, 1953 as Terry Bollea in Augusta, Georgia; 6'7"; 302 lbs.; lives in Tampa, Florida. First man to body slam Andre the Giant (Hogan was afraid Andre was going to turn on him in that fixed match, but he did pick him up; no mean feat) in WrestleMania III (1987). Began wrestling in 1977; still active, as of this writing, but he was fired from and blacklisted by the WWE for alleged "scandalous remarks" he had made in 2007. The Hulk appeared in a number of movies, including "Rocky III" (1982) with Sylvester Stallone, "No Holds Barred" (1989) with Kurt Fuller, and "Suburban Commando" (1991) with Christopher Lloyd.

"Iron" Mike Mazurki—b. Dec. 25, 1907 as Mikhail Mazuruski (another source spells it Mazurkevych), in Austria-Hungary, now the Ukraine; d. Dec. 9, 1990 in Glendale, California; wrestler and actor; appeared in more than 100 movies, including "Cheyenne Autumn (1964) with Richard Widmark, "Donovan's Reef" (1963) with John Wayne, and "Challenge to be Free" (1975) with Fritz Ford; 6'5"; 240lbs.

Iron Sheik, The—b. June 9, 1926 as Edward George Farhat in Lansing, Michigan; d. January 18, 2003 in Williamston, Michigan. 5'11"; 253 lbs. Wrestled 1949-98.

Ivan Rasputin, the Mad Russian—b. June 3, 1912 as Hyman Fishman in Chelsea, Massachusetts; d. September 25, 1976 in Riverside, California. Uncredited role in "Mighty Joe Young" (1949) with Ben Johnson.

Ivan "The Russian Bear" Koloff—b. Aug. 24, 1942 as Oreal Perras; 5'9½"; beat Bruno Sammartino on Jan. 18, 1971; retired 1994.

Jay S. York—b. Aug. 4, 1938; d. Oct. 7, 1995 in Los Angeles, California. Wrestled in the 1960s under the name The Alaskan Bear. Acted in "Paradise Alley" (1978) with Sylvester Stallone, "Tall Tale" (1995) with Patrick Swayze and "Kinjite: Forbidden Subjects" (1989) with Charles Bronson); briefly a member of the rock group *Delaney & Bonnie*.

Jesse "The Body" Ventura—b. Jul. 15, 1951 as James Janos in Minneapolis, Minnesota; 6'4"; Vietnam vet; wrestled from 1975-86; former governor of Minnesota (1999-2003). He appeared in "Predator" (1987) with Arnold Schwarzenegger. WWE Hall of Famer; author .

Junkyard Dog—b. Dec. 13, 1952 as Sylvester Ritter in Charlotte, North Carolina; d. Jun. 2, 1998 of a car accident near Forest, Mississippi (fell asleep at the wheel); 6'4". Wrestled 1977-93.

Kamala the Ugandan Giant—b. May 28, 1950 as James Harris in Senatobia, Mississippi; 6'7"; 380 lbs. Wrestled from 1974-2011; also an author.

Killer Karl Davis—b. Apr. 16, 1908 in Ohio; d. Jul. 1, 1977 in San Bernardino County, California; 6'2"; wrestler and actor; wrestled in the 1940s; as an actor he appeared in "Mighty Joe Young" (1949) with Terry More, "The Road to Denver" (1955) with John Payne, and "Apache Warrior (1957) with Keith Larsen.

Killer Kowalski (Tarzan Kowalski in 1947)—b. Oct. 13, 1926 in Windsor, Ontario, California as Edward Spulnik; d. Aug. 30, 2008 in Malden, Massachusetts; 6'7"; 280 lbs. Wrestled 1947-77.

King Kong Bundy—b. Nov. 7, 1957 as Christopher Pallies Atlantic City, New Jersey; 6'4"; 440-502 lbs. Wrestled from 1981-2006. Appeared as an actor in "Moving" (1988) with Richard Pryor and "Fight the Panda Syndicate" (2008) with Sam Rocco.

Lou Albano—see Captain Lou Albano

"Macho Man" Randy Savage—b. Nov. 15, 1952 as Randy Poffo in Columbus, Ohio; wrestled 1973-2005; d. May 20, 2011 in Seminole, Florida of a heart attack; 6'2"; 239 lbs.; manager/wife (1984-92; divorced) **"Miss" Elizabeth Hulette** (b. circa 1961, d. May 1, 2003). Appeared as an actor in "Ready to Rumble" (2000) with Oliver Platt, "Spider-Man" (2002) with Tobey Maguire, and did a voiceover for "Bolt" (2008) with John Travolta.

263

Mae Young—b. Mar. 12, 1923; d. Jan. 14, 2014; wrestler; 5'3"; usually wrestled with the Fabulous Moolah. Became well known for preferring to actually fight than act it out.

Man Mountain Dean—b. Jun. 30, 1891 as Frank Leavitt in NYC, New York; d. May 29, 1953 in Norcross, GA; 6' +; 300 + lbs. Did some acting, fought in WWI and WWII. Wrestled c. 1914-1937. Appeared as an actor in "Mighty Joe Young" (1949) with Ben Johnson, "The Gladiator" (1938) with Joe E. Brown, and "The Private Life of Henry VIII" (1933) with Charles Laughton.

Max, the Iron Man—wrestler born Ian Batchelor, May 24, 1910 in Petaluma, California; d. August 10, 1986 in Torrance, California; he had an uncredited part in "Mighty Joe Young" (1949) with Terry Moore.

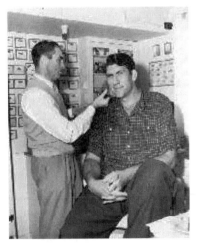

Max Edmund Palmer *(in photo he's on the right)* **("Paul Bunyan")**—b. Nov. 2, 1927 in Randolph, Mississippi; d. May 7, 1984 in St. Louis, Missouri. Tallest wrestler ever; claimed 8'2"; he acted in "Invaders From Mars" (1953) with Jimmy Hunt, "Killer Ape" (1953) with Johnny Weissmuller, and "Stone" (1974) with Ken Shorter. He was an evangelist preacher from 1963-84.

Mike Lane—b. Jan. 6, 1933 in Washington, D. C. Wrestled at 6'8" and 275 lbs. from 1952-59 as Tarzan Mike and Dick Holbrook. Also acted, appeared in "The Harder They Fall" (1956, photo, l., with Humphrey Bogart and Jan Sterling from Columbia Pictures; also starred former boxing greats Max Baer and Jersey Joe Wolcott). Acted in many movies and TV shows and also produced.

Mr. Clean ("Tiger" Joe Marsh)—b. Joseph Marusich (Josip Marušić) on Aug. 25, 1911 in Chicago, IL; 3000 matches; 6'1", 262 lbs.; was world heavyweight wrestling champ in 1937; wrestled until 1954; acted in movies (gate guard in "Escape to Witch Mountain"), "The Cat from Outer Space" and "On the Waterfront"; d. May 9, 1989.

Mr. T—b. May 21, 1952 as Lawrence Tureaud in Chicago, Illinois; 5'10", 255 lbs.; wrestled from 1985-86 & 1994-95. He began his career as a bouncer in a night club; he began his trademark of wearing gold chains, rings, and bracelets at this club, the result of customers losing said items. Later he was a bodyguard for ten years for such well-known figures as Steve McQueen, Michael Jackson, Joe Frazier, and Diana Ross. He adopted his distinctive hairstyle after seeing it in "National Geographic" on an African Mandinka warrior. Acted in many movies including "Rocky III" (1982) with Sylvester Stallone. From 1983-87 he co-starred with George Peppard in the hugely popular TV series, "The A-Team." In 1995 Mr. T had a bout with T-cell lymphoma but recovered. He gave up wearing his gold as a sign of respect to "the people who lost so much" (quote Mr. T) in the Hurricane Katrina disaster (2005). He currently does commercials and makes personal appearances.

"Nature Boy" Buddy Rogers—b. Feb. 20, 1921 as Herman Rohde Jr. in Camden, New Jersey, d. Jun. 26 (some sources say Jun. 22), 1992; billed at 6'2" and 227 lbs. but (according to some sources) was actually 5'11" and 195 lbs. Wrestled from 1939 to 1963 and was a two-time world champ.

Ox Baker—b. Apr. 19, 1934 as Douglas Baker in Sedalia, Missouri; d. Oct. 20, 2014 in Hartford, Connecticut; 6'5"; 342 lbs.; was Kurt Russell's on-screen wrestling opponent in "Escape From New York" in 1981. Famous for his heart punch in the ring. Allegedly caused the death of ring opponent Ray Gunkel in 1972. Ox Baker died from a heart attack in 2014.

Primo Carnera (The Ambling Alp)—b. Oct. 26, 1906 in Sequals, Italy; d. Jun. 29, 1967 in his hometown in Italy from liver disease; wrestler and world heavyweight boxing champ (1933-34); pro boxer from 1928-45; 6'7 1/2", 270 lbs.; nicknamed "The Ambling Alp." Appeared in "Mighty Joe Young" (1949) with Ben Johnson and "Hercules Unchained" (1959) with Steve Reeves.

Professor Toru Tanaka—b. Jan. 6, 1930 in Honolulu, Hawaii as Charles Kalani (he was full-blooded Hawaiian, not Japanese); d. Aug. 22, 2000 from heart failure; 6'2"; wrestler, Army vet and actor; appeared in "An Eye for an Eye" (1981) with Chuck Norris and "The Running Man" (1987) with Arnold Schwarzenegger.

Ravishing Rick Rude—b. Dec. 7, 1958 as Richard Rood in Robbinsdale (another source says St. Peter), Minnesota; d. Apr. 20, 1999 of cardiac arrest; 6'4". Wrestled from 1982 to 1994.

Rowdy Roddy Piper—b. Apr. 17, 1954 in Saskatoon, Saskatchewan, Canada as Roderick Toombs; died Jul. 30, 2015 in Hollywood, California. wrestled from 1973-87; 6' tall; acted in "They Live" (1988) and other films.

Sammy Stein—(photo, 1937) b. Apr. 1, 1905 as Samuel Stein in NYC, New York; d. Mar. 30, 1966 in Las Vegas, Nevada; wrestler, football player, and actor in "The Lost Patrol" (1934) with Boris Karloff, "Remember Pearl Harbor" (1942) with Don "Red" Barry, and "Mighty Joe Young" (1949) with Terry Moore; 6' tall.

Sgt. Slaughter—b. Aug. 27, 1948 as Robert Remus in Detroit, Michigan; 6'6"; 305 lbs. Actually was a sergeant in the US Marine Corps. Did a voice over for the animated movie, "G. I. Joe: The Movie" (1987). NWA champ and NWA Tag Team champ. His persona was used by Hasbro for the original G. I. Joe toy.

Slammin' Sammy (b. Frank) Menacker—b. May 13, 1914 as Frank Menacker in NYC, New York; d. Jan. 7, 1994 in Auburn, Illinois; was a catcher for the NY Yankees before he wrestled in the 1940s; also wrestling commentator and actor; was in "Mighty Joe Young," (1949) with Ben Johnson. Served during WWII and rose to the rank of Major.

Stu Hart—b. May 3, 1915 as Stewart Hart, d. Oct. 16, 2003; 5'10", 231 lbs.; mostly amateur wrestler; father of Bret Hart; trained many wrestlers including son Bret Hart, Roddy Piper, and Junkyard Dog. WWE Hall of Famer.

Super Swedish Angel—Tor Johnson, wrestler and actor; b. Oct. 19, 1903 as Karl Oscar Tore Johansson in Kallmar, Sweden, d. May 12, 1971; 6'3"; 387 lbs. (1956 weight). As an actor he appeared in "Bride of the Monster" (1955) with Bela Lugosi and the infamously mundane "Plan 9 from Outer Space" (1959) with Gregory Walcott. Despite his formidable appearance and terrifying roles, co-stars said he was really a gentle soul and quite friendly.

Superfly Jimmy Snuka—b. May 18, 1943 in Fiji Islands as James Reiher; 5'10". Wrestler and author; WWE Hall of Famer. In 2013 a new probe was started to reinvestigate the suspicious death of Snuka's former girl friend, Nancy Argentino, 23, who died mysteriously in their Whitehall Township, Pennsylvania hotel room in May 1983. An investigation at that time said she had died from traumatic brain injuries and three dozen cuts and bruises consistent with being hit with a stationary object. Snuka said that he had been away at that time at a WWF taping at the Allentown, Pennsylvania Fairgrounds. Currently, Snuka, 73, was charged last year with Argentino's death but has been declared incompetent to stand trial because he had dementia. Lehigh County, Allentown Judge Kelly Banach thinks he might be faking. Only time will tell.

Swedish Angel—b. in 1908 as Phil Olafsson; d. Feb. 10, 1974; wrestled in the 1940s; his bizarre appearance was caused by a disease called acromegaly; he had an uncredited part in "Mighty Joe Young" (1949) with Ben Johnson.

Terry Funk—b. Jun. 30, 1944 as Terrence Funk in Hammond, Indiana; son of wrestler Dory Funk; two-time wrestling world champ; acted in "Paradise Alley" (1978) with Sylvester Stallone and "Beyond the Mat" (1992); 6'1" and 247 lbs.

Wee Willie Davis–b. Dec. 7, 1906 as William Davis in NYC, New York; d. Apr.9, 1981; wrestled in the 1930s; 6'5"; appeared in "Mighty Joe Young" (1949) with Terry Moore and "The Asphalt Jungle" (1950) with Sterling Hayden.

RON EBNER was born in rural Glendon, Pennsylvania in 1948. THE WINDS OF HELL a horror novel, was his first publication. He has also published NOVA, a science fiction novel; PLAGUE WORLD, a horror novel; and two short story collections—OTHERWORLDLY TALES and OTHERWORLDLY TALES 2: FROM THE GRIM REAPER. He also wrote the non-fiction work, HOLLYWOOD CELEBRITIES: WHERE ARE THEY NOW? His last release was the non-fiction work, SOCIOPATHS: AMERICA'S PSYCHO KILLERS (now out of print), followed by SOCIOPATHS 2: AMERICA'S PSYCHO KILLERS: Updated and Expanded. For many years he was an independent writer for LOST TREASURE, a metal-detecting magazine. Mr. Ebner lives with his wife, Carol, and their obstreperous cat, Sassy, in northwestern Arizona.

www.ron-ebner.com

Made in the USA
San Bernardino, CA
11 October 2017